The Kennedy Reader

The Kennedy Reader

Edited by Jay David

The Bobbs-Merrill Company, Inc.
A Subsidiary of Howard W. Sams & Co., Inc.
Publishers • *Indianapolis* • *Kansas City* • *New York*

Designed by Martin Stephen Moskof
Printed in the United States of America

Acknowledgments

"Their Men Not in Havana" Apr. 22, 1961; "A Tragedy for the World," Nov. 23, 1963. By permission of the *Guardian*, Manchester, England.

Book review of *Why England Slept* by Thomas C. Linn, Aug. 3, 1940. Copyright © 1940 The New York Times Company. Reprinted by permission.

Book review of *Why England Slept* by S. T. Williamson, Aug. 11, 1940. Copyright © 1940 The New York Times Company. Reprinted by permission.

"A Communication," Nov. 25, 1963, *The Washington Post*. Copyright © 1963 by John Kenneth Galbraith.

From *The Founding Father* by Richard J. Whalen. Copyright © 1964 by Richard J. Whalen. Reprinted by arrangement with The New American Library, Inc., New York.

"A Eulogy: John Fitzgerald Kennedy" from the *Saturday Evening Post*, December 14, 1963. Copyright © by Arthur Schlesinger, Jr.

"In Arlington Cemetery" by Stanley Koehler, "Elegy for the New Year" by Jack Marshall, and "November 22, 1963" by Lewis Turco from *Of Poetry and Power*, edited by Edwin Glikes and Paul Schwaber. "In Arlington Cemetery" copyright © 1964 by Stanley Koehler. "Elegy for the New Year" copyright © 1964 by Jack Marshall (first published in the *Hudson Review*). "November 22, 1963" copyright © 1965 by Lewis Turco (originally published in *Poetry*). Reprinted by permission of the authors and the editors.

From *John F. Kennedy, President* by Hugh Sidey. Copyright © 1963, 1964 by Hugh Sidey. Reprinted by permission of Atheneum Publishers.

"Upon Education Rests the Fate of the Nation" by John F. Kennedy. Copyright © January 1958 by the *NEA Journal*.

"Sportsman Kennedy Emphasized Participation" from the Paris edition of the *New York Herald Tribune*, November 25, 1963. By permission of the Associated Press.

*I would like to express sincere gratitude
to my fine staff—
Managing Editor David Curtis,
Catherine Johnston, Elaine Crane,
and Janice Van Raay—
for their invaluable assistance in the
preparation of this book.*

Table of Contents

Introduction

It has become an historical commonplace to assert that only a half-century or more of hindsight will lend us the objectivity with which to judge John Fitzgerald Kennedy in proper perspective. Cliché or not, this assertion is probably quite sound—although it could be argued that, as President, John F. Kennedy may have been largely responsible for ensuring that we do, indeed, survive those requisite fifty years. Be that as it may, however, it is certain that historians of the twenty-first century will have at their disposal a greater volume of material about their subject than have any of their predecessors. For John F. Kennedy himself not only wrote and published more than most public figures, but also inspired—and continues to inspire —an outpouring of writings of all kinds that is nothing short of phenomenal.

In *The Kennedy Reader,* I have attempted to collect the best that has thus far been written about and by the man who was our thirty-fifth President. The material has been selected from a wide range of sources, including books, magazines, newspapers, the President's public papers, essays, poems, and more. The selections span three decades and four continents, because John F. Kennedy was a man who made his presence known early in life and throughout the world.

In compiling this anthology, I have attempted to reconstruct in full neither the public history of John F. Kennedy the politician-statesman, nor the personal history of John F. Kennedy the man. Political portraits, Presidential histories, and personal biographies are available elsewhere. Rather, I have attempted to select only those writings which provide the clearest insights into particular aspects of his life or character. The nature of the man was such that his public and private selves were closely interwoven—he was not one to be known by his acts alone.

In fact, it has been said that John F. Kennedy was so complex, so deep, and so innately guarded in his personal relationships that no one ever fully "knew" him. Although he did manage to bring a remarkable amount of his "private" personality to his public office, much of that personality was necessarily and properly submersed in carrying out the duties of President. Yet, there were several who did get to know John F. Kennedy well, and who have written well about him from several viewpoints. Among those whose works are represented in this volume are Theodore Sorensen, Arthur Schlesinger, Jr., Pierre Salinger, Tazewell Shepard, Jr., John K. Galbraith, Everett Dirksen, Evelyn Lincoln, and Maud Shaw.

Many of the selections tell us a good deal about the kinds of ideals that John Kennedy cherished. Much can be learned about a man from understanding his sense of values. He was not an idle dreamer, but he did have a dream, a reasoned vision of the way things should be—and, hopefully, could be. He was a "pragmatic idealist," and if this seems a contradiction in terms, President Kennedy embodied that contradiction. From his rewarding study of history he had gained an abiding faith in the ideals upon which his nation had been founded, the belief that these ideals could be translated into effective action, and the conviction that a people that did not at least make the effort was fated to stagnate. John F. Kennedy called upon his people to arise in the pursuit of certain goals. In the final analysis, it may be that his most significant contribution was not the specific group of goals and ideals to which he asked us to aspire, but that he asked us to aspire at all.

President Kennedy was a great politician and a great statesman, but he had not always been so. In fact, he came to politics not a little reluctantly and largely out of a sense of personal loyalty and family pride after an untimely air crash had killed his older brother Joe, who seemed doubtlessly destined for the White House. Once committed, however, Kennedy characteristically put forth his total effort. The story of his dramatic rise to power is well told by Richard T. Whalen.

In America, the word "politician" frequently has a disreputable ring, connoting a man who engages in political activity for private or partisan gain. It evokes images of smoke-filled rooms, clandestine dealings, deceiving half-truths, and insincere promises. Hence, to call a man a "great politician" is not wholly to praise him —and John F. Kennedy *was* a great politician. Politics for him was a game with rules which, however distasteful, simply had to be followed. And John Kennedy played that game as he played every other: with vigor, skill, and a fierce determination to win. But winning was not the end, only the means, and as to what extent his true ends justified those means, each of us must be his own judge.

John F. Kennedy's career in the sphere of international diplomacy, more than any other, epitomizes his growth as a President. If a word could characterize his handling of the Bay of Pigs debacle, it might be "naïveté"; if another could characterize his handling of the Cuban missile incident, it would be "sophistication." Certainly the latter action required great courage, but John Kennedy always had courage. Somewhere between the two Cubas he had picked up a knowledge of the realities of international relations, and this, coupled with the understanding of his adversary gained at the Vienna Conferences, enabled him to tread the narrow path to triumph.

That "victory" in 1962 earned Kennedy the final grudging respect of Khrushchev, paving the way to what may be remembered as Kennedy's single most important contribution as President: the Nuclear Test Ban Treaty. World peace was always one of John F. Kennedy's most cherished goals, and a test ban always one of the top-priority steps toward achieving that peace. It meant a great deal to him, for he saw nuclear testing not only as a dire threat to the civilization of the present, but also as an unpardonable crime against the unborn generations of the future.

The quality of decisive action in a leader is all too rarely combined with a scholar's love of learning, but President Kennedy possessed them both. The term "scholar" is not one to be used lightly, for it implies more than moderate learning and modest literary pretensions; it describes a certain attitude toward knowledge, an understanding of its virtues, its limitations, and its uses. John Kennedy displayed that attitude early in life, when he wrote *Why England Slept,* an analysis of the factors explaining Great Britain's sluggishness in reacting to the forces leading to World War II. Written as the young Kennedy's undergraduate thesis at Harvard, the book was hailed not only for its incisive and perceptive observations, but also for its mature and professional handling of the historical data involved. Later, as a Senator, while recovering from a back operation that had brought him near death, Kennedy undertook the painstaking research for *Profiles in Courage.* One inspiring chapter of this perennial best-seller is included in this anthology.

All of Kennedy's serious writings reveal the depth of his abiding interest in history, in the people and events that shaped history, and in the special virtue of courage displayed by those caught up by history and fated to stand isolated in a wracking moment of decision. Understanding what Kennedy wrote as well as why and how he wrote it provides a useful key to his multi-faceted character.

John F. Kennedy was a man who seems to have been at once bewilderingly complex and engagingly simple. He understood and had mastered the cold realities of political power, yet never surrendered his essential magnanimity and his attachment to the fundamental values of human life. Thus, it is not enough to understand his decisions during the Bay of Pigs fiasco or the Cuban missile crisis; we must also understand his decision to revitalize the White House Rose Garden. It cannot suffice to stress that John Kennedy loved poetry and patronized all the arts; it must be added that he loved football and publicly championed the cause of physical fitness. And it is not enough to watch him at the helm of state during his grim confrontation with Premier Khrushchev in Vienna; we must also see him manning the tiller of his sailboat with his wife and children off beloved Hyannis Port.

The international trauma of the assassination of any President is bound to elicit an enormous flood of analysis and tribute. But that accorded to John F. Kennedy was surely extraordinary both for its volume and for its distinctly personal nature. I hope that the selections in this volume may help readers to understand better the deep complexity and the warm simplicity of a man whose Presidency marked a turning point in the history of the world, and whose life gave hope to millions of its people.

Jay David
New York City

A Communication

By John Kenneth Galbraith

The Washington Post
November 25, 1963

In these last few hours hundreds, thousands of men have tried to write about John F. Kennedy. This is not wholly a ritual of the modern newspaper, one of the final rites of the great. Millions of people on this dark and sombre weekend want to read of, and then to reflect on this man who was so profoundly a part of their lives. This wish the papers are seeking to serve.

My justification for this brief word is not that of a friend but of a writer who knew the President a trifle better than most of those who must tell of him in these days.

No one knew the President well. In a sense no one could, for it is part of the character of a leader that he cannot be known. The rest of us can indulge in our moments when we open the shutters to our soul. We are granted also our moments of despair—the despair, indeed, that we felt on Friday when that incredible flash came in from Dallas. But a Kennedy or a Roosevelt can never turn the palms of his hands outward to the world and say: "Oh God. What do we do now?" That armor which insures confidence in power and certainly in command may never be removed even for a moment. No one ever knew John Kennedy as other men are known.

But he carried his armor lightly and with grace, and one sometimes thought with the knowledge of having it without escape; at least it need not be a barrier before his friends and associates. He surprised even friends with the easy candor with which he spoke of touchy problems, half-formed plans, or personal political dangers. Without malice or pettiness he contemplated the strengths and weaknesses of high officials and influential politicians. He was constantly and richly amused by the vanities of men in high places. He freely discussed ideas the mention of which would make most men shudder. Last summer during the visit of President Sarvepalli Radhakrishnan of India, in a social moment before a formal dinner, mention was made of some woman politician. He turned and asked me why there had been so few women politicians of importance—whether women were poorly adapted to the political art. Here surely was a politically ticklish subject: women are half the voting population and might not react well to wonder at their political shortcomings. I struggled to come up with examples—the first Elizabeth, Mrs. F.D.R., one or two others. The President admitted of the exceptions but good-humoredly returned to the rule. He knew he could discuss an interesting point without anyone proceeding to argue that he was against the Nineteenth Amendment.

"The political campaign won't tire me," he said in the spring of 1960, "for I have an advantage. I can be myself." He had learned one of the hardest lessons of life, which is that we all have far more liberty than we use. And he knew beyond this, that others because they admired it would respect the informality with which he passed through life. No President ever said so much to so many friends and acquaintances and so rarely had to disavow or explain.

John F. Kennedy was much interested in writing. This I think provides one small clue to understanding. Good writing requires a sense of economy and of style and the absence of vanity which allows a man to divorce his writing at least a little from himself. A writer can be interesting when he is speaking to others; he is rarely, if ever, interesting when he is speaking to himself except to himself.

Mr. Kennedy hated verbosity. Though he rejoiced in politics he hated the wordiness of the political craft. He never, at least in his adult life, opened his mouth without having something to say. Never even in conversation did he speak for the pleasure of hearing his own words and phrases. Many of us have a diminished interest in the words of others. Mr. Kennedy was the rare case of the man who applied the rules with equal rigor against himself.

The Kennedy style, though it involved detachment from self, involved no self-deprecation. In the early years when he was enlisting followers, he did not offer a program for universal salvation. He was suspicious of all resonant formulae from whatever source— he rightly regarded some of the liturgy of American liberalism as corrupt. It is trundled out at election time, as once were the candidate's trains, urged in a torrent of words and then put away for four years. His case again had the merit of candor. He said essentially, I am a man worth following, you can count on me to be honestly better at the art of government than any other possible contender, and, an important detail, I know how to get elected.

That he was qualified in the art of government there will never be any question. His style called for unremitting good taste and good manners. It called also for a profound commitment to information and reason. He did not think that man had been civilized as an afterthought; he believed it was for a purpose. Perhaps there are natural men; those who have the original gift of art and insight. Mr. Kennedy without being so rude as to say so would believe such pretension to be an excuse for laziness. His reliance was on what men had learned and had come to know. What Mr. Kennedy had come to know about the art and substance of

American Government was prodigious. I first knew Jack Kennedy 25 years ago when I was a young tutor and he was an undergraduate at Winthrop House at Harvard. He was gay, charming, irreverent, good looking and far from diligent. What no one knew at the time was that he had the priceless notion that education never stops. Some of us who later worked with him on economic issues—farm policy, interest rates, Federal Reserve policy, the control of inflation, other arcane or technical matters—used to say that we had observed three stages in his career in the House and more particularly in the Senate: the first was when he called up to ask how we thought he should vote; the second was when he telephoned to ask 15 or 20 quick questions as to what lay behind the particular action or measure; the third was when he did not call at all or inquired as to why, as he had gleaned from an article or a letter to *The Times,* we seemed to be acting on some misinformation. My colleague Prof. Carl Kaysen, who has worked in the White House these last years, has said that when asked who is the most knowledgeable of the President's advisers he always felt obliged to remind his questioner that none was half so well-informed as the President himself.

Mr. Kennedy knew that knowledge was power: no one, of course, will ever imagine that this was his sole reliance. Knowledge without character is worthless—or worse.

Departments and individuals in approaching the President invariably emphasize the matters which impress them most. Mr. Kennedy knew how to make the appropriate discounts without anyone quite realizing they were being made. He had a natural sense for all of the variables in a problem: he would not be carried away by anyone.

Like all men of deep intelligence—he respected the intelligence of others. That was why he did not talk down to the American people: it was why he was contemptuous of the arm-waving circus posturing of the American politician which so many American newspapermen so much admire right up to the moment of final defeat.

4

The President faced a speaker with his wide gray-blue eyes and total concentration. So also a paper or an article. And so far as one could tell, once it was his it was his forever. This, of course, was not all.

Knowledge is power. But knowledge without character and wisdom is nothing, or worse. These the President also had, and also the highly practical capacity to see when part of an argument, being advanced by a department, bureau or zealot, was being presented as the whole. But I come back to the grasp of issues, the breadth of information and the power of concentration. Perhaps these come naturally. I suspect, in fact, that few men in history have ever combined natural ability with such powers of mental self-discipline.

John F. Kennedy's Inaugural Address was an excellent one—
although Kennedy had, after reading Thomas Jefferson's
Inaugural the evening before, remarked with humility, "Better
than mine." Firm but not dogmatic, optimistic but not irresponsible,
tough but not belligerent, it was a rallying cry to the nation
and a notice—not a threat—to the world. It was a pledge, a plea,
a prayer, and more: it was a reaffirmation of the principles upon
which the nation had been founded, and upon which President
Kennedy hoped to base his efforts toward creating a better world.

Inaugural Address

January 20, 1961

*Vice President Johnson, Mr. Speaker, Mr. Chief Justice, President
Eisenhower, Vice President Nixon, President Truman, Reverend
Clergy, fellow citizens:*

We observe today not a victory of party but a celebration of
freedom—symbolizing an end as well as a beginning—signifying
renewal as well as change. For I have sworn before you and Almighty
God the same solemn oath our forebears prescribed nearly a century
and three quarters ago.

The world is very different now. For man holds in his mortal
hands the power to abolish all forms of human poverty and all forms
of human life. And yet the same revolutionary beliefs for which our
forebears fought are still at issue around the globe—the belief that

the rights of man come not from the generosity of the state but from the hand of God.

We dare not forget today that we are the heirs of that first revolution. Let the word go forth from this time and place, to friend and foe alike, that the torch has been passed to a new generation of Americans—born in this century, tempered by war, disciplined by a hard and bitter peace, proud of our ancient heritage—and unwilling to witness or permit the slow undoing of those human rights to which this nation has always been committed, and to which we are committed today at home and around the world.

Let every nation know, whether it wishes us well or ill, that we shall pay any price, bear any burden, meet any hardship, support any friend, oppose any foe to assure the survival and the success of liberty.

This much we pledge—and more.

To those old allies whose cultural and spiritual origins we share, we pledge the loyalty of faithful hands. United, there is little we cannot do in a host of cooperative ventures. Divided, there is little we can do—for we dare not meet a powerful challenge at odds and split asunder.

To those new states whom we welcome to the ranks of the free, we pledge our word that one form of colonial control shall not have passed away merely to be replaced by a far more iron tyranny. We shall not always expect to find them supporting our view. But we shall always hope to find them strongly supporting their own freedom—and to remember that, in the past, those who foolishly sought power by riding the back of the tiger ended up inside.

To those peoples in the huts and villages of half the globe struggling to break the bonds of mass misery, we pledge our best efforts to help them help themselves, for whatever period is required—not because the communists may be doing it, not because we seek their votes, but because it is right. If a free society cannot help the many who are poor, it cannot save the few who are rich.

To our sister republics south of our border, we offer a special pledge—to convert our good words into good deeds—in a new alliance for progress—to assist free men and free governments in casting off the chains of poverty. But this peaceful revolution of hope cannot become the prey of hostile powers. Let all our neighbors know that we shall join with them to oppose aggression or subversion anywhere in the Americas. And let every other power know that this Hemisphere intends to remain the master of its own house.

To that world assembly of sovereign states, the United Nations, our last hope in an age where the instruments of war have far outpaced the instruments of peace, we renew our pledge of support—to prevent it from becoming merely a forum for invective—to strengthen its shield of the new and the weak—and to enlarge the area in which its writ may run.

Finally, to those nations who would make themselves our adversary, we offer not a pledge but a request: that both sides begin anew the quest for peace, before the dark powers of destruction unleashed by science engulf all humanity in planned or accidental self-destruction.

We dare not tempt them with weakness. For only when our aims are sufficient beyond doubt can we be certain beyond doubt that they will never be employed.

But neither can two great and powerful groups of nations take comfort from our present course—both sides overburdened by the cost of modern weapons, both rightly alarmed by the steady spread of the deadly atom, yet both racing to alter that uncertain balance of terror that stays the hand of mankind's final war.

So let us begin anew—remembering on both sides that civility is not a sign of weakness, and sincerity is always subject to proof. Let us never negotiate out of fear. But let us never fear to negotiate.

Let both sides explore what problems unite us instead of belaboring those problems which divide us.

Let both sides, for the first time, formulate serious and precise proposals for the inspection and control of arms—and bring the absolute power to destroy other nations under absolute control of all nations.

Let both sides seek to invoke the wonders of science instead of its terrors. Together let us explore the stars, conquer the deserts, eradicate disease, tap the ocean depths and encourage the arts and commerce.

Let both sides unite to heed in all corners of the earth the command of Isaiah—to "undo the heavy burdens . . . (and) let the oppressed go free."

And if a beach-head of cooperation may push back the jungle of suspicion, let both sides join in creating a new endeavor; not a new balance of power, but a new world of law, where the strong are just and the weak secure and the peace preserved.

All this will not be finished in the first one hundred days. Nor will it be finished in the first one thousand days, nor in the life of this Administration, nor even perhaps in our lifetime on this planet. But let us begin.

In your hands, my fellow citizens, more than mine, will rest the final success or failure of our course. Since this country was founded, each generation of Americans has been summoned to give testimony to its national loyalty. The graves of young Americans who answered the call to service surround the globe.

Now the trumpet summons us again—not as a call to bear arms, though arms we need—not as a call to battle, though embattled we are—but a call to bear the burden of a long twilight struggle, year in and year out, "rejoicing in hope, patient in tribulation"—a struggle against the common enemies of man: tyranny, poverty, disease and war itself.

Can we forge against these enemies a grand and global alliance, North and South, East and West, that can assure a more fruitful life for all mankind? Will you join in that historic effort?

In the long history of the world, only a few generations have been granted the role of defending freedom in its hour of maximum danger. I do not shrink from this responsibility—I welcome it. I do not believe that any of us would exchange places with any other people or any other generation. The energy, the faith, the devotion which we bring to this endeavor will light our country and all who serve it—and the glow from that fire can truly light the world.

And so, my fellow Americans: ask not what your country can do for you—ask what you can do for your country.

My fellow citizens of the world: ask not what America will do for you, but what together we can do for the freedom of man.

Finally, whether you are citizens of America or citizens of the world, ask of us here the same high standards of strength and sacrifice which we ask of you. With a good conscience our only sure reward, with history the final judge of our deeds, let us go forth to lead the land we love, but knowing that here on earth God's work must truly be our own.

America's Voice

The London Times
January 21, 1961

When President Kennedy stood up yesterday to speak for the first
time to the republic and the world he can scarcely have been without
a thought of that other famous inauguration just a hundred years
ago. He did not refer to the anniversary. But something of the
cadence of Abraham Lincoln's oratory can be heard in the sentences
of his address, and underlying them Lincoln's sense of the spiritual
mission of the great presidential office. President Kennedy was voic-
ing the American people's historic dedication to declared ideals and
defined Christian standards—"the belief that the rights of man
come not from the generosity of the State but from the hand of God"
—and this is something which the American people of today will
echo. Therewith goes the implication, as clear to Mr. Kennedy as

13

it was to Lincoln, that in 1961 as in 1861 the great principles enshrined in the American political scriptures of the Founding Fathers stand in a crisis of history, full of menace but full of hope.

The President's exalted hopes give warmth and colour to the whole speech, but over against them he sets the shadow, *corruptio optimi pessima*, man's expanding opportunity to master his environment as never before matched by his equal power to destroy it and himself. Mr. Kennedy held out the right hand of America's fellowship to all who would grasp it and cooperate, using the new scientific resources to release humanity from poverty and all other ancient ills. He reaffirmed his country's fidelity to "those old allies whose cultural and spiritual origins we share." He gave a welcome to the newly emancipated members of the international community. He pledged his country to the continued support of the Pacific Authority of the United Nations. And he made a new appeal or "request" to "those nations who would make themselves our adversaries" to join with America in the search for peace before the forces of destruction can finally prevail.

Mr. Kennedy, however, made it very clear that the peace for which America will work, with all other nations of good will, can be only a peace of the strong. Giving a special pledge of economic help to "our sister republics south of The Border," he added a warning that they must not be allowed to become the prey of hostile powers. The Monroe Doctrine, which has of late seemed to be called in question, was by implication reasserted: "This hemisphere intends to remain master of its own house." The emancipated nations must bear the responsibility of freedom, not allow themselves to succumb to new forms of tyranny. And, much as the President's conscience revolts against that schism of the world in which both sides are "racing to alter that uncertain balance of terror that stays the hand of mankind's final war," sincerely as he proclaims his readiness to pursue by negotiation the development of the things that unite East and West instead of "belaboring" the things that divide, he yet declares in the plainest terms that while the arms race continues there is no course for America and her friends but to remain so invincibly strong that their strength need never be deployed.

It so happens that, by coincidence, the Central Committee of the Soviet Communist Party published on the same day a statement in which they too expressed their country's determination to go on working for peaceful coexistence between socialist and capitalist states, though they on their side added that Russia's defence potential must be kept up pending the realization of disarmament. In the mood of the President's address it is permissible to dwell rather on the echo of pacific intent than on the parallel defensive reservations, though there is something ominous in the further declaration that it is the international duty of the Russian people to give allout aid to people fighting for "liberation from imperialist and colonial oppression." According to a former American tradition, such words might have found a place in the Inaugural Address. Nothing like them is there: instead, Mr. Kennedy undertakes to help the underdeveloped countries to help themselves, in the freedom they already possess, to lift themselves out of their backward conditions. In so speaking he shows himself more aware than his Soviet rivals that he is living in the contemporary world.

There is little in the speech that bears upon domestic politics; no appeal to commercial self-interest; no promise of easier days; no reference to the unsettled conflicts of interest up and down the country which beset the election campaign. That does not convey any suggestion that Mr. Kennedy is unconscious of the practical urgencies or irresolute to grapple with them. Soon enough the new Administration will be required to descend into the mundane business of the market place. But it and the people it rules and serves will be the better equipped to meet their workaday cares for having taken an hour off to listen to the noble words—generous, vigorous, leaderlike, resolute, and devout. Great ceremonial occasions have their indispensable place in the life of a nation, and it is right that they should be used to uplift the hearts and call the people to service to the loftiest ideals. To such appeals to their native altruism Americans always respond. As what free people does not?

from The Kennedy Wit

by Bill Adler

During the 1960 Presidential campaign, there was only one occasion in which candidate Kennedy and candidate Nixon appeared at the same dinner. It occurred at the Alfred Smith Memorial Dinner at the Waldorf-Astoria Hotel in New York. These were Mr. Kennedy's opening remarks:

> I am glad to be here at this notable dinner once again, and I am glad that Mr. Nixon is here, also. Now that Cardinal Spellman has demonstrated the proper spirit, I assume that shortly I will be invited to a Quaker dinner honoring Herbert Hoover.
>
> Cardinal Spellman is the only man so widely respected in American politics that he could bring together, amicably, at the same banquet table, for the first time in this campaign, two political leaders

17

who are increasingly apprehensive about the November election, who have long eyed each other suspiciously, and who have disagreed so strongly, both publicly and privately—Vice President Nixon and Governor Rockefeller.

Mr. Nixon, like the rest of us, has had his troubles in this campaign. At one point even the *Wall Street Journal* was criticizing his tactics. That is like the *Osservatore Romano* criticizing the Pope.

One of the inspiring notes that was struck in the last debate was struck by the Vice President in his very moving warning to the candidates against the use of profanity by Presidents and ex-Presidents when they are on the stump. And I know after fourteen years in the Congress with the Vice President, that he was very sincere in his views about the use of profanity. But I am told that a prominent Republican said to him yesterday in Jacksonville, Florida, "Mr. Vice President, that was a damn fine speech." And the Vice President said, "I appreciate the compliment but not the language." And the Republican went on, "Yes sir, I liked it so much that I contributed a thousand dollars to your campaign." And Mr. Nixon replied, "The hell you say."

However, I would not want to give the impression that I am taking former President Truman's use of language lightly. I have sent him the following wire:

"Dear Mr. President: I have noted with interest your suggestion as to where those who vote for my opponent should go. While I understand and sympathize with your deep motivation, I think it is important that our side try to refrain from raising the religious issue."

Alfred Smith Memorial Dinner
New York City
October 19, 1960

John F. Kennedy: Man of the Sea,
by Tazewell Shepard, Jr.

Tazewell Shepard, Jr., was John Kennedy's Naval Aide during the President's entire term of office. The author, whose long Navy career includes the Navy Cross for "extraordinary heroism" in World War II, has written this work as "both a personal narrative and an unofficial history of [John F. Kennedy's] involvement with the Sea Services, as viewed from the White House." Reproduced here is Shepard's account of Kennedy's early association with the sea, out of which grew the abiding love and respect which were to shape his later life.

John F. Kennedy:
Man of the Sea

by Tazewell Shepard, Jr.
Captain, United States Navy

Chapter II
Child of the Sea

"I have been interested in the sea from my earliest boyhood. . . . My earliest recollections of the United States Navy go back to the days when as a small boy I used to be taken to the U.S.S. *Constitution* in Charlestown, Massachusetts. The sight of that historic frigate with all its tall spars and black guns stirred my imagination and made history come alive for me."

From the Introduction by John F. Kennedy to *Old Ironsides: The Story of the U.S.S. Constitution* by Thomas P. Horgan.

The President, Mrs. Kennedy has said, loved the sea "as a child, boy, and man." The summers of his childhood were spent beside it, playing in the grass on the restlessly shifting dunes of Cape

Cod, wading among the rushes that grew in the warm waters of Nantucket Sound in front of the big white house in Hyannis Port, digging at low tide the clams that lived exactly nine inches below the surface of the sand in the sheltered coves nearby. The austere and rugged beauty of the Cape caught the imagination of the young Kennedy. He especially loved Hyannis Port and continued to do so until the day he died. And, indeed, it is an exceedingly pleasant place. The comfortable house overlooks a long beach, a tennis court, and a green and spacious lawn for games. Boats of the summer people ride at anchor behind the breakwater that juts from the shore. The place couldn't have been better suited to a boy in love with the sea.

The child began to sail when he was still so small that his head barely showed above the gunwales of his sailboat. For the Kennedy family, sailing was the number one water sport, and it was several years before they owned a power boat. During Jack's childhood the family acquired a Wianno Junior, a sixteen-footer with a jib and a mainsail, which was named *Tenovus* because the family of Joseph Patrick Kennedy consisted of his wife, Rose, and eight children. After Edward was born in 1932 the family acquired a second Wianno Junior and named it *Onemore*. The family also acquired in those years a Star boat, *Flash II,* and a Wianno Senior, a centerboard sloop that Jack named *Victura* "because it means something about winning." So that their children could cope with the increasing number of sailboats, the Kennedys hired a sailing instructor named Eric, who insisted that they master the smallest boat before progressing to the larger ones. . . .

Summers found Jack Kennedy back at Hyannis Port, sailing on the Sound and becoming an increasingly accomplished swimmer and sailor. Eric had started all the children racing at an early age, when he was allowed to crew for them but was forbidden to touch the tiller. Eric was determined that his charges should win, however, and other children would sometimes claim a foul on the grounds that Eric had pushed on the tiller with his foot.

Regardless of Eric and long after he had left the family service,

Jack Kennedy was a consistent winner, probably because he was all business in any race. LeMoyne Billings, his Choate roommate, first learned the hardships of competitive sailing with the Kennedys when he raced from Hyannis Port to Nantucket in the *Victura*. Joe Kennedy was the skipper that day and Jack, Lem and another friend crewed. To the novice Billings, the stern discipline of the race, the lack of congenial talk, and five hours' shivering in the cold spray as they beat their way across the Sound did not seem much like fun.

Jack did not really like to crew; he preferred the greater challenge of command, where the competition was more keenly felt. His behavior in a race contrasted sharply with his usual witty and lighthearted attitude; racing was a serious matter, and a laggard performance by one of his crew did not pass without comment. Jack Kennedy loved best to race *Flash II*. Star boats were exceedingly tricky to sail because of their tall masts and narrow hulls, but *Flash II* was an especially fast boat and in it Jack Kennedy became an exceptional sailor, winning many races at the Wianno and Hyannis Port Yacht Clubs. Jack's victories in the *Flash II* were the cause of much good-natured bantering between him and his favorite opponent, Jock Kiley of Wianno. Kiley attributed Jack's success to the *Flash II,* which was the fastest Star boat around. The Kennedys maintained, of course, that it was just a question of skill. Finally, to settle the matter, Jack Kennedy and Jock Kiley switched boats for one race. *Flash II* with Jock Kiley at the helm jumped to an early lead. The boat was running true to form, when in the middle of the race both boats were becalmed. As a little breeze began to stir, Jack took a different tack, as he often did. In the trailing position, he was the first to feel the effect of the wind. He hugged the shore line where the breeze was freshest and began to close the distance, managing to pull ahead at the end and—just barely—to win the race. There was no more switching of boats after that. Jack Kennedy at the helm of *Flash II* went on to win the Nantucket Sound championship in 1936 and represented the Sound in the Atlantic Coast championships, where he won one of the four races but not the title. In the *Victura,* however, which was a Wianno Senior, the man to beat was Jack Dailey, from whom John F. Kennedy later bought his house in Hyannis Port.

When John Kennedy entered Harvard in 1936, he weighed 149 pounds, which was not much flesh for the six-foot-plus frame of an active nineteen-year-old. He won a place on the swimming team and pursued the sport with a passion. Just before he was to try out for a place on the squad for the Yale meet, he was in the infirmary at Harvard with influenza. Afraid that the hospital diet would leave him too weak to compete successfully, he persuaded his roommate to smuggle steaks and chocolate malted milkshakes to him. Fever notwithstanding, he sneaked out of the infirmary for the tryouts and swam with vigor, but he lost. . . .

Although the President's earliest memories of the Navy went back to his boyhood days in Massachusetts and his visits to "Old Ironsides," his first official connection with it began in October 1941, two months before the United States entered the war, when he was appointed an ensign in the United States Naval Reserve. For the Navy and for John F. Kennedy, it was a felicitous meeting.

He saw the coming of war in Europe and he was certain that the United States would soon be involved in it. In the meantime, he took a few courses at Stanford, where he also registered for the draft. The Selective Service law had just been passed, and at the end of October 1940 John F. Kennedy was number eighteen on the draft-board rolls in Palo Alto, California. His serial number was 2,748. He was among the first in the country to be called, but because of an injury to his back, incurred in football at Harvard, he was rejected. He wanted to get in the Navy, and he spent five months exercising his back in order to pass the Navy physical examination, which he did in September 1941. He reported for duty at the Navy Department in Washington the following month and began working on a daily news digest for Naval Intelligence. After the Japanese attacked Pearl Harbor, he applied for sea duty but was sent instead to Charleston, South Carolina, to work on plans to protect our defense plants against enemy bombing. The job was less than exciting. After several months in Charleston, he was sent to the Naval Reserve Officers' Training School at Northwestern University. While he was at Northwestern, Lieutenants John Bulkeley and John Harlee came by to seek recruits for PT (patrol torpedo) boats, and they interviewed Ensign Kennedy. Lieutenant Bulkeley had just received the Congressional Medal of Honor as commander of the PT boat that had rescued General Douglas MacArthur and his wife and young son from the Philippines when their capture by the Japanese had seemed certain. The PT boats had also sunk an auxiliary Japanese cruiser in Subic Bay and gained in luster and fame at a time when all else seemed tarnished with defeat. It was just the sort of duty that would appeal strongly to an active young man, and Jack Kennedy had all the qualifications: he was an athlete and a good swimmer, he had extensive experience in handling small craft, and he was intelligent. Accordingly, he applied, was accepted, and entered the Motor Torpedo Boat Squadron Training Center at Melville, Rhode Island, on October 1, 1942, for eight weeks of training at Narragansett Bay. He was also promoted from ensign to lieutenant, junior grade.

Lieutenant Kennedy completed the course in good shape—such good shape, in fact, that he was ordered to stay there to train others instead of being sent into action as he had hoped. Despite his vigorous objections, this assignment stuck. His instructors regarded him as a sincere and hard-working student with particular aptitude for boat handling—just the kind of man they needed to train others—and Lieutenant Kennedy was made commanding officer of *Motor Torpedo Boat 101,* a training boat in M.T.B. Squadron Four. Later that winter some of the boats, including Lieutenant Kennedy's, were ordered to Panama. When the young officer heard rumors that the boats would be stationed in Panama for some time, he grew desperate, for he feared that this would keep him out of the combat area, preventing his getting into action. Massachusetts Senator David I. Walsh was then Chairman of the Senate Naval Affairs Committee and easily the most powerful man in the Senate as far as the Navy was concerned. Through him Jack Kennedy achieved his goal. Senator Walsh wrote the Navy Department requesting that John F. Kennedy be assigned to a war zone. Shortly thereafter, instead of going to Panama, he was pulled out of Squadron Four and ordered to the Solomon Islands as an officer replacement. He shipped out of San Francisco on March 6, 1943, for the South Pacific, where the course of the war was beginning to change slowly, with the turning back of the long Japanese advance. For six months, Lieutenant Kennedy had been learning how to handle the speedy, brittle PT boats, and by late April he was playing a part in the Pacific War as commanding officer of *PT 109*. Before that came to pass, however, the young lieutenant had been tried in battle.

A few minutes after noon on April 7, 1943, *LST 449* was approaching Guadalcanal, en route from Espiritu Santo in the New Hebrides to Tulagi in the Solomons, with a group of Naval officers and various supplies. Lieutenant Kennedy, a passenger on the LST, was below, reading in his bunk, when suddenly an alert was flashed: the Japanese were launching their greatest attack since Pearl Harbor. One hundred and seventy-seven Japanese fighters and dive bombers were winging toward Guadalcanal from Rabaul in New Britain. Shortly after three that afternoon, a Japanese plane dived from the tropical sky and dropped a 500-pound bomb off the port bow of *LST 449*. The explosion was tremendous, knocking the ship into a twenty-degree list to starboard and lifting the stern entirely out of the water. When Lieutenant Kennedy stumbled to the deck, he saw nine enemy planes attacking the LST and its escort, the destroyer *Aaron Ward*. Bombs were falling all around the LST, but none scored a direct hit. The *Aaron Ward*, however, took a bomb in its engine room. With that torn apart and both firerooms flooded, the ship could not survive, and it sank three miles off Florida Island.

During the course of the battle, *LST 449* went to the rescue of a Japanese pilot who had parachuted from his burning plane. As was often the case, the pilot resisted capture. He slipped out of his life jacket and began to swim away. Only his right hand was visible; he kept his left underwater. The LST drew closer and threw him a line, but the Japanese pilot suddenly pulled his left hand from the water and fired two pistol shots at his rescuers. Instantly the pilot's shots were answered with a fusillade from the boat, and although his shots went wide of the mark, the returning fire did not. The flier threw up his arms and collapsed face forward into the sea. Thus Lieutenant Kennedy was initiated into war.

Many years after this battle, a letter arrived at the White House. What it said tells a great deal about John F. Kennedy and about war:

October 3rd, 1961

The President
The White House
Washington 25, D.C.

My dear Mr. President:

I have written you several times concerning this matter, but as yet, I haven't received a reply. I realize that you're a busy man, but I would appreciate hearing from you.

On April 7th, 1943 entering the bay at Guadalcanal, on the U.S.S. L.S.Q. 449, we were attacked by dive bombers. They sank the Arran Ward, a destroyer who was escorting us at the time.

We had a passenger on board by the name of Kennedy, who at that time was a junior grade officer.

At this particular time I was only sixteen years old and scared to death. Our ship had just been straddled by bombs and our gun tub was knee deep in water. I wanted to run but gained strength by the courage shown by Mr. Kennedy. This was either you or one of your brothers.

The ironic thing about this, was that we previously made fun and called you a sissy. This due to the fact that you were a rich man's son.

When you stood there and helped pass those shells to our gun tub, I gained a new perspective in life.

Being from the hills of South Carolina and a poor man's son, I thought everyone was against me. I later realized that it's what you make of yourself and not what you're born with. I sincerely think you did this for yourself. In my opinion you would have become President regardless.

I voted for you because of the courage I saw you display on April 7th, 1943. We need a man who has this type of courage. Please let me know if this person and you are the same.

Very respectfully yours,
Ted Guthrie

The President, who had said on another occasion that the events of that day remained one of his most vivid memories, answered Mr. Guthrie's letter on October 16. "I greatly appreciate the kind of things which you said in your letter," he wrote. "Those were perilous times for us all, but the times in which we now live are no less serious. Just as your wartime service was essential for victory in that conflict, so now is the unremitting support, understanding, and sacrifice of all our people, if we are to win our longterm struggle with Communism. Your pledge of that support is heart-warming to me." (We had no record at the White House of the previous correspondence Mr. Guthrie mentioned.)

Three weeks after the sinking of the *Aaron Ward,* Lieutenant Kennedy was putting together a crew for the PT boat to which he had been assigned. Its number was 109, and its story and that of its skipper, Lieutenant (junior grade) John Fitzgerald Kennedy, have become part of American folklore.

*Robert J. Donovan is a former Chief of the Washington Bureau
of the New York* Herald Tribune, *and former president
of the White House Correspondents' Association. His* PT 109 *was
a national success both as a book and later as an exciting
motion picture. The following chapter details the courageous
heroics of Lieutenant John F. Kennedy and his crew after their boat
had been sunk by a Japanese vessel and they had made their way
to one of the smaller Solomon Islands.*

from

PT 109

by Robert J. Donovan

Chapter IX

Plum Pudding Island is an oval of green with a band of white sand around it like a life preserver, holding it afloat in water that blends from sapphire, where it is deep, to the color of mint where it washes the coral reefs. The island is about a hundred yards long and seventy yards wide at the middle. A few palms rattle in the breeze, but the place is dominated by tall casuarina trees with long needles. The branches form an unbroken canopy over the sandy ground, carpeted with dead needles. Mats of decaying leaves from the naqi naqi trees give off a sweet odor. Coral fragments lie scattered under the white flowering kidokidoga bushes. On the beach are nautilus shells and kauri shells, which because of their cartographic markings are called by the natives, in their own tongue, map-of-the-village shells. Hermit crabs scurry about like tiny Atlases with the world in the form of their shells on their shoulders. Birds, however, are the chief inhabitants. White wading birds waddle along the shore. Frigate birds wheel overhead, and in the evening thousands of black gulls fly back from their searches of the sea to nest in the trees.

Near sundown on August 2 Kennedy and Pat McMahon half drifted up on the southeastern rim of Plum Pudding Island. Reaching the clean white sand seemed to be the ultimate limit of Kennedy's endurance. His aching jaws released the strap of McMahon's kapok, the end of which was pocked with Kennedy's tooth marks. For a time Kennedy lay panting, his feet in the water and his face on the sand. He would have been completely at the mercy of a single enemy soldier, but the island was deserted. His feet blistered, McMahon crawled out of the water on his knees and feebly helped Kennedy up. Swimming with the strap in his teeth Kennedy had swallowed quantities of salt water. When he stood he vomited until he fell again in exhaustion. McMahon's hands were swollen grotesquely. Every move he made tortured him. He knew, however, that as long as they were on the beach they would be exposed to view. He tried to drag Kennedy across the ten feet of sand, yet he could scarcely drag himself. He found he could crawl, and as Kennedy's strength returned he too crawled across the beach in stages with McMahon until the two of them collapsed under the bushes. After a while Kennedy was strong enough to sit up and watch the others as they neared the beach on their two-by-eight plank.

It took the eleven survivors fully four hours to swim the three and a half miles across Blackett Strait from the overturned hulk of *PT 109* to Plum Pudding Island. At the start they were all close together, but gradually Kennedy pulled ahead with McMahon in tow. Kennedy had swum the backstroke on the Harvard swimming team and was generally a strong swimmer. Towing McMahon he would move in spurts, swimming the breast stroke vigorously for ten or fifteen minutes and then pausing to rest.

"How far do we have to go now?" McMahon would inquire. Kennedy would assure him that they were making good progress.

"How do you feel, Mac?" he would ask, and McMahon would invariably reply, "I'm okay, Mr. Kennedy, how about you?"

Being a sensitive person, McMahon would have found the swim unbearable if he had realized that Kennedy was hauling him through three miles or so of water with a bad back. He was miserable enough without knowing it. Floating on his back with his burned hands trailing at his sides, McMahon could see little but the sky and the flattened cone of Kolombangara. He could not see the other men, though while all of them were still together, he could hear them puffing and splashing. He could not see Kennedy but he could feel the tugs forward with each stretch of Kennedy's shoulder muscles and could hear his labored breathing.

McMahon tried kicking now and then but he was extremely weary. The swim seemed endless, and he doubted that it would lead to salvation. He was hungry and thirsty and fearful that they would be attacked by sharks. The awareness that he could do nothing to save himself from the currents, the sharks or the enemy oppressed him. His fate, he well knew, was at the end of a strap in Kennedy's teeth. At that stage of his life it never occurred to him to pray. His sole reliance was on Kennedy's strength. . . .

Their worries increased as they neared the island. They couldn't be sure they were not swimming into a Japanese trap. As yet they did not know how Kennedy and McMahon had fared. With only a couple of hours of daylight left their hopes of rescue before another night were fading.

As they approached the island finally, Kennedy waved to them from under the trees. When they saw him they felt the relief of men who had come safely through the first round of danger. There was enough of a current flowing by the island to cause them some difficulty in bringing the plank in to the beach. The nastiest part was getting through the coral. Coral antlers jabbed their shins. Coral spurs cut their feet. Coral knobs bruised their thighs. At times the men slipped and cut themselves against beautiful abrasives. At other times the surge of water swept them involuntarily against a coral spike. When they finally dragged the plank up on the beach they looked every inch the part of nine shipwrecked sailors.

The men ducked under the trees near Kennedy and McMahon. There was little conversation. Pulling off their kapoks they all sat breathing heavily and staring across Blackett Strait at Kolombangara.

From his knob five or six miles directly across from them Lt. Evans was getting off his last message of the day. Having seen a flight of Allied planes and assuming they were looking for the survivors, he asked Ken:

WILL YOU PLEASE ADVISE RESULT OF SEARCH BY P FORTYS OVER GIZO

He received no answer that night. . . .

The three officers, Kennedy, Thom, and Ross, drew aside and conferred among themselves. The question was simply put by Kennedy. "How are we going to get out of here?" As they hashed over the problem, their theory of rescue boiled down almost exclusively to the idea of intercepting the PT boats in Ferguson Passage, difficult though it would be for a swimmer to attract their attention in the dark. Quietly Kennedy said that he would swim out into the passage that night and see what he could do with his revolver and the battle lantern. Ross thought this was absurd. Nevertheless Kennedy broke up the conference and told the other men his plans. To McMahon they seemed suicidal. Maguire urged Kennedy not to go. Kennedy ordered that a watch be kept on the beach during the night.

"If I find a boat," he said, "I'll flash the lantern twice. The password will be 'Roger'; the answer will be 'Willco.' "

He stripped down to his skivvies and strapped the rubber life belt around his waist. He wore shoes to protect his feet on the reefs. He hung the .38 from a lanyard around his neck. The revolver swung at his waist, the muzzle pointing down. He wrapped the battle lantern in kapok to float it.

Dusk had settled over Blackett Strait when he stepped into the water. He knew that the PT boats would be leaving Rendova Harbor at just about this time. What he did not know was that Warfield had dispatched the boats to the southern tip of Vella Lavella. They would be operating that night not in Ferguson Passage but in Gizo Strait miles to the north.

Through the trees the men watched Kennedy make his way from the shore to the reef. His departure depressed them and made them feel lonelier than ever. Under the direction of Ensign Thom a watch was set up on the beach. Two men would be on at a time, each for two hours. They would crouch on the beach with one man looking in one direction and the other looking the opposite way. Before long Kennedy was a speck disappearing in the water.

The line of the reef bends southward from Plum Pudding along the arm of the anchor, past Three Palm Islet to Leorava, the sandbar next to Naru. Thence, curving around into the outer arm of the anchor, it forms the upper boundary of Ferguson Passage. Kennedy's objective was to follow the reef until, near Leorava, it touches Ferguson Passage and then to leave it and swim out into the passage. The depth of the water along the way varies. Sometimes Kennedy could walk in water waist-deep or shoulder-deep. At other times the reef would fall away and he would have to swim until his foot touched it again. Now and then he would lie on the water and grasp coral outcroppings and pull himself along to spare his legs.

As darkness came on it was an eery trek. Often when he put his foot down something darted away in the water. He could tell that the reef was alive with creatures strange to him. Once he saw a huge fish and winced at the recollection of tales he had heard of the mutilation of men by sharks and barracuda. He flashed his light and thrashed his arms and legs. The fish swam away. The coral bottom was slippery. Occasionally Kennedy would slip against a fascicle of coral and cut his leg. At other times he would step unwittingly into a deep hole and go under.

After nightfall Blackett Strait was lonelier than a desert. As landmarks disappeared, Kennedy's sense of direction blurred. Phosphorescent particles blinked at him from the water. The only sounds were the whistle of the breeze and the lapping of the waves. Though the water was warm, Kennedy would often feel cold. The blotting out of points of reference by the darkness made it difficult for him to know how fast he was moving, how far he had gone, how far he had yet to go. His only map was the reef. When he would reach a break in it he would have to swim through deep water, hoping that in the blackness he could pick it up again on the other side of the gap.

Stumbling, slipping, swimming along, he finally reached Ferguson Passage after having traveled a distance of between two and three miles. Pausing to rest, he took off his shoes and tied them to his life belt. Then he floated off the reef and struck out for the center of Ferguson Passage, towing the battle lantern along in the kapok. With the .38 trailing below him in the water, the lanyard tugged at his neck as he swam.

Out in the Ferguson Passage he treaded water, looking toward the Solomon Sea and listening. It was his intention, when the PTs came through, to fire a recognition signal of three shots into the air, and flash his light at the nearest boat. The skipper would be the most surprised sailor in the South Pacific to find Jack Kennedy paddling around by himself in the middle of the Passage. This comforting dream never came true. Instead of PT boats, Kennedy saw only aerial flares beyond Gizo. Did this mean, he wondered, that the boats had gone up west of Gizo and were operating in Gizo Strait? As hours passed and none appeared he concluded that this must be the case.

Foggy and tired from his long hours in the water, he faced back toward the reefs and started swimming again. His limbs were lifeless. To lighten his burden he untied his shoes from the life belt and let them sink, though he knew what a slashing his feet would take when he got back on the reef. As he swam he wondered, however, whether he was ever going to get back. He moved on and on through the darkness but he never seemed to come to the reef. What was happening apparently was that a current through Ferguson Passage was carrying him sideways into Blackett Strait.

On the beach at Plum Pudding sometime after midnight, Harris, while standing watch, thought he saw a light on the water and was electrified by hope that Kennedy had attracted a PT boat and was coming to their rescue. In all probability Kennedy was miles away and the light was phosphorescence or the reflection of a star. It was not necessarily a product of Harris's imagination alone, however, because when he roused the other men some of them saw it too—or thought they did. Thom strode out into the water, calling, "Jack! Jack!" Some thought a voice answered. As the minutes passed the men began to ask themselves whether what they had seen and heard was real, or whether they had seen and heard what they had wanted. In any case time went by and Kennedy did not come. Faintly in the distance they could hear the pounding of the ocean on the reef beyond Naru. A shower drenched the island and the thirsty men licked the leaves. The rainwater tasted bitter. The leaves were coated with bird droppings. In days to come the survivors would give Plum Pudding, or Kasolo, Island a third name—Bird Island.

The discovery Kennedy made with his weary wits when daylight came was that in spite of a debilitating expenditure of energy he was still wallowing about at the confluence of Ferguson Passage and Blackett Strait. As dawn spread a pale light on the water, he was able to reorient himself. He had just enough strength left to make it back to Leorava. Crawling up on the sands of the tiny island with one tree and a patch of bushes, he collapsed in a deep slumber.

During the long dark hours that Kennedy had been swimming through the wastes of Ferguson Passage the Japanese had landed from two to three hundred more soldiers at Kequlavata Bay on the northern coast of Gizo Island. Some of the Gizo Scouts—the natives who were working for Lt. Evans—had a camp at Sepo Island, between Plum Pudding and the site of the landing, and they spotted the Japanese reinforcements. They knew that they must carry this intelligence to the coastwatcher. Early on the morning of Tuesday, August 3, therefore, Biuku Gasa and Eroni Kumana climbed into a dugout canoe and paddled down Blackett Strait on a mission as simple as any in the greatest of all wars could possibly be. Yet by a most extraordinary combination of circumstances this mission was destined to result in the saving of eleven officers and men of the United States Navy, one of whom would become the President of the United States within the lifetime of Biuku and Eroni.

Biuku and Eroni were ebony-colored Melanesians of slight stature but superb form. Eroni's face wore a stern, intense expression, while Biuku looked blithe and gentle. Both youths were around nineteen. Biuku had been born on Wana Wana Island and briefly had attended a Methodist mission school run by the Australians. Religion affected him. Although he understood little English, he could say, "In God we trust" with more meaning than the phrase carries on most lips. Eroni was born in Lale Village on Ganongga Island and also had received instructions before the war in a Methodist school. Like Biuku, he was loyal to the British and was willing to help Britain's allies when war burst into the Solomon Islands. . . .

As Biuku and Eroni were on their way to Kolombangara Kennedy woke up in broad daylight on Leorava. He felt cold and utterly ragged and still had a mile and three-quarters to swim to return to his men. He tried the battle lantern but it did not light, so he tossed it aside. His shoes having been discarded the night before, he waded back into the water in his skivvies with only his life belt and revolver. The coral cut his bare feet as he started back up the reef.

When Kennedy had failed to return at daybreak, the men grew discouraged. They feared he had drowned. Johnston was still in a haze, and McMahon's pain was awful. Periodically he soaked his burns in salt water. It stung like fire, but he felt he had to try something. Mauer, nagged by hunger and thirst, decided to try climbing a tall palm to get some coconuts. Part way up a large red ant bit his leg and he had to slide down and pull the ant off like a chigger. On the next attempt he made it to the top and twisted off three unripe coconuts, one of which, upon returning to the ground, he pried open with great effort with his knife. Parched from his exertions, he drank the bland, warm milk. Johnston asked if he could give McMahon a drink.

"Yeah, there are two of them," Mauer replied, pointing to the other coconuts on the ground.

When Mauer had finished drinking, Thom gave him a cutting look and asked sarcastically, "Have you had enough?" At that Mauer glanced down at the uncomplaining McMahon, and realizing that neither Johnston nor McMahon had the strength to open a coconut, he was covered with remorse. He could not understand what had happened to him, that he had not offered them a drink.

Harris had been concerned over the lack of oil for the pistols, and the coconuts gave him an idea. He knew there was oil in coconut meat, so he disassembled all the .45s and rubbed it on the moving parts. The experiment was not successful because the coconut meat has a gummy effect on steel.

As the men were lying in the bushes late in the morning idly watching the gulls fish in Blackett Strait, Maguire suddenly exclaimed, "Here's Kirksey!" When he looked again he saw that it was not Kirksey but Kennedy swimming in from the reef. Thom ordered the men to stay under cover while he and Ross went to meet him. Ross threw his arms around Kennedy, but Kennedy fell to the beach, retching. He looked skinny, bedraggled and exhausted. He had a beard. His hair was matted over his forehead. His circled eyes were bloodshot. His sun tan had taken on a yellowish hue. Thom and Ross dragged him across the sand into the bushes. When Maguire asked him how he felt, he grunted. After a while someone inquired whether he had seen any PT boats.

"No," he said. He muttered something about being unable to control his movement in the currents. He became very sick and then fell asleep. The others could think of nothing to do. They sat there as the afternoon wore on. Once Kennedy woke, looked up at Ross and said, "Barney, you try it tonight," and then went back to sleep.

Ross was convinced of the futility of swimming into Ferguson Passage, but he obeyed. Warned by Kennedy's ordeal, he set out at four o'clock in order to reach the passage while it was still daylight. The channel was just a marking on charts to him, and he wanted to get his bearings so he could surely find his way back. That was his chief worry. He was afraid he would get lost among the islands. He told the others not to expect him that night unless he succeeded in signaling a boat. If his mission should prove unfruitful, he would remain on one of the reef islands until daylight. He took Kennedy's Smith & Wesson on the lanyard. Also, to reduce the risk of attracting sharks by the white shade of his legs he donned khaki pants. As he slithered and swam along the reef, he was appalled to see some sand sharks three or four feet long. When he reached Ferguson Passage dusk was falling. Since it was still too early to go out, he swam about until his foot touched a coral head where he could stand in chest-deep water outside the reef. Depressed by the silence, he occupied himself by making mental note of the seascape to guide him back.

Soon it was not only lonely and silent but pitch-dark. Waves washed him off his pedestal, but he would grope his way back to wait until he guessed it was time for the PTs to approach. He dreaded the thought of swimming by himself into Ferguson Passage. He might not have done so had Kennedy not done it the night before. "If he can to it I can do it," kept running through Ross's mind.

He swam for about twenty minutes. He was not sure whether he had gone far enough, but he feared going too far. He treaded water and waited. He did not know, of course, though he began to suspect it, that the PT boats had again gone up to Vella Lavella. He hauled the .38 out of the water and pulled the trigger. The revolver fired, but the shot sounded flat against the broad surface of the water. At intervals he fired twice more. After a long wait he swam back to the reefs and was happy to discover that he had come in near an islet, which was Leorava, Kennedy's resting place the night before. He went ashore and promptly fell asleep.

On the morning of Wednesday, August 4, he awoke in the warm sun feeling fine. Boyishly, he felt like an emperor of his own realm. He wished the other men could see him and relished the thought of how he would tell people back home about his South Pacific adventures after the war. It was just like a magazine cartoon of a man shipwrecked with a blonde. Except there was no blonde, he reflected. Standing on the sand barefoot in rumpled pants, his hair unkempt and a black beard sprouting from ear to ear, he magnificently confirmed the judgment of the Princeton Class of '41 when it had voted him "Worst dressed."

By the time Ross started swimming back to Plum Pudding, Biuku and Eroni had reached Evans's hilltop with the news of the Japanese landing at Kequlavata Bay. Evans asked them if they had seen or heard of any PT boat survivors in the islands around Gizo. They said they had not, whereupon the coastwatcher at 10:25 A.M. messaged PWD:

NO SURVIVORS FOUND AT GIZO

As they left to return to Sepo Island, the native scouts were reminded by Evans that there might be PT survivors in the Gizo area. At 11:30 A.M. Evans received a message from KEN:

WHERE WAS HULK OF BURNING PT BOAT LAST SEEN X IF STILL FLOATING REQUEST COMPLETE DESTRUCTION X ALSO REQUEST INFORMATION IF ANY JAPS WERE ON OR NEAR FLOATING HULK

Because of other traffic Evans did not reply until 5:05 P.M. when he messaged KEN:

CANNOT CONFIRM OBJECT SEEN WAS FLOATING HULK OF PT X OBJECT LAST SEEN APPROX TWO MILES NE BAMBANGA DRIFTING SOUTH X NOT SEEN SINCE PM

SECOND X P FORTYS FLEW LOW OVER IT AND GIZO
SCOUTS HAVE NO KNOWLEDGE OBJECT OR ANY JAPS
THAT VICINITY

Ross had no trouble finding Plum Pudding. When he arrived
during the morning he discovered that Kennedy was feeling better,
although the second consecutive failure to make contact with the
PT boats had a dispiriting effect on everyone. Johnston, showing
signs of recovery, was now frightened but tried not to show it.
Sharkey was deeply discouraged. He was assailed by doubts as
to whether he had done the right thing by his family when he en-
listed. His brain seethed with questions about the merits of the
Navy, the aims of the United States in the war and his own
purposes in life.

With some quietly, with others openly, bitterness toward the
Navy was growing. "Where are the boats, anyway?" the men asked.
To the other officers, Thom and Ross, Kennedy betrayed his anger
at Lumberi for not making a greater effort at rescuing them. To
the men he did not show it. He never made light of their predicament, but now and then he would get off some remark about it
that would force a laugh. "What I would give for a can of grapefruit
juice!" he said to Zinser. Now that he had overcome his exhaustion
he kept purposely active. Without exhorting, he tried to give the
men the feeling that he was optimistic, that things would turn out
well.

Because of his burned arms Zinser would sometimes feel sorry
for himself—until he looked at McMahon. McMahon's pitiable
condition made everyone ashamed to complain. It broke Kennedy's
heart to look at him. Scabs forming over his burned eyelids made
it difficult for him to see. The palms of his hands were swollen to
a thickness of three inches. They were cracked like burned bacon,
and he could look deeply into his own flesh. His misery was redou-
bled because his burns were giving off a terrible stench, which he
knew was offensive to the others. He did not seek the help of God,
but in his pain he reflected that if he ever got home, he would

do things differently. Still, he was less sure than ever that he would see his home again.

The men were hungry. Mauer had last fed them late on Sunday afternoon, and it was now midday Wednesday. Partly because he wanted more coconuts for the crew to eat and partly because he wished to be nearer Ferguson Passage and the boats, Kennedy decided after Ross's return that they would move to Olasana Island, situated close to the bottom of the anchor shaft and only one island removed from the passage. Olasana lies a mile and three-quarters inward from Plum Pudding in a southwesterly direction.

Again the men dragged the plank into the water, and once more Kennedy took the strap of McMahon's kapok in his teeth and towed him. Kennedy was running the risk of leaving a safe island for one occupied by Japanese. They had not noticed any activity around Olasana, however, and they could see that it abounded in coconut palms. In their weariness the water felt good. Even McMahon was hopeful this time that at least they would reach their destination. It took a few hours to make the crossing. The current seemed stronger among the islands than it was in Blackett Strait. After Kennedy and McMahon were ashore on Olasana, the men had trouble working their way to a point on the beach within a few hundred yards of them. Nearing the island, Albert had left the plank and swum ahead. When he called back to the others they were furious because they feared his voice might be heard by Japanese.

The eleven survivors gathered in the trees behind the curved beach on the southeastern tip of Olasana, whence they could look straight across another half-mile of water to Naru Island bordering Ferguson Passage. They talked the situation over, this time in hushed voices, and asked themselves whether they should explore Olasana. It appeared about twice the size of Plum Pudding. "Why go looking for trouble?" someone inquired. This logic was accepted, and none of them ever saw more than a corner of the island about fifty yards square. They gathered coconuts but after eating them, some of the men, Kennedy and McMahon among them, became ill. Partly as a joke Ross ate a live snail, which tasted terrible. One of the men caught a land crab, but no one was hungry enough yet for that. He tossed it back on the beach. Zinser tried digging for fresh water, only to split his fingernails on coral. He worried that the Navy would report him missing in action and subject his wife to the anguish of fearing he was dead.

By dark all were weary from the long swim. For the first time in three nights no one went into Ferguson Passage. For the first time in three nights the boats came through Ferguson Passage and were on station in Blackett Strait by 9:30 P.M. . . .

Kennedy went down the beach a short distance from the men and beckoned Thom and Ross. "What do we do now?" he asked them. They had swum into Ferguson Passage at night. They had changed islands. They had posted lookouts for boats or planes. Was there anything more they could do to help themselves? Kennedy was restless. He did not want just to sit in the shade all day. To keep up the morale of the men, if for no other reason, they must do something that at least would give the appearance of striving for a way out. He looked across to Naru Island. It was only a half-mile swim. The far side of it faced Ferguson Passage, but what of that? No Allied vessels would be operating there in daylight. Kennedy had no scheme into which a visit to Naru fitted. But more or less on the spur of the moment he said to Ross, "Let's take a look at this one anyway."

At practically the same time Biuku Gasa and Eroni Kumana got into their canoe on Wana Wana Island to cross Ferguson Passage and head back up Blackett Strait to return to their station on Sepo Island. After making their report to Evans the previous day, they had left Kolombangara and passed the night at the native village of Raramana on Wana Wana. Now, after taking leave of friends there, they started paddling on the most direct route to Sepo, which would take them close by Naru, opposite Ferguson Passage from Raramana.

Compared with their earlier swims Kennedy and Ross found the crossing to Naru easy. It was shortly after noon when they crawled up on the white beach of the narrow, four-hundred-yard-long island at the base of the anchor. Black butterflies flitted about the heavy foliage. The ground was pockmarked with crab holes. Thunder from the reefs echoed through the tall palms and casuarina. Kennedy and Ross crept cautiously toward the Ferguson Passage side. Of all the islands in the group, this would be the most logical one for the Japanese to man because of its outlook on the passage. Moreover, just before Kennedy and Ross had left Olasana they had seen some New Zealand P-40s make a strafing attack on the Ferguson Passage side of Naru. They feared that the target of this attack might have been a Japanese outpost and so they moved very carefully through the bushes on Naru.

The distance across the island is short, and they reached the Ferguson shore quickly. Looking out from the fringe of trees, they could see Rendova Peak in its full outline. It was still nearly thirty-eight miles away, but across open water and low islands it looked exasperatingly accessible. Certainly there must be some way, they thought, for eleven men to get to it.

They started along the beach to their left. On the reef about a mile or so from the shore they spied the wreckage of a small Japanese vessel, which is probably what the P-40s had been strafing, and a short distance farther they came upon what appeared to be cargo washed ashore. With the greedy curiosity of a couple of beachcombers they ripped open a rope-bound crate, which to their delight contained hard candy in the shape of tear drops. For a few moments it was like Christmas morning on Naru Island. Briefly, the troubles of war and shipwreck faded. Sucking on hard candy, the two moved on in higher spirits, and Kennedy said that after their exploration was over they would take the candy back to the men. This manna alone would have made the trip to Naru a smashing success. Ross wondered how two swimmers were going to get a crate of candy across a half-mile of salt water.

They had barely gone another twenty yards when they found a dugout canoe that someone had left in the bushes with a large tin of rainwater. Without knowing it they had come upon one of the caches the native scouts had scattered among the islands. They sat down by the canoe and sparingly drank some of the water.

As Biuku and Eroni neared the Naru side of Ferguson Passage they too noticed the Japanese wreckage on the reef and decided to see whether it contained anything of interest. Reaching the reef they anchored their canoe a short distance away and climbed into the hulk. While Kennedy and Ross were quenching their thirst with a can of rainwater, Biuku and Eroni were satisfying their own curiosity by poking through the gear, charts and utensils of one sort and another that were strewn about the deck. The only booty that interested them was Japanese rifles. They each took one and stepped back down on the reef just as Kennedy and Ross re-emerged on the beach.

Across a mile of water both pairs of men instantly spotted one another. Eroni and Biuku, terrified that the two on the beach were Japanese stranded by the wreck and might shoot them, splashed along the roof and tumbled into the canoe, Eroni in his haste dropping his rifle. Kennedy and Ross, thoroughly alarmed that they had been sighted at last by the Japanese, dived into the bushes. Who were those men? Had they actually seen Kennedy and Ross? Would the Japanese garrison soon be alerted to search the islands? The trip to Naru that had begun so auspiciously was now filled with dismaying possibilities.

Eroni and Biuku paddled furiously away from Naru toward Blackett Strait. Once they had rounded the sandbar of Leorava they were headed in the direction of Sepo Island and away from the eleven Americans. If they had just kept going, they would have reached their headquarters several miles away and perhaps forgotten all about the two figures on Naru. At that moment their only interest in the two men was to get away from them and their only mission was to return to Sepo. Had they kept going as they were for just a short distance farther, eleven men on a small Pacific island might never have been heard from again. But at the last moment, they veered clear off their course and headed for Olasana Island.

Biuku had become thirsty from the exertions of their sprint from Naru and persuaded Eroni, who was paddling in the stern, to turn in to Olasana for coconuts. So they took a sharp turn to the left and paddled for the closest point of Olasana, which was the beach at the southeastern tip of the island.

When Kennedy had departed for Naru with Ross he left Thom in charge of the other men. All nine were resting in the bushes behind the beach waiting to hear what the skipper had found on the other island when almost simultaneously three or four of them saw the canoe approaching with the two natives. The men were stunned. After all they had been through, was capture to be their fate? Capture and perhaps torture and finally death? Everyone started to whisper at once. These strangers looked like boys. Perhaps they were scouts for the Japanese on Gizo. If not, there was still no basis on which the men could safely assume that the natives would be friendly. The Americans still had time to fire on them or to slip deeper into the jungle. They probably could avoid detection even now. Biuku and Eroni might get their drink and be off again without seeing them.

At this point, however, Thom made a fateful decision. In a gamble that involved all their lives he stood up and walked out on the beach in sight of the strangers, who were now within thirty feet of the shore.

The sudden apparition of the tattered and bedraggled giant with the blond beard astounded Biuku and Eroni. Nothing in their experience had prepared them for the sight of such a man. In sheer fright they back-paddled as fast as their arms would go. Thom ran out to the water's edge and beckoned them with his right hand. "Come, come," he called. Fearful again that they had happened upon Japanese, the natives turned their canoe about, thereby bringing a crisis for the Americans. Self-preservation itself might demand that these men be stopped, with bullets if necessary, from going off and possibly reporting their presence to the Japanese. But if the bullets failed to halt them, the very act of firing would arouse their hostility and might provoke them into reporting them.

And, either way, the flight of the natives might end the only chance of rescue.

"Navy, Navy," Thom pleaded. "Americans, Americans." Eroni and Biuku were a sufficiently safe distance away to pause and listen. The trouble was they didn't understand what Thom was saying. Sensing their doubts, he said, "Me no Jap" and rolled up his right sleeve and showed them his white skin. Biuku and Eroni still remained dubious. Thom tried another tack. "Me know Johnny Kari," he said. John Kari was the headman at Wana Wana, who was known to the PT men through his visits to Lumberi as a native scout. Still no response from Biuku and Eroni. Then Thom got an inspiration.

"White star," he said, pointing to the sky. "White star." At last Biuku and Eroni understood. Now they were reassured that Thom and the men who were emerging from the trees behind him were allies. Slowly the two natives paddled ashore. The insigne on American aircraft was a white star set in a white bar. The coastwatchers instructed their native scouts that airmen who crashed or parachuted from planes bearing the white star were to be treated well and brought with all possible haste to a coastwatcher's station.

The survivors helped Biuku and Eroni drag their canoe across the narrow beach and conceal it between two palm trees. When they all gathered together in the bushes, the meeting was awkward, because the natives were uncomprehending and shy, and few of the sailors really trusted them. Little by little the Americans learned to communicate with Biuku and Eroni. When they understood what the two were trying to say they were shocked. The natives pointed to Naru and indicated the island contained Japanese—meaning Kennedy and Ross. This filled the men with grim doubts as to whether they would ever see the two officers again. . . .

After a long and apprehensive wait in the bushes, Kennedy and Ross, seeing no further signs of the two men in the canoe, resumed their exploration of Naru without making any more discoveries. With the canoe that they had found in the bushes earlier

Kennedy now felt much more mobile. He decided to venture out into Ferguson Passage that night, believing he would have a better chance of intercepting the PT boats in a canoe than if he were swimming.

While it was still light, however, he wanted to take the candy and water back to the men on Olasana. He tore a slat off the crate for a paddle and suggested that Ross wait for him. When he left, Ross fell asleep on the beach.

Thom's men also had a canoe now, and they had a long discussion of how they might use it to save themselves. Thom finally decided that he and Starkey and one of the natives would try paddling all the way to Rendova Harbor to organize a rescue party. It would be a long, hard paddle, but the trip seemed perfectly feasible otherwise. When the idea was conveyed to the natives they shook their heads in dissent. Thom was insistent, however, and the natives did not put up any resistance. Biuku got into the canoe with Thom and Starkey. It was not until they were outside the protection of Naru that the two Americans realized that a heavy sea was running in Ferguson Passage. The waves rocked the canoe dangerously. Biuku protested and wanted to return to Olasana. Thom and Starkey nevertheless pushed stubbornly on until they too could see that the canoe would capsize long before they ever reached Rendova. Reluctantly they returned to the island.

At about the same time Kennedy arrived from Naru, to the inexpressible relief of the men. He was surprised to find the two natives, not realizing, of course, that these were the same two men he and Ross had seen. And he was at a loss to know why Biuku and Eroni should be so certain that there were Japanese on Naru.

The only thing Japanese he had found on the island was wreckage and candy, and he proceeded to distribute the candy among the nine ravenous men. He also took the tin of water out of the canoe and left it with them before rejoining Ross for the paddle into Ferguson Passage. His hopes would have been high indeed if he could have known that Warfield had ordered the boats through Ferguson Passage that night to patrol in Blackett Strait.

From the outset, however, Kennedy and Ross were in difficulty.

The waves that had turned Thom, Starkey and Biuku back were now smashing over the reef, and the wind was rising. Ross thought it foolhardy to pit a canoe against such weather at night and said so. "Barney, I think we ought to go on," Kennedy replied. Once beyond the reef the sea ran too high for them. With slats for paddles they could not keep the bow into the waves. Water splashed over the gunwales. In the stern Ross tried bailing with a coconut shell, but more water poured into the canoe. As they were shouting to each other about turning back a five-foot wave capsized them. They splashed about in the dark until they got a grip on the overturned canoe.

"Sorry I got you out here, Barney," Kennedy called.

"This would be a great time to say I told you so, but I won't," Ross answered.

Spun around by the foaming water, they found their sense of direction confused, but they could see the dark outline of an island, and worked toward it; the reef, when they returned to it, blocked their progress at first, as they swung back and forth in the waves that piled up against the barrier. The swings grew higher and higher until finally Kennedy, Ross, the canoe and tons of water were hurled across the reef in the air. From the deep channel they crashed painfully into shallows jagged with coral. Kennedy lost Ross in the blackness. "Barney," he called. No answer came back. Pierced by the thought that he was responsible for Ross's predicament, he yelled at the top of his lungs, "Barney!" "I'm over here," Ross answered. The canoe had survived the crash intact, and the slats were floating near them.

(Dugout canoes are thick, sturdy craft, hewn with an adze from the trunk of a single tree, preferably a goliti tree. When the natives set out to make a canoe they put a coconut on a stick nearby, and traditionally the job is supposed to be finished when the coconut sprouts in two months.)

On lacerated feet Kennedy and Ross made their way ashore on Naru, sometimes holding the slats down to walk on over rough coral. When they reached the beach they lay down in exhaustion and slept. . . .

from The Kennedy Wit

by Bill Adler

On a trip to the West Coast, President Kennedy was asked by a little boy, "Mr. President, how did you become a war hero?"

It was absolutely involuntary. They sank my boat.

Washington is a city of Southern efficiency and Northern charm.
Quoted by William Manchester in Portrait of a President

A Thousand Days, by A. M. Schlesinger, Jr.

Arthur M. Schlesinger, Jr., was Special Assistant to President Kennedy, his position bringing him into close and prolonged contact with the President and his associates. Already an accomplished historian, Schlesinger was thus afforded a precious insider's look at the process of executive decision-making in action.

Midway through October, 1962, U.S. Intelligence sources had amassed conclusive evidence of a rapid Soviet buildup of medium-range nuclear missiles in Cuba. President Kennedy's long-deliberated decision was to order a naval quarantine or blockade of the island. In the following pages Schlesinger records the incredibly tense and dramatic events of the crisis that ensued, and the remarkable poise and responsibility of the President who guided his nation through to safety.

from

A Thousand Days

by Arthur M. Schlesinger, Jr.

Chapter XXXI
The Great Turning

Within the Kremlin, so far as one could tell, there was confusion. The Russians had obviously anticipated neither the quick discovery of the bases nor the quick imposition of the quarantine. Their diplomats across the world were displaying all the symptoms of improvisation, as if they had been told nothing of the placement of the missiles and had received no instructions what to say about them. Ambassador Anatoly Dobrynin himself gave every indication of ignorance and confusion. As late as Wednesday a message to Robert Kennedy from Mikoyan repeated that Cuba was receiving no weapons capable of reaching the United States. Georgi Bolshakov, who transmitted the message and who had seemed to us all an honest fellow, assured the Attorney General that he believed this himself.

In New York on Wednesday Stevenson was continuing the battle for the American resolution in the United Nations. John J. McCloy, whom the President had summoned from a business trip to Germany to give the U.N. presentation a bipartisan flavor, was adding his weight to our councils. Then U Thant made an unexpected intervention, proposing that the Soviet Union suspend its arms shipments and the United States its quarantine to allow an interlude for negotiations. Khrushchev accepted this thought at once and with evident pleasure; but from our viewpoint, it equated aggression and response, said nothing about the missiles already in Cuba, permitted work to go forward on the sites and contained no provisions for verification. Still, while New York and Washington agreed in rejecting U Thant's proposal, the manner of the rejection caused debate. Some in Washington appeared to fear any response which would "entrap" us in a negotiating process; it seemed to us in New York that they must be bent to clear the road for an air strike and an invasion. Stevenson and McCloy strongly recommended a response to U Thant which would keep the diplomatic option alive.

1. WAITING

On Wednesday night, as we were pondering these matters at the U.S. Mission in New York, I received a telephone call from Averell Harriman. Speaking with unusual urgency, he said that Khrushchev was desperately signaling a desire to cooperate in moving toward a peaceful solution. Harriman set forth the evidence: Khrushchev's suggestion of a summit meeting in his reply to Bertrand Russell; his well-publicized call on the American singer Jerome Hines the night before after a Moscow concert; his amiable if menacing talk with an American businessman, William Knox of Westinghouse International; the indications that afternoon that the nearest Soviet ships were slowing down and changing course. This was not the behavior of a man who wanted war, Harriman said; it was the behavior of a man who was begging our help to get off the hook. Khrushchev had sent up similar signals after the U-2 affair in

1960, Harriman continued, and Eisenhower had made the mistake of ignoring him; we must not repeat that error now. "If we do nothing but get tougher and tougher, we will force him into counter-measures. The first incident on the high seas will engage Soviet prestige and infinitely reduce the chance of a peaceful solution." The key to it all, he went on, lay in Khrushchev's two remarks during the recent visit of Robert Frost and Stewart Udall to the Soviet Union—his observation to Frost that the democracies were too liberal to fight* and his observation to Udall that the Soviet Union must be treated as an equal. "We must give him an out," Harriman said again. "If we do this shrewdly, we can downgrade the tough group in the Soviet Union which persuaded him to do this. But if we deny him an out, then we will escalate this business into a nuclear war."

These words from the most experienced of all American diplomats seemed utterly convincing to me. I asked him whether he had made these points at the State Department. He said, "They never ask my advice about anything outside the Far East. I haven't been in on this at all." Accordingly I sent Harriman's views along to the President. Kennedy called him the next morning, and I imagine that Harriman's counsel may have strengthened his own inclination to go farther along the diplomatic road. At any rate, his reply to U Thant on Thursday, while stressing that the "threat was created by the secret introduction of offensive weapons into Cuba, and the answer lies in the removal of such weapons," authorized Stevenson to continue discussions on whether satisfactory arrangements could be assured to this end. This was a second vital decision. . . .

There were other portents, and to them our intelligence com-

---

* Actually Khrushchev never made this remark; it was Frost's interpretation in a New York press conference after a transatlantic flight of an anecdote cited by Khrushchev from Gorki's memoirs where Tolstoy described himself as "too weak and too infirm to do it but still having the desire." Khrushchev was applying this to nations: the United States as old, the Soviet Union as young. Frost, yielding to prejudices of his own, transposed it into a remark about liberals. See Franklin D. Reeve, *Robert Frost in Russia* (Boston, 1964), 115, 120-123.

munity turned like Roman haruspices to the entrails of a sacrificial victim. For the first time all that long week Soviet diplomatic behavior across the world was beginning to conform to a pattern; this indicated that Moscow had at least sent out instructions. . . .

But despite these gestures the situation was still loaded with danger. Work continued on the sites; unless this was stopped, the missiles would soon be on their launching pads. Nor had the Soviet Union yet admitted the presence of nuclear missiles in Cuba at all. On Thursday evening at the UN Stevenson returned to the debate in the Security Council. He crisply dismissed the communist argument that the United States had created the threat to the peace: "This is the first time that I have ever heard it said that the crime is not the burglary, but the discovery of the burglar." As for those who thought the quarantine too extreme a remedy: "Were we to do nothing until the knife was sharpened? Were we to stand idly by until it was at our throats?. . .The course we have chosen seems to me perfectly graduated to meet the character of the threat."

Zorin made a cocky but evasive reply. Now Stevenson took the floor again. Ironically regretting that he lacked his opponent's "talent for obfuscation, for distortion, for confusing language and for double-talk," saying sternly, "those weapons must be taken out of Cuba," he turned on the Russian with magnificent scorn:

Do you, Ambassador Zorin, deny that the USSR has placed and is placing medium and intermediate-range missiles and sites in Cuba? Don't wait for the translation. Yes or no?

Zorin muttered something about not being in an American courtroom. Stevenson, cold and controlled:

You are in the courtroom of world opinion. You have denied they exist, and I want to know if I understood you correctly. I am prepared to wait for my answer until hell freezes over. And I am also prepared to present the evidence in this room—now!

It was a moment of tremendous excitement. At Stevenson's order, aerial photographs were wheeled on easels into the council chamber, showing the transformation of San Cristóbal from a peaceful country spot into a grim nuclear installation. Other pictures added further evidence. Zorin wanly denied the authenticity of the display. Stevenson wondered savagely why the Soviet Union did not test its denial by permitting a United Nations team to visit the sites.

Then, in a moment, Stevenson concluded: "We know the facts and so do you, sir, and we are ready to talk about them. Our job here is not to score debating points. Our job, Mr. Zorin, is to save the peace. And if you are ready to try, we are."

The Stevenson speech dealt a final blow to the Soviet case before world opinion.

2. THE LETTERS

But on Friday work still continued on the sites. In Florida the American army prepared for invasion. In Washington the pressure to attack mounted as each passing moment brought the installations closer to operation. And in Moscow there must have been deep anxiety and bitter debate.

Khrushchev had now evidently abandoned the effort to bring in more nuclear weapons. But some of the men around him—perhaps the Soviet military—were apparently determined to make the missiles already there operational as speedily as possible. Indeed, this group may have gone along with the pacific gestures of Wednesday and Thursday precisely to gain time to complete the sites. In any case, once the missiles were on launching pads, Moscow might be able to drive a better bargain.

Khrushchev himself, however, seems to have reached a different position. He knew by now that his essential gamble had failed. Whatever he had once supposed, the Americans were ready to fight. His own options were narrowing before his eyes. If he were to strike at Berlin, he would only expose the Soviet Union to nuclear attack. If he did not compose matters quickly in the Caribbean, then the great army, massing so visibly in Florida, would descend on Cuba; "on the morning of [Saturday] October 27," as he told the Supreme Soviet in December, "we received information that the invasion would be carried out in the next two or three days." If an invasion began, Khrushchev either would have to use the rockets he liked to boast about so jovially or else desert the only communist state in the Americas and condemn himself as a *fainéant* before the international communist movement. It was now beyond the realm of tactical maneuver: all roads led to the abyss. The Soviet Chairman and the American President were the two men in the world with ultimate responsibility for nuclear war. Like Kennedy, Khrushchev had peered into the abyss before. "Immediate action," as he later told the Supreme Soviet, "was needed to prevent an invasion of Cuba and to preserve peace."

At one-thirty on Friday John Scali, the State Department correspondent for the American Broadcasting Company, received a call from Aleksander Fomin, a counselor at the Soviet Embassy, insisting on an immediate meeting. Scali, who had lunched occasionally with Fomin in the past, joined him at once at the Occidental Restaurant. The usually phlegmatic Russian, now haggard and alarmed, said, "War seems about to break out. Something must be done to save the situation." Scali replied that they should have thought of that before they put the missiles in Cuba. The Russian sat in silence for a moment. Then he said, "There might be a way out. What would you think of a proposition whereby we would promise to remove our missiles under United Nations inspection, where Mr. Khrushchev would promise never to introduce such offensive weapons into Cuba again? Would the President of the United States be willing to promise publicly not to invade Cuba?" When Scali said he did not know, Fomin begged him to find out immediately from his State Department friends. Then, reaching for a pencil, he wrote down his home telephone number: "If I'm not at the Embassy, call me here. This is of vital importance."

Scali carried the proposal to Roger Hilsman, and Hilsman carried it to Rusk. After discussion with the Executive Committee, Rusk asked Scali to tell the Russian that we saw "real possibilities" for a negotiation but they must understand that time was short—no more than forty-eight hours. At seven-thirty Friday evening Scali passed this word along. They met this time in the coffee shop of the Statler Hilton. Fomin, once he had satisfied himself about the authenticity of Scali's message and after a brief attempt to introduce the idea of UN inspection of Florida as well as Cuba, rose and, in his haste to get the word back, tossed down a five-dollar bill for a thirty-cent check and speeded off without waiting for the change.

Two hours later a long letter from Khrushchev to the President began to come in by cable. The Soviet leader started by insisting that the weapons shipments were complete and that their purpose was defensive. Then he declared his profound longing for peace; let us, he said with evident emotion, not permit this situation to get out of hand. The enforcement of the quarantine would only drive the Soviet Union to take necessary measures of its own. But if the United States would give assurances that it would recall its fleet from the quarantine, this would immediately change everything. Then the necessity for the Soviet presence in Cuba would disappear. The crisis, Khrushchev said, was like a rope with a knot in the middle: the more each side pulled, the more the knot would tighten, until finally it could only be severed by a sword. But if each side slackened the rope, the knot could be untied.

The letter was not, as subsequently described, hysterical. Though it pulsated with a passion to avoid nuclear war and gave the impression of having been written in deep emotion, why not? In general it displayed an entirely rational understanding of the implications of the crisis. Together with the Scali proposal, it promised light at the end of the cave. And in New York on Friday we heard that Zorin had advanced the same proposal to U Thant, and that the Cubans at the UN were beginning to hint to unaligned delegates that the bases might be dismantled and removed if the United States would guarantee the territorial integrity of Cuba. The President probably had his first good night's sleep for ten days; certainly the rest of us did.

But when the Executive Committee assembled on Saturday morning, prospects suddenly darkened. The Moscow radio began to broadcast a new Khrushchev letter containing, to everyone's consternation, an entirely different proposition from the one transmitted through Scali and embodied in Khrushchev's letter of the night before. The Soviet Union now said it would remove its missiles from Cuba and offer a non-aggression pledge to Turkey if the United States would remove its missiles from Turkey and offer a non-aggression pledge to Cuba. The notion of trading the Cuban and Turkish bases had been much discussed in England; Walter Lippmann and others had urged it in the United States. But Kennedy regarded the idea as unacceptable, and the swap was promptly rejected. The proposal was perplexing enough; but, far more alarming, word soon came that a U-2 was missing over Cuba, presumably shot down by the Russians (piloted, indeed, by the brave South Carolinian, Major Rudolf Anderson, Jr., who had first photographed the installations on October 14). American planes had thus far flown over the missile sites without interference. The Soviet action now, some felt, could only mean one thing: that the confrontation was entering its military phase. The bases were becoming operational, and the Russians were evidently determined to use force to maintain them. We had no choice, it was argued, but a military response; and our tactical analysis had already shown that strikes at the bases would be little use without further supporting action, so, once the process began, it could hardly stop short of invasion.

The President declined to be stampeded. Obviously, if they shot down U-2s, we would have to react—but not necessarily at once. Again he insisted that the Russians be given time to consider what they were doing before action and counteraction became irrevocable. There remained the Khrushchev letters, and the Executive Committee turned to them again with bafflement and something close to despair. . . .

Later that afternoon the Executive Committee met again. Robert Kennedy now came up with a thought of breathtaking sim-

plicity and ingenuity: why not ignore the second Khrushchev message and reply to the first? Forget Saturday and concentrate on
Friday? This suggestion may, indeed, have been more relevant
than anyone could have known. For, as Henry Pachter has argued,*
the so-called second letter, from internal evidence, appears to have
been initiated as the immediate follow-on of Khrushchev's reply
to U Thant; it began with a reference to Kennedy's reply to U Thant
on Thursday and took no note of events on Friday. Moreover, its
institutional tone suggested that it was written in the Foreign Office. Might it not have been drafted in Moscow on Thursday and
Friday with an eye on Saturday morning release in New York?
Then the so-called first letter, which reflected the movement of
events well beyond the U Thant proposal and which was clearly
written by Khrushchev himself, may well have been composed
late Friday night (Moscow time) and transmitted immediately to
Kennedy while the "second" letter was deep in the bureaucratic
pipelines. Knowing heads of state and foreign office bureaucrats,
one could take anything as possible.

At any rate, on October 27, Kennedy now wrote Khrushchev,
"I have read your letter of October 26th with great care and welcomed the statement of your desire to seek a prompt solution." As
soon as work stopped on the missile bases and the offensive weapons were rendered inoperable under UN supervision, Kennedy
continued, he would be ready to negotiate a settlement along the
lines Khrushchev had proposed. Then, in a sentence expressive
of his desire to retrieve something out of the crisis, he added: "If
your letter signifies that you are prepared to discuss a detente affecting NATO and the Warsaw Pact, we are quite prepared to consider
with our allies any useful proposals."

And so the message shot inscrutably into the night. Robert
Kennedy carried a copy that evening to the Soviet Ambassador,
saying grimly that, unless we received assurances in twenty-four

---

* In his brilliant essay on the missile crisis, *Collision Course* (New York, 1963),
67-68.

hours, the United States would take military action by Tuesday. No one knew which Khrushchev letter superseded the other; no one knew whether Khrushchev was still in power. "We all agreed in the end," Robert Kennedy said afterward, "that if the Russians were ready to go to nuclear war over Cuba, they were ready to go to nuclear war, and that was that. So we might as well have the showdown then as six months later." Saturday night was almost the blackest of all. Unless Khrushchev came through in a few hours, the meeting of the Executive Committee on Sunday might well face the most terrible decisions.

Sunday, October 28, was a shining autumn day. At nine in the morning Khrushchev's answer began to come in. By the fifth sentence it was clear that he had thrown in his hand. Work would stop on the sites; the arms "which you described as offensive" would be crated and returned to the Soviet Union; negotiations would start at the UN. Then, no doubt to placate Castro, Khrushchev asked the United States to discontinue flights over Cuba. (As for the errant U-2 which had strayed over Russia the day before, he warned that "an intruding American plane could be easily taken for a nuclear bomber, which might push us to a fatal step.") Looking ahead, he said, "We should like to continue the exchange of views on the prohibition of atomic and thermonuclear weapons, general disarmament, and other problems relating to the relaxation of international tension."

It was all over, and barely in time. If word had not come that Sunday, if work had continued on the bases, the United States would have had no real choice but to take action against Cuba the next week. No one could discern what lay darkly beyond an air strike or invasion, what measures and countermeasures, actions and reactions, might have driven the hapless world to the ghastly consummation. The President saw more penetratingly into the mists and terrors of the future than anyone else. A few weeks later he said, "If we had invaded Cuba . . . I am sure the Soviets would have acted. They would have to just as we would have to. I think there are certain compulsions on any major power." The compulsions opened up the appalling world of inexorability. The trick was to cut the chain in time. When Kennedy received Khrushchev's reply that golden October morning, he showed profound relief. Later he said, "This is the night to go to the theater, like Abraham Lincoln." . . .

6. AFTERMATH

. . . .The ultimate impact of the missile crisis was wider than Cuba, wider even than the Western Hemisphere. To the whole world it displayed the ripening of an American leadership unsurpassed in the responsible management of power. From the moment of challenge the American President never had a doubt about the need for a hard response. But throughout the crisis he coolly and exactly measured the level of force necessary to deal with the level of threat. Defining a clear and limited objective, he moved with mathematical precision to accomplish it. At every stage he gave his adversary time for reflection and reappraisal, taking care not to force him into "spasm" reactions or to cut off his retreat.

Moreover, despite strong pressure to take action repugnant to our national traditions, he always linked his use of power to the ideals of the country and to the necessities of the world which would have to go on after the conflict. By his own composure, clarity and control, he held the country behind him. It was almost as if he had begun to reshape the nation in his own image, for the American people, so many of whom had been in a frenzy about air-raid shelters a year before, so many of whom still longed for total solutions, went through the Cuba week without panic or hysteria, with few cries of "better red than dead" and fewer demands (until the crisis was safely over) for "total victory."

In a toast to Chancellor Adenauer two weeks afterward, Kennedy spoke of "an important turning point, possibly, in the history of the relations between East and West." He meant, as he later explained, that this was the first time that the United States and the Soviet Union had ever directly challenged each other with nuclear weapons as the issue; and in his sense of "a climactic period" he associated the missile crisis with the growing conflict between China and Russia and the Chinese attack on India. All this, he said, was "bound to have its effects, even though they can't be fully perceived now."

He did not exaggerate the significance of the Cuban victory in itself. He recognized that he had enjoyed advantages in this specific contest—because Cuba did not lie within the reach of Soviet conventional power or within the scope of Soviet vital interests, and because the Russians knew they could not sustain this particular course of deceit and irresponsibility before the world. These conditions might not be present the next time. But he hoped that he had made to Khrushchev in the Atlantic in October 1962 the point he had failed to make sixteen months before in Vienna— that neither side dare tamper carelessly with the delicate and complex equilibrium of world power. "If we suffer a major defeat, if they suffer a major defeat," he mused with newspapermen at Palm Beach on the last day of the year, "it may change the balance of power. . . . It also increases possibly the chance of war."

This was why, when Khrushchev backed down, Kennedy refrained from calling the American victory a victory or the Russian rout a rout. "Every setback," Kennedy said later, "has the seeds of its own reprisal, if the country is powerful enough." So the German invasion of Czechoslovakia in the winter of 1939 had led to the British guarantee of Poland. "We tried to make their setback in Cuba not the kind that would bring about an increase in hostility but perhaps provide for an easing of relations."

It was this combination of toughness and restraint, of will, nerve, and wisdom, so brilliantly controlled, so matchlessly calibrated, that dazzled the world. Before the missile crisis people might have feared that we would use our power extravagantly or not use it at all. But the thirteen days gave the world—even the Soviet Union—a sense of American determination and responsibility in the use of power which, if sustained, might indeed become a turning point in the history of the relations between East and West.

The Soviet Arms Buildup in Cuba

Radio and Television Report
to the American People

October 22, 1962

[Delivered from the President's Office
at 7 P.M.]

Good evening, my fellow citizens:

This Government, as promised, has maintained the closest surveillance of the Soviet military buildup on the island of Cuba. Within the past week, unmistakable evidence has established the fact that a series of offensive missile sites is now in preparation on that imprisoned island. The purpose of these bases can be none other than to provide a nuclear strike capability against the Western Hemisphere.

Upon receiving the first preliminary hard information of this nature last Tuesday morning at 9 A.M., I directed that our surveillance be stepped up. And having now confirmed and completed our evaluation of the evidence and our decision on a course of action, this Government feels obliged to report this new crisis to you in fullest detail.

The characteristics of these new missile sites indicate two distinct types of installations. Several of them include medium range ballistic missiles, capable of carrying a nuclear warhead for a distance of more than 1,000 nautical miles. Each of these missiles, in short, is capable of striking Washington, D.C., the Panama Canal, Cape Canaveral, Mexico City, or any other city in the southeastern part of the United States, in Central America, or in the Caribbean area.

Additional sites not yet completed appear to be designed for intermediate range ballistic missiles—capable of traveling more than twice as far—and thus capable of striking most of the major cities in the Western Hemisphere, ranging as far north as Hudson Bay, Canada, and as far south as Lima, Peru. In addition, jet bombers, capable of carrying nuclear weapons, are now being uncrated and assembled in Cuba, while the necessary air bases are being prepared.

This urgent transformation of Cuba into an important strategic base—by the presence of these large, long range, and clearly offensive weapons of sudden mass destruction—constitutes an explicit threat to the peace and security of all the Americas, in flagrant and deliberate defiance of the Rio Pact of 1947, the traditions of this nation and hemisphere, the joint resolution of the 87th Congress, the Charter of the United Nations, and my own public warnings to the Soviets on September 4 and 13. This action also contradicts the repeated assurances of Soviet spokesmen, both publicly and privately delivered, that the arms buildup in Cuba would retain its original defensive character, and that the Soviet Union had no need or desire to station strategic missiles on the territory of any other nation.

The size of this undertaking makes clear that it has been planned for some months. Yet only last month, after I had made clear the distinction between any introduction of ground-to-ground missiles and the existence of defensive antiaircraft missiles, the Soviet Government publicly stated on September 11 that, and I quote, "the armaments and military equipment sent to Cuba are designed exclusively for defensive purposes," that, and I quote the Soviet Government, "there is no need for the Soviet Government to shift its weapons . . . for a retaliatory blow to any other country, for instance Cuba," and that, and I quote their government, "the Soviet Union has such powerful rockets to carry these nuclear warheads that there is no need to search for sites for them beyond the boundaries of the Soviet Union." That statement was false.

Only last Thursday, as evidence of this rapid offensive buildup was already in my hand, Soviet Foreign Minister Gromyko told me in my office that he was instructed to make it clear once again, as he said his government had already done, that Soviet assistance to Cuba, and I quote, "pursued solely the purpose of contributing to the defense capabilities of Cuba," that, and I quote him, "training by Soviet specialists of Cuban nationals in handling defensive armaments was by no means offensive, and if it were otherwise," Mr. Gromyko went on, "the Soviet Government would never become involved in rendering such assistance." That statement also was false.

Neither the United States of America nor the world community of nations can tolerate deliberate deception and offensive threats on the part of any nation, large or small. We no longer live in a world where only the actual firing of weapons represents a sufficient challenge to a nation's security to constitute maximum peril. Nuclear weapons are so destructive, and ballistic missiles are so swift, that any substantially increased possibility of their use or any sudden change in their deployment may well be regarded as a definite threat to peace.

For many years, both the Soviet Union and the United States, recognizing this fact, have deployed strategic nuclear weapons with great care, never upsetting the precarious status quo which ensured that these weapons would not be used in the absence of some vital challenge. Our own strategic missiles have never been transferred to the territory of any other nation under a cloak of secrecy and deception; and our history—unlike that of the Soviets since the end of World War II—demonstrates that we have no desire to dominate or conquer any other nation or impose our system upon its people. Nevertheless, American citizens have become adjusted to living daily on the bull's-eye of Soviet missiles located inside the U.S.S.R. or in submarines.

In that sense, missiles in Cuba add to an already clear and present danger—although it should be noted the nations of Latin America have never previously been subjected to a potential nuclear threat.

But this secret, swift, and extraordinary buildup of Communist missiles—in an area well known to have a special and historical relationship to the United States and the nations of the Western Hemisphere, in violation of Soviet assurances, and in defiance of American and hemispheric policy—this sudden, clandestine decision to station strategic weapons for the first time outside of Soviet soil—is a deliberately provocative and unjustified change in the status quo which cannot be accepted by this country, if our courage and our commitments are ever to be trusted again by either friend or foe.

The 1930's taught us a clear lesson: aggressive conduct, if allowed to go unchecked and unchallenged, ultimately leads to war. We are also true to our word. Our unswerving objective, therefore, must be to prevent the use of these missiles against this or any other country, and to secure their withdrawal or elimination from the Western Hemisphere.

Our policy has been one of patience and restraint, as befits a peaceful and powerful nation which leads a worldwide alliance. We have been determined not to be diverted from our central concerns by mere irritants and fanatics. But now further action is required—and it is under way; and these actions may only be the beginning. We will not prematurely or unnecessarily risk the costs of worldwide nuclear war in which even the fruits of victory would be ashes in our mouth—but neither will we shrink from that risk at any time it must be faced.

Acting, therefore, in the defense of our own security, and in that of the entire Western Hemisphere, and under the authority entrusted to me by the Constitution as endorsed by the resolution of the Congress, I have directed that the following *initial* steps be taken immediately:

First: To halt this offensive buildup, a strict quarantine on all offensive military equipment under shipment to Cuba is being initiated. All ships of any kind bound for Cuba from whatever nation or port will, if found to contain cargoes of offensive weapons, be turned back. This quarantine will be extended, if needed, to other types of cargo and carriers. We are not at this time, however, denying the necessities of life as the Soviets attempted to do in their Berlin blockade of 1948.

Second: I have directed the continued and increased close surveillance of Cuba and its military buildup. The foreign ministers of the OAS, in their communique of October 6, rejected secrecy on such matters in this hemisphere. Should these offensive military preparations continue, thus increasing the threat to the hemisphere, further action will be justified. I have directed the Armed Forces to prepare for any eventualities; and I trust that in the interest of both the Cuban people and the Soviet technicians at the sites, the hazards to all concerned of continuing this threat will be recognized.

Third: It shall be the policy of this Nation to regard any nuclear missile launched from Cuba against any nation in the Western Hemisphere as an attack by the Soviet Union on the United States, requiring a full retaliatory response upon the Soviet Union.

Fourth: As a necessary military precaution, I have reinforced our base at Guantanamo, evacuated today the dependents of our personnel there, and ordered additional military units to be on a standby alert basis.

Fifth: We are calling tonight for an immediate meeting of the Organ of Consultation under the Organization of American States, to consider this threat to hemispheric security and to invoke Articles 6 and 8 of the Rio Treaty in support of all necessary action. The United Nations Charter allows for regional security arrangements—and the nations of this hemisphere decided long ago against the military presence of outside powers. Our other allies around the world have also been alerted.

Sixth: Under the Charter of the United Nations, we are asking tonight that an emergency meeting of the Security Council be convoked without delay to take action against this latest Soviet threat to world peace. Our resolution will call for the prompt dismantling and withdrawal of all offensive weapons in Cuba, under the supervision of U.N. observers, before the quarantine can be lifted.

Seventh and finally: I call upon Chairman Khrushchev to halt and eliminate this clandestine, reckless, and provocative threat to world peace and to stable relations between our two nations. I call upon him further to abandon this course of world domination, and to join in an historic effort to end the perilous arms race and to transform the history of man. He has an opportunity now to move the world back from the abyss of destruction—by returning to his government's own words that it had no need to station missiles outside its own territory, and withdrawing these weapons from Cuba—by refraining from any action which will widen or deepen the present crisis—and then by participating in a search for peaceful and permanent solutions.

This Nation is prepared to present its case against the Soviet threat to peace, and our own proposals for a peaceful world, at any time and in any forum—in the OAS, in the United Nations, or in any other meeting that could be useful—without limiting our freedom of action. We have in the past made strenuous efforts to limit the spread of nuclear weapons. We have proposed the elimination of all arms and military bases in a fair and effective disarmament treaty. We are prepared to discuss new proposals for the removal of tensions on both sides—including the possibilities of a genuinely independent Cuba, free to determine its own destiny. We have no wish to war with the Soviet Union—for we are a peaceful people who desire to live in peace with all other peoples.

But it is difficult to settle or even discuss these problems in an atmosphere of intimidation. That is why this latest Soviet threat

—or any other threat which is made either independently or in response to our actions this week—must and will be met with determination. Any hostile move anywhere in the world against the safety and freedom of peoples to whom we are committed—including in particular the brave people of West Berlin—will be met by whatever action is needed.

Finally, I want to say a few words to the captive people of Cuba, to whom this speech is being directly carried by special radio facilities. I speak to you as a friend, as one who knows of your deep attachment to your fatherland, as one who shares your aspirations for liberty and justice for all. And I have watched with deep sorrow how your nationalist revolution was betrayed—and how your fatherland fell under foreign domination. Now your leaders are no longer Cuban leaders inspired by Cuban ideals. They are puppets and agents of an international conspiracy which has turned Cuba against your friends and neighbors in the Americas—and turned it into the first Latin American country to become a target for nuclear war—the first Latin American country to have these weapons on its soil.

These new weapons are not in your interest. They contribute nothing to your peace and well-being. They can only undermine it. But this country has no wish to cause you to suffer or to impose any system upon you. We know that your lives and land are being used as pawns by those who deny your freedom.

Many times in the past, the Cuban people have risen to throw out tyrants who destroyed their liberty. And I have no doubt that most Cubans today look forward to the time when they will be truly free—free from foreign domination, free to choose their own leaders, free to select their own system, free to own their own land, free to speak and write and worship without fear or degradation. And then shall Cuba be welcomed back to the society of free nations and to the associations of this hemisphere.

My fellow citizens: let no one doubt that this is a difficult and dangerous effort on which we have set out. No one can foresee precisely what course it will take or what costs or casualties will

be incurred. Many months of sacrifice and self-discipline lie ahead
—months in which both our patience and our will will be tested
—months in which many threats and denunciations will keep us
aware of our dangers. But the greatest danger of all would be to
do nothing.

The path we have chosen for the present is full of hazards, as
all paths are—but it is the one most consistent with our character
and courage as a nation and our commitments around the world.
The cost of freedom is always high—but Americans have always
paid it. And one path we shall never choose, and that is the path of
surrender or submission.

Our goal is not the victory of might, but the vindication of
right—not peace at the expense of freedom, but both peace *and*
freedom, here in this hemisphere, and, we hope, around the world.
God willing, that goal will be achieved.

Thank you and good night.

Khrushchev Misjudged Spirit of U.S., Character of Kennedy

*Never Understood American Policy
on Bay of Pigs—Acted on Assumption
That President Was Weak.*

The New York Times

by James Reston

It is now fairly obvious that Nikita Khrushchev, in planning Soviet policy in Cuba, misjudged the spirit of America and the character of President Kennedy.

This is a common European habit, reaching from George III of Great Britain to Adolf Hitler, and in Khrushchev's case it is easy to explain.

He never understood the President's policy on the invasion of the Bay of Pigs in Cuba in April 1961. As he has said in numerous private conversations, he would have understood a hands-off policy by the United States in Cuba at that time or an effective strike that would have brought Castro down, as Moscow moved on Hungary or the Baltic states, but he could not understand how the United States could get involved in that exercise without seeing it through to a successful conclusion.

Accordingly, he has been acting ever since on the assumption that President Kennedy was weak. He tried to bully him when they met in Vienna in June 1961. He has been saying to almost every Western visitor to the Soviet Union since then that the United States would not fight, even in the defense of its vital interest, and he has obviously based his policy in Cuba on this assumption.

The dispatch of missiles to Cuba that could strike most of the continental United States was the result. This was the test of Khrushchev's assumption, and the feeling of well informed diplomats here is that he had two objectives in mind.

First, if his assumption were right that Mr. Kennedy would not regard this as a cause of war, the Soviet Union would have demonstrated that it could defy the United States in the Western Hemisphere and establish an effective base in the Caribbean for the exploitation of Latin America's social and political instability.

Second, even if this assumption proved wrong and Mr. Kennedy reacted with an invasion of Cuba, the Soviet Union could go to the United Nations, argue that Moscow was doing no more in Cuba than the United States was doing in Turkey and Italy, and use the crisis to arrange a deal for the destruction of bases in Cuba, Turkey and maybe even Berlin.

President Kennedy, however, has not fallen in with this plan. He has neither ignored the Soviet missiles nor plunged into Cuba to destroy them. He has, instead, chosen a middle course of blockading Cuba, and the first reaction to this has been better than was generally expected.

The other members of the Organization of American States have approved the President's action. The North Atlantic allies have been impressed by the evidence of Soviet missiles in Cuba and have gone along. Even the Soviet Union's response has been polemical but milder than was expected. And the political leaders of both parties in the United States have backed the President.

Incidentally, this approval of the political leaders at home was not easy. When President Kennedy called them to the White House this week, their complaint was not that the President was going too far, but that he was not going far enough.

Even in the middle of what has been a fairly savage congressional election campaign, the complaint in the private meeting at the White House was that the President was proposing to stop Communist ships in a long blockade instead of launching an attack at once against the missile sites in Cuba.

It is unfortunate that the Russians, who do not understand the limitations of political debate in America, could not have a transcript of that meeting in the White House between the President and his political allies and opponents.

For, as usual, when outside pressures are applied, something happens here. Politicians who have been condemning the President suddenly begin to support him. Allies, who regret our lack of style and proportion, overcome their doubts in the crisis.

This is the point Khrushchev has missed. Since the end of the last war, Washington and Moscow have accommodated themselves, however unwillingly, to a series of compromises in Korea, Vietnam, Germany, the Formosa Straits, the Middle East, Eastern Europe, and Middle Africa.

Rather than force the issues in these places to the point of war, both sides have accepted the principle of truce. Thus, the United States did not press for a decisive victory at the Yalu in Korea, but settled for an accommodation at the Thirty-Eighth Parallel. Similarly, the Soviet Union tolerated Nato bases in Turkey, and the United States did not intervene even in the melancholy revolution in Hungary.

But in Cuba, Khrushchev has forced the issue. He has sought to tip the balance of power, and the instinct of this country has forced the President to oppose him.

The question now is whether Khrushchev will persist in this dangerous course, or whether he will pause and re-examine the assumptions of his policy.

from The Kennedy Wit

by Bill Adler

President Kennedy was asked to comment on the press treatment of his administration thus far:

Well, I'm reading more and enjoying it less.

May 9, 1962

Question: Mr. President, you have said, and I think more than once, that heads of government should not go to the summit to negotiate agreements but only to approve agreements negotiated at a lower level. Now it's being said and written that you're going to eat those words and go to a summit without any agreement at a lower level. Has your position changed, sir?

President Kennedy: Well, I'm going to have a dinner for all the people who've written it and we'll see who eats what.

March 7, 1962

Kennedy Without Tears, by Tom Wicker

Tom Wicker is the White House reporter for the New York Times, *and covered most of the principal events of the Kennedy Administration. His* Kennedy Without Tears, *the first section of which follows, is his attempt to portray John F. Kennedy as he really was, before the American penchant for myth-making totally beclouded the truth. For, as Arthur Krock notes in his foreword, "the truth explains what the gathering myth obscures—that Kennedy was endearingly and admirably human."*

from

Kennedy Without Tears
The Man Beneath the Myth

By Tom Wicker

Shortly after President Kennedy was shot, the following inscription appeared on a plaque in one of the private bedrooms of the White House:

> *In this room Abraham Lincoln slept during his occupancy of the White House as President of the United States, March 4, 1861–April 13, 1865.*
>
> *In this room lived John Fitzgerald Kennedy with his wife Jacqueline Kennedy during the two years, ten months, and two days he was President of the United States, January 20, 1961–November 22, 1963.*

Before many years pass, that deliberate linkage of two Presidents, that notice chiseled upon history by Jacqueline Kennedy, may seem as inevitable as the Washington Monument. Already, airports and spaceports and river bridges and a cultural center have been named for her husband. Six months after his death books about him, even phonograph records, were at floodtime; many more were being written or planned. *Profiles in Courage* seemed destined to be a perennial best-seller. It was almost as if he had never called businessmen sons of bitches, sent troops to Ole Miss, the refugees to the Bay of Pigs, or kicked the budget sky-high.

Thus, John F. Kennedy is certain to take his place in American lore as one of those sure-sell heroes out of whose face or words or monuments a souvenir dealer can turn a steady buck. There he soon will stand, perhaps in our lifetime—cold stone or heartless bronze, immortal as Jefferson, revered as Lincoln, bloodless as Washington. One can imagine the graven words on his pedestal:

Ask not what your country can do for you. Ask what you can do for your country.

What his country inevitably will do for John Kennedy seems a curious fate for the vitality and intensity, the wry and derisive style of the man who was the Thirty-fifth President of the United States. His wit surely would have seared the notion of John F. Kennedy International Airport, much less Cape Kennedy—for this was the man who once told the great-great-grandson of John Adams, "It is a pleasure to live in your family's old house, and we hope that you will come by and see us."

One suspects the Eternal Flame might have embarrassed him as much as the Navy did that brilliant Pacific day when the strutting admirals put him literally on a flagdraped pedestal aboard an aircraft carrier while the band played "Hail to the Chief" and the jets screamed overhead on taxpayers' money; one of his favorite quips, after all, was that he had gone from Lieutenant J.G. to Commander-in-Chief without any qualifications at all.

I can almost hear that amused Boston voice inquiring, as he once did after reading a favorable Gallup Poll, where all those peo-

ple who admired him so much were when Congress turned down
his school bill in 1961. Staring from Valhalla at himself cast in stone
in the middle of some downtown Washington traffic circle, he might
well whisper to earthly passersby what he once told 12,000 Democrats in Harrisburg, Pennsylvania:

"I will introduce myself. I am Teddy Kennedy's brother."

And when children rise reverently in some future Fourth of
July pageant to recite the chiastic prose of the Kennedy Inaugural
Address—the stirring words that raced so many pulses among
that "new generation of Americans" to which he appealed—some
may recall instead the same rhythm, the same rhetoric, but different words and a more subtle imagination at work:

"We observe tonight not a celebration of freedom but a victory
of party, for we have sworn to pay off the same party debt our
forebears ran up nearly a year and three months ago. Our deficit
will not be paid off in the next hundred days, nor will it be paid
off in the first one thousand days, nor in the life of this Administration. Nor, perhaps, even in our lifetime on this planet. But let us
begin—remembering that generosity is not a sign of weakness
and that ambassadors are always subject to Senate confirmation.
For if the Democratic party cannot be helped by the many who are
poor, it cannot be saved by the few who are rich. So let us begin."

In much the same vein were Kennedy's remarks at a dinner
of the White House Correspondents Association in April, 1962.
The organization had just raised its dinner ticket prices—and
Kennedy had just forced the steel companies to rescind a somewhat more important price increase.

"The sudden and arbitrary action of the officers of this association," he said to the correspondents, "in increasing the price of
dinner tickets by $2.50 over last year constitutes a wholly unjus-
tifiable defiance of the public interest. . . . In this serious hour in
our nation's history, when newsmen are awakened in the middle
of the night to be given a front page story, when expense accounts
are being scrutinized by Congress, when correspondents are required to leave their families for long and lonely weekends at Palm

Beach, the American people will find it hard to accept this ruthless decision made by a tiny handful of executives. . . ."

Now a politician who could laugh at parodies of his noblest speech and his moment of most spectacular success—let alone make the parodies himself, as Kennedy did the foregoing—obviously was something more intricate in life than the mere sum of the virtues symbolized by the Eternal Flame: purity, steadfastness, warmth, light. A President delighted by the political caricature of Everett McKinley Dirksen, but impatient with the solemn earnestness of Chester Bowles, obviously had a wide streak of Honey Fitz down his spine; yet that same President, confronted with an adulatory mob of hundreds of thousands of cheering Europeans, could not bring himself to respond with more than a halfhearted jab of the arm from the chest—something like a halfback straight-arming a tackler, apologetically. But let us not imagine that he was merely unemotional; those who saw it are not likely to forget his flashing anger when a reporter asked him at a news conference about two "security risks" in the State Department.

In the early days of Kennedy's New Frontier (there was bound to be something roguish about a man who could bring the Ivy Leaguers—and himself—to Washington with a slogan that evoked echoes of the Wild West, which appalled most of them), I thought Richard Nixon was perhaps a more interesting *man* than Kennedy. I thought Nixon was, as Conrad wrote of Lord Jim, "one of us." But Kennedy, I thought then, for all his charm and fire and eloquence, was a straightforward political man, who listened to his own rhetoric, contrived his "image" in the comforting faith that a statesman had to get elected before he could do anyone any good, and believed sincerely that his causes were not only right but actually offered solutions to human problems. I thought Kennedy had what someone has called the perfect mentality—that of a football coach, combining the will to win with the belief that the game is important.

Now, I think that what Kennedy really had of that mentality was a rather peculiar form of the will to win. He wanted power, all right, but something more; "This ability," he once said, "to do things well, and to do them with precision and with modesty, attracts us all." It was a theme to which he often returned—the pursuit of excellence. And as the probability of his political canonization turns toward certainty, and the sad calcification of his humanity into stone and bronze continues, there is not much football coach in the man Kennedy who recalls himself to me most strongly.

If that human Kennedy still seems to me to have been altogether too detached and too controlled to have been, as were Nixon and Lord Jim, "one of us," with all those fascinating hesitancies and inadequacies, and torments out of which literature is made, nevertheless he *was* a man "of few days and full of trouble," and for all I know he may even have played "such fantastic tricks before high heaven as to make the angels weep." But the statues will tell us nothing of that. . . .

As Arthur Schlesinger has written, "the Eisenhower administration . . . bequeathed the new President a force of Cuban exiles
under American training in Guatemala, a committee of Cuban
politicians under American control in Florida and a plan to employ
the exiles in an invasion of their homeland and to install the committee on Cuban soil as the provisional government of a free Cuba."

On April 17, 1961, that invasion took place in the Zapata
Swamp at Cuba's Bay of Pigs. It was—militarily, politically, and
diplomatically—a total disaster. The Cuban exile forces were
overwhelmed by Fidel Castro's troops in less than three days; at
home, President Kennedy was roundly criticized by responsible
politicians and statesmen as well as the more militant dissent
groups; and abroad, full propaganda advantage was taken of what
seemed to many to be a clear violation of our avowed policy of
non-intervention in the internal affairs of independent nations.

President Kennedy immediately and publicly accepted full
blame for the fiasco, but privately he asked, "How could everybody
involved have thought such a plan would succeed?" Yet the question of the distribution of the blame for the Bay of Pigs is
secondary. It happened, and the reactions of the press which follow
indicate just how great a mistake it was. The incident is a dramatic
starting point for the study of John F. Kennedy's foreign policy,
for it provides a background against which the later triumphs are
raised into high relief.

Lessons of Failure

Cuban Fiasco Focuses Attention on
The Weaknesses of U.S. Policy

by Arthur Krock

Washington, April 22—Some of the damages to the interests of the United States in the world, and especially in the Western Hemisphere, that were inflicted by the failure of the attempt by anti-Communist Cubans to secure a firm foothold on the island are already apparent. Obvious as these are, because the expedition was encouraged and to an extent aided by the United States Government, they carry the potential of developing others more serious.

But there are beneficial aspects to the disaster. President Kennedy not only has expressed a determination to recoup the losses by a "re-examination and re-orientation of [the] forces, tactics, and institutions" which showed themselves so vulnerable to such grevious errors. He also, as in the prompt recall to duty of Gen. Maxwell Taylor and its purpose, has indicated the capacity to detect and to remove the points of vulnerability in Government policy, act and judgment.

As exposed by the episode in Cuba, the principal weak points are:

(1) The invocation of half-measures to effect paramount policies, one of which in the words of the Monroe Doctrine which has been absorbed in the Pan-American treaty structure, is that: "Any attempt on the part of these powers [outside the Western Hemisphere] to extend their system to any part of this Hemisphere" shall be considered as "dangerous" to its "peace and safety." And when this policy became official throughout the Western Hemisphere, "attempt" was specified as covering internal subversion, as well as outside aggressions, in behalf of an external system.

By signing this protocol, however, the United States committed itself to repel such "attempts" only in concert with its hemispheric neighbors. And when it became apparent that Premier Castro was turning Cuba into a member of the Communist police-state system which is dominated by Soviet Russia, several other signers of the protocol refused to concede its violation in Cuba, or were afraid to challenge it because of Communist influence within their boundaries, or fell victim to the Moscow-Havana propaganda that "American imperialists" sought to deny the Latin peoples the right of independence of the United States and to government of their free choice.

The result was that the United States, enchained by its commitment and not yet persuaded that hemispheric and its own security were sufficiently endangered in Cuba to risk the consequences in "world opinion" of acting unilaterally, dallied with half-measures in equipping the anti-Castro Cubans for their dangerous venture. And when Washington reluctantly faced the fact that the danger incarnated by Castro was real and great and Castro had not yet been powerfully rearmed by Communist nations, President Eisenhower was naturally unwilling to commit the incoming Mr. Kennedy to a forceful unilateral program.

While President Kennedy was getting his bearings, the program of limited assistance to the anti-Castro rebels continued. But this would not have culminated in the recent invasion and its failure if it had not been for Washington's Vulnerable Point No. 2.

(2) This was the conclusion by official intelligence authorities, and accepted on his own final responsibility by the President, that the timing of the proposed expedition was favorable and that the United States should equip and transport the rebels it had trained. The conclusion was founded on reports from United States intelligence agents in Cuba and elsewhere that the rebels would be joined by considerable segments of Castro's army and the Cuban people. The intelligence estimate proved to have been gravely in error.

(3) This point of vulnerability is principally the product of the State Department, the White House and the United States Information Agency. Although it was well-known in all these quarters that the landing force numbered only a few hundred Cubans, they permitted publications to go unchallenged for days that "thousands" were involved. One report widely published in Washington put the number at "five thousand." The consequence was, of course, that Castro's repulse of a minor invading force, undertaken primarily to land supplies and make contact with the rebels in the Cuban mountains, was successfully represented to the world audience as a victory of major proportions. Although the U.S.I.A. expanded its Latin-American broadcasting programs by many hours, it failed to correct the widespread overestimate of the numbers involved, stressing only that they were "volunteers."

(4) This point of weakness is created by the influence over United States policy granted to the Afro-Asian bloc and India in the United Nations by the Eisenhower Administration and extended by President Kennedy. This influence was reflected in President Kennedy's assurance to Castro, Soviet Russia and the world

at large that the United States "under no conditions" would make a military intervention in Cuba.

(5) This is a long enduring point of vulnerability: the dual function of the Central Intelligence Agency that authorizes it to collect information on which high policy is based, and also operate on the policy. This in turn has led to ideological policy-making by the C.I.A. such as was represented by the exclusion of some radical anti-Castro groups able to render vital assistance.

Perhaps he cannot eliminate another weakness any more successfully than his predecessors: the "leaks" to reporters by Government officials to portray their principals as those who were right all along and others all wrong in instances of failure like the Cuban episode. The fact, however, is that all top level members of the Administration supported both the concept and the timing of the landing.

Despite all this the President in his speech to the editors freed our policy from its greatest weakness—the restraint from protecting the hemisphere and this nation imposed by the treaty commitment never to intervene unilaterally.

Kennedy's First Defeat: How Will He React?

By James Reston

The New York Times
Sunday, April 23, 1961

Washington, April 22—For the first time in his life, John F. Kennedy has taken a public licking. He has faced illness and even death in his 43 years, but defeat is something new to him, and Cuba was a clumsy and humiliating one, which makes it worse.

How he reacts to it may very well be more important than how he got into it. For this will be a critical test of the character and perspective of the new President, and of the brilliant young men he has brought to the pinnacle of American political power.

The temptation to lash back and "get even" in Cuba is very great. The politician's natural reaction to a dramatic defeat is to try for a dramatic victory as soon as possible. He has the power to do so. No doubt, the proud spirit of the country would support his landing the Marines in Cuba.

Moreover, former President Eisenhower, who knows the agony of choosing between desperate courses of action, would undoubtedly support him. Former Vice-President Nixon is quoted as saying publicly that he would go along even if this meant putting United States forces on the beaches of Cuba. And some of the President's closest advisers deeply involved in the defeat are eager to recoup the losses of the last few days.

Nevertheless, this is no time for sudden action, but for a little more careful reflection and staff work than went into the original decision to allow the Cuban refugees to engage the prestige of the United States.

Cuba is not a present danger to the United States. Even if and when it gets the 150 Communist MIG fighter planes and the Cuban pilots now being trained in Czechoslovakia—the fear of which played such an important part in the decision to launch this week's adventure—this is no serious menace to the security of the Republic.

As the President said in his press conference yesterday, the threat of the rising power and ideology of Cuba is more of a menace to the other states of the Caribbean and the rest of Latin America than it is to the United States, but if Castro tries to use his military power against any other state in the Caribbean or the hemisphere, then the issue will be clear. At that point, the United States can wipe him out, with the requisite sanction of law on its side.

After all, the mere presence of military force in a weak country is not necessarily a threat to a strong country. Turkey, for example, has been getting from the United States far more power than Castro ever dreamed of getting from the Russians. The United States power, including even rockets with nuclear warheads, has been situated in Turkey for a long time, but the Russians, while annoyed by this fact, have not felt obliged to use their power to invade Turkey.

It all depends on how President Kennedy looks at all this. He can look at it in personal and political terms and concentrate on redressing the blunders of the last few weeks by landing two or three divisions in Cuba. In other words, he can put the immediate situation ahead of all the other world-wide social and economic programs he has been working so hard to emphasize ever since he came to power.

On the other hand, he can look at the wider world picture, now greatly darkened by the events in Laos and the sudden insurrection of the French Army that has broken out in Algeria.

He can try to deal with social and economic problems in Cuba by military means, and risk the whole inter-American and United States systems in the process.

But it does come back to his personal decision. He has the authority to act in historic and world terms or in terms of the limited immediate problems of the Cuban crisis.

Either way the decision will involve risks. This is a gloomy and impatient city this week-end. It is acting as if it were the last half of the ninth inning and Cuba were vital to the security of the United States, whereas the facts are that this is merely the first half of the first inning and Cuba can be dealt with at whatever time the President likes.

Kennedy, in short, is now facing not only Castro and Khrushchev but the history and meaning of the American story, and how he reacts to it will tell a lot about the kind of leadership he has in mind to offer for the United States and the free world.

Their Men Not in Havana

The Manchester Guardian
Saturday, April 22, 1961

American policy toward Cuba has led to a resounding and deserved humiliation. On the evidence so far available the Kennedy Administration appears to be guilty of deliberate intervention in the internal affairs of another country. The anti-Castro forces may have timed their invasion on their own initiative; but there is little doubt that they were sustained and helped by the United States before the invasion took place. There is no doubt at all that in giving open encouragement to the rebel forces, the United States has ignored her obligations under the Pan American Convention of 1928. Article 1 of that Convention binds the signatories to "use all the means at their disposal to prevent the inhabitants of her territory, nationals, or aliens, from participating in gathering elements, crossing the boundary, or sailing from their territory for the purpose of starting or promoting civil strife." The United States has done very nearly the opposite.

As a result, she has made Dr. Castro stronger than he was before; she has made his regime still more repressive and dictatorial; and she has thrown him still farther into the arms of the Soviet Union. Worse still, President Kennedy has gravely diminished the moral standing of his Administration, begun with such high hopes only three months ago. Neutral governments have universally condemned him. Even in the Western alliance he has wantonly thrown away much of the goodwill he previously enjoyed. Worst of all, American policy has given Mr. Khrushchev the chance to pose as the protector of small nations struggling to free themselves from foreign tutelage. Thus President Kennedy has achieved the exact opposite of what he set out to do. He has strengthened the appeal of communism in Latin America, Africa, and Asia; he has made the watchwords of democracy sound like the camouflage of imperialism.

These disasters are the natural outcome of the assumption on which American policy appears to have been based. The United States has been as blind to the realities of the twentieth century as Britain was at Suez or France in Indo-China. She has justified herself by appealing to the Monroe Doctrine and by claiming that Dr. Castro had succumbed to an "alien ideology." But ideologies know no frontiers; and the Monroe Doctrine was not signed in heaven. The second justification offered by the United States is that Dr. Castro is a dictator. That is a dangerous argument indeed. Are we now to expect American intervention against Guatemala, against Portugal, against Spain, against Yugoslavia, against Turkey, against Pakistan? And if not, why not?

The most distressing feature of the whole affair is that President Kennedy seems totally unwilling to learn from his mistakes. His speech to the American Society of Newspaper Editors was unrepentant and defiant. His reference to "outside Communist penetration that becomes a threat to the security of the United States or the safety of this hemisphere" apparently brought cheers from his audience; elsewhere, it will bring nothing but alarm. As elucidated later by the White House, the passage is said to have meant that the United States will intervene in Cuba if the Communists get missile launching pads; if Cuba joins the Warsaw Pact; if Cuba becomes "the focal point of political infection"; or if Cuba attacks the American naval base or conducts a campaign of terror against American citizens there.

The fourth of these conditions is morally justifiable. The other three are not. Cuba is a sovereign state, and as such legally entitled to join what defensive alliances she pleases. Politically, no doubt, Mr. Khrushchev would be extremely foolish to ask for missile pads in Cuba. Morally, however, Russian missile bases in Cuba are no more objectionable than American bases in Greece and Turkey. As for Cuba's becoming the "focal point of political infection," that condition would allow the United States to intervene whenever she felt inclined to do so. What exactly is "political infection" and how can it be measured? And how does one distinguish between the "focal points" of infection and the places to which infection is carried? The phrase reveals abysmal ignorance of the nature of communism and the sociological reasons for its appeal. The chief source of the appeal of communism in the underdeveloped world is not poverty; it is that communism seems to offer a path to national liberation. By seeming to lay down in advance that the peoples of Latin America are not to be allowed to choose communism even if they want to, President Kennedy increases the appeal of communism for every self-respecting Latin-American patriot. We must hope that most of them take a more sophisticated view than he does.

from The Kennedy Wit

by Bill Adler

On this matter of experience, I had announced earlier this year that if successful I would not consider campaign contributions as a substitute for experience in appointing Ambassadors. Ever since I made that statement I have not received one single cent from my father.

Alfred E. Smith Memorial Dinner
New York City
October 19, 1960

I have just received the following telegram from my generous Daddy. It says, "Dear Jack: Don't buy a single vote more than is necessary. I'll be damned if I'm going to pay for a landslide."

Gridiron Dinner
Washington, D.C.
1958

97

History Will Be Our Judge

*Courage, Perceptive Judgment, Integrity
and Dedication Are Imperative*

By John F. Kennedy,
President-Elect of the United States

[Delivered before the Massachusetts
Legislature, Boston, Massachusetts,
January 9, 1961.]

I have welcomed this opportunity to address this historic body, and, through you, the people of Massachusetts to whom I am so deeply indebted for a lifetime of friendship and trust. For fourteen years I have placed my confidence in the citizens of Massachusetts —and they have generously responded by placing their confidence in me.

Now, on the Friday after next, I am to assume new and broader responsibilities. But I am not here to bid farewell to Massachusetts. For forty-three years—whether I was in London, or in Washington, or in the South Pacific, or elsewhere—this has been my home; and God willing, wherever I serve, this shall remain my home.

It was here my grandparents were born—it is here I hope that my grandchildren will be born.

I speak neither from false provincial pride nor artful political flattery. For no man about to enter high office in this country can ever·be unmindful of the contribution which this state has made to our national greatness. Its leaders have shaped our destiny since long before the great Republic was born.

Its principles have guided our footsteps in times of crisis as well as in times of calm. Its democratic institutions—including this historic body—have served as beacon-lights for other nations as well as your sister states. For what Pericles said to the Athenians has long been true of this commonwealth:

"We do not imitate—but we are a model to others."

And so it is that I carry with me from this state to that high and lonely office to which I now succeed more than fond memories and fast friendships. The enduring qualities of Massachusetts—the common threads woven by the Pilgrim and the Puritan, the fisherman and the farmer, the Yankee and the immigrant—will not and could not be forgotten in this nation's executive mansion. They are an indelible part of my life, my conviction, my view of the past, and my hopes for the future.

Allow me to illustrate: During the last sixty days I have been engaged in the task of constructing an administration. It has been a long and deliberate process. Some have counseled greater speed. Others have counseled more expedient tests.

But I have been guided by the standard of John Winthrop, set before his shipmates on the flagship *Arabella* 331 years ago, as they, too, faced the task of building a new government on a new and perilous frontier.

"We must always consider," he said, "that we shall be as a city upon a hill—the eyes of all people upon us."

Today, the eyes of all the people are truly upon us—and our Government, in every branch, at every level, national, state and local, must be as a city upon a hill—constructed and inhabited by men aware of their grave trust and their great responsibilities.

For we are setting out upon a voyage in 1961, no less hazardous than that undertaken by the *Arabella* in 1630. We are committing ourselves to tasks of statecraft no less awesome than that of governing the Massachusetts Bay Colony, beset as it then was by terror without and disorder within.

History will not judge our endeavors—and a government cannot be selected—merely on the basis of color or creed or even party affiliation. Neither will competence and loyalty and stature, while essential to the utmost, suffice in times such as these.

For of those to whom much is given, much is required. And when at some future date the high court of history sits in judgment on each one of us—recording whether in our brief span of service we fulfilled our responsibilities to the state—our success or failure, in whatever office we may hold, will be measured by the answers to four questions:

First, were we truly men of courage—with the courage to stand up to one's enemies—and the courage to stand up, when necessary, to one's own associates—the courage to resist public pressure as well as private greed? Secondly, were we truly men of judgment—with perceptive judgment of the future as well as the past—of our own mistakes as well as the mistakes of others—with enough wisdom to know what we did not know, and enough candor to admit it?

Third, were we truly men of integrity—men who never ran out on either the principles in which they believed or the people who believed in them—men whom neither financial gain nor political ambition could ever divert from the fulfillment of our sacred trust?

Finally, were we truly men of dedication—with an honor mortgaged to no single individual or group, and compromised by no private obligation or aim, but devoted solely to serving the public good and the national interest?

Courage—judgment—integrity—dedication—these are the historic qualities of the Bay Colony and the Bay State—the qualities which this state has constantly sent to this chamber here on Beacon Hill here in Boston and to Capitol Hill back in Washington.

And these are the qualities which, with God's help, this son of

Massachusetts hopes will characterize our Government's conduct in the four stormy years that lie ahead.

Humbly I ask His help in this undertaking—but aware that on earth His will is worked by man, I ask for your help and your prayers, as I embark on this new and solemn journey.

John Kennedy was such a fine thinker that it is easy to forget that he was also an excellent athlete. He loved sports, especially those associated with the water, and was a tough competitor, as those who competed against (or with) him in sailing or touch football can testify. He never forgot the importance of good physical conditioning, and even when his duties as President precluded normal physical activity, he attempted to stay in shape. The next two pieces illustrate this side of John F. Kennedy's nature and evidence his concern for the physical well-being of his nation.

Sportsman Kennedy
Emphasized Participation

The New York Herald Tribune
(Paris Edition)
November 25, 1963

Boston, Nov. 24—John F. Kennedy, onetime scrub football player and ardent fan, was one of the best friends American sports ever had.

The man who munched a hot dog in the Orange Bowl and opened three American League baseball seasons with the traditional first pitch emphasized participation to the spectator public.

President Kennedy did not merely stress physical well-being with touch-football games on the White House lawn, sailing and swimming offshore near his Hyannis Port, Mass., summer home, and golf games wherever his ailing back permitted.

He also created a Council on Youth Fitness under the supervision of Oklahoma's football coach and athletic director, Bud

Wilkinson. The program was encouraged throughout all primary public schools in the country.

And when the bitter power struggle between the Amateur Athletic Union and National Collegiate Athletic Association over control of amateur athletics threatened the U.S. Olympic program earlier this year, the vigorous young President stepped in strongly.

He appointed Gen. Douglas MacArthur the final-say arbitrator in the dispute and the five-star general hammered out a truce.

For outstanding service to football President Kennedy received a gold medal award from the National Football Foundation. He had surrounded himself with football men, feeling they were rounded citizens best trained to meet today's problems.

Byron (Whizzer) White, the famed Colorado halfback of the late 1930's, became a Supreme Court justice.

There were football men among his advisers, including former Harvard captain Kenneth O'Donnell, and when racial strife broke out in Birmingham, Ala., one of Mr. Kennedy's choices as a Federal mediator was Earl (Red) Blaik, former Army and Dartmouth football coach.

Although his younger brother gained more football prominence at Harvard, President Kennedy was an end on the freshman and junior varsity squads and a swimmer.

United States Attorney General Robert Kennedy and Sen. Ted Kennedy were Harvard varsity football players.

A freshman teammate of the then future President recalled he "was a tall, rangy end and he was pretty good, though he never made a varsity letter."

President Kennedy called on his early swimming training during the war when the PT boat he skippered was sliced in two by a Japanese destroyer in the South Pacific.

He managed to tow a crewman from the wreck to shore, a distance of three miles, in five hours. Later, he spent a week swimming from island to island seeking aid.

Mr. Kennedy attended the last three Army-Navy games, the first as President-elect. In one he departed from planned procedure by walking to the near sideline for the toss of the coin by the team captains rather than have them come to the Presidential box.

Two years ago the man of vigor shed his coat and sat in shirt-sleeves at the Army-Navy game when the temperature in Philadelphia soared to 60.

President Kennedy loved to mingle in crowds with a minimum of fanfare. His last football game was Oct. 19 on the campus of his alma mater when he entered Harvard Stadium virtually unannounced two plays after the kickoff of the Columbia game.

Fans got their first notion of his presence when the Harvard band suddenly struck up "Hail to the Chief."

A subject of gentle ribs from the Crimson band, President Kennedy heard the musicians play "Hit the Road, Jack" at halftime.

As he rose to leave for a speaking engagement he stopped and took time to shake hands with and beam at an excited woman spectator.

While his motorcade sped back toward his hotel, the President made an unscheduled stop to get a malted milk. One man, sitting near the spot where Mr. Kennedy had been, refused to believe the Chief Executive had been there.

He was that kind of man. Events of his life were often as hard to believe as was the shocking news of his death.

Only the crisis in Vietnam kept President Kennedy from attending the Army-Air Force game in Chicago three weeks ago.

For those who were privileged to cover Army-Navy and Orange Bowl games, the President was such a familiar sight that he became almost a personal friend.

The memories include his applause for Navy against Missouri, his greeting to a blushing cheerleader from Oklahoma, a surprise pregame stroll through the Oklahoma players' dressing room and informal halftime walks between lines of rigid Cadets and Midshipmen in Philadelphia.

from the address in New York City at

The National Football
Foundation and Hall of
Fame Banquet

December 5, 1961

Mr. LaRoche [Chester J. LaRoche, President of the National Football Foundation], *ladies and gentlemen:*

I want to express my thanks to you for this award. Politics is an astonishing profession—it has permitted me to go from being an obscure lieutenant serving under General MacArthur to Commander in Chief in 14 years, without any technical competence whatsoever; and it's also enabled me to go from being an obscure member of the junior varsity at Harvard to being an honorary member of the Football Hall of Fame.

Actually, there are not so many differences between politics and football. Some Republicans have been unkind enough to suggest that my election, which was somewhat close, was somewhat similar to the Notre Dame-Syracuse game. But I'm like Notre Dame, we just take it as it comes and we're not giving it back. . . .

I am delighted to be here tonight and participating with you. This is a great American game. It has given me, personally, some of the most pleasant moments of my life—from last Saturday when I had a chance to see the Army-Navy game to a Harvard-Yale game I saw 40 years before. . . .

I do see a close relationship between sports and our national life and I sometimes wonder whether those of us who love sports have done as much as we should in maintaining sports as a constructive part of this country's existence.

I will not enter into a debate about whether football or baseball is our national sport. The sad fact is that it looks more and more as if our national sport is not playing at all—but watching. We have become more and more not a nation of athletes but a nation of spectators.

Professional athletes—professional athletics—I believe has a great place in our national life, but I must confess that I view the growing emphasis on professionalism and specialization in amateur sports without great enthusiasm. Gibbon wrote two centuries ago that professionalism in amateur sports was one of the early evidences of the decline and fall of the Roman Empire.

Football today is far too much a sport for the few who can play it well. The rest of us—and too many of our children—get our exercise from climbing up to the seats in stadiums, or from walking across the room to turn on our television sets. And this is true for one sport after another, all across the board.

The result of this shift from participation to, if I may use the word, "spectation," is all too visible in the physical condition of our population.

Despite our much-publicized emphasis on school athletics, our own children lag behind European children in physical fitness. And astonishingly enough, when Dr. Kraus and Dr. Weber recently went back, after ten years, to Europe they found a sharp decline in the physical fitness of European children, because in the last decade mechanization had begun to get at them too. . . .

I find this situation disturbing. We are under-exercised as a nation. We look, instead of play. We ride, instead of walk. Our existence deprives us of the minimum of physical activity essential for healthy living. And the remedy, in my judgment, lies in one direction; that is, in developing programs for broad participation in exercise by all of our young men and women—all of our boys and girls.

I do not say this in order to decry excellence in sports or anywhere else. But excellence emerges from mass participation. This is shown by the fact that in some areas of our Olympic Games, we have steadily fallen behind those nations who have stressed broad participation in a great variety of sports.

I believe that as a nation we should give our full support, for example, to our Olympic development program. We will not subsidize our athletes as some nations do, but we should as a country set a goal, not in the way the Soviet Union or the Chinese do, but in the kind of way Australia and other countries do—perhaps in our own way—to emphasize the most important part of life, the opportunity to exercise, to participate in physical activity, and generally to produce a standard of excellence for our country which will enable athletes to win the Olympics—but more importantly than that, which will give us a nation of vigorous men and women.

There are more important goals than winning contests, and that is to improve on a broad level the health and vitality of all of our people.

We have begun this year to make progress toward this goal with the new President's Council of Youth Fitness. The idea behind our youth fitness program is to give as many American boys and girls as possible a chance for a healthy physical development.

Coach Bud Wilkinson, who shook off the Washington—after losing his first five games finally got out of our atmosphere and went on to win the next five—and the Council staff, in cooperation with the Nation's leading educators and medical organizations, have worked out a basic physical fitness program for our elementary and secondary schools. Pilot projects have been set up in a number of cities. . . .

I hope that every school district in this country will adopt our minimum program. I urge every parent to support the program and his own children's participation in it. I urge our colleges and universities to lay down basic standards of physical fitness. I urge the Nation's community recreation centers to provide more opportunity for those who are no longer attending school. And finally, I urge organizations such as this, with all of the prestige and influence which you bring to American life, to help establish more programs for participation by American boys and girls—by Americans young and old. In short, what we must do is literally change the physical habits of millions of Americans—and that is far more difficult than changing their tastes, their fashions, or even their politics.

I do not suggest that physical development is the central object of life, or that we should permit cultural and intellectual values to be diminished, but I do suggest that physical health and vitality constitute an essential element of a vigorous American community.

No one knew this better than the men of Greece, to whom our civilization owes so much. The Greeks sought excellence not only in philosophy and drama and sculpture and architecture, but in athletics. The same people who produced the poetry of Homer, the wisdom of Plato and Aristotle—they also produced the Olympic Games. The Greeks understood that mind and body must develop in harmonious proportion to produce a creative intelligence. And so did the most brilliant intelligence of our earliest days, Thomas Jefferson, when he said, "Not less that two hours a day should be devoted to exercise." If a man who wrote the Declaration of Independence, was Secretary of State, and twice President could give it two hours, our children can give it ten or fifteen minutes.

There's no reason in the world—and we've seen it tonight—why Americans should not be fine students and fine athletes. When

I was young, Barry Wood used to play with Ben Ticknor football for Harvard—and hockey and baseball and tennis. He was a ten-letter man—and also the First Marshal of Phi Beta Kappa. And since then he has combined a life of leadership in the medical profession.

I have in Washington, as you know—and he is a friend of many of you—the Deputy Attorney General, Byron White, who was simultaneously a Rhodes scholar and a halfback for the Detroit Lions, and the year that he led the league in ground gained rushing, was also number one man in his class at the Yale Law School. We can combine and must combine intellectual energy and physical activity.

Theodore Roosevelt once said, "The credit belongs to the man who is actually in the arena—whose face is marred by dust and sweat and blood . . . who knows the great enthusiasms, the great devotions—and spends himself in a worthy cause—who at best if he wins knows the thrills of high achievement—and if he fails at least fails while daring greatly—so that his place shall never be with those cold and timid souls who know neither victory nor defeat."

The athletes in this room—you gentlemen—and your colleagues across the country have known victory and defeat, and have accepted both. I salute you.

from The Kennedy Wit

by Bill Adler

Ladies and gentlemen, I was warned to be out here in plenty of time to permit those who are going to the Green Bay Packers game to leave. I don't mind running against Mr. Nixon but I have the good sense not to run against the Green Bay Packers.

Green Bay, Wisconsin
October, 1960

Eulogy

by Senator Everett McKinley Dirksen

Minority Leader of the Senate

[Delivered in Support of the Senate's Resolution
upon the Death of President Kennedy.]

The memory of John Fitzgerald Kennedy lingers in this forum
of the people. Here we knew his vigorous tread, his flashing smile,
his ready wit, his keen mind, his zest for adventure. Here with
quiet grief we mourn his departure. Here we shall remember him
best as a colleague whose star of public service is indelibly in-
scribed on the roll of the United States Senate.

And here the eternal question confronts and confounds us.
Why must it be? Why must the life of an amiable, friendly, aggressive young man, moved only by high motives, lighted on his way
by high hopes, guided by broad plans, impelled by understanding
and vision, be brought to an untimely end with his labor unfinished?

And why, in a free land, untouched by the heel of dictatorship
and oppression, where the humblest citizen may freely utter his

grievances, must that life be cut short by an evil instrument, moved by malice, frustration and hate? This is the incredible thing which leaves us bewildered and perplexed.

One moment there is the ecstasy of living when one can hear the treble cries of scampering children over the White House lawn, the pleasure of receiving a Thanksgiving turkey which I presented to him but three days before the evil deed, the pleasure of conversation over many things including his hopes for the future, the exciting fact of sunshine and green grass in late November, the endless stream of citizens coming to the President's house, the strident voice of the city rising from the hum of traffic, the animation of saluting crowds, and then the sudden strangling death rattle of dissolution. Who shall say, save that there is a divinity which shapes our ends and marks our days.

As the tumult and grief subside, as the nation resumes and moves forward, and his own generation measures his works and achievements, what shall we say who knew him well—we in this forum where he spent eight years of his life—we who knew him best not as Mr. President but simply as Jack?

We saw him come to the Senate at age thirty-five. We saw him grow. We saw him rise. We saw him elevated to become the Chief Magistrate of this nation. And we saw him as the leader of both branches of this Republic assembled to deliberate over common problems.

In this moment when death has triumphed, when hearts are chastened, when the spirit reels in sheer bewilderment, what do we say, now that the book of life has been closed?

Let me say what we always said when he was alive, gay, happy, friendly, ambitious and ready to listen.

He had vision that went beyond our own. His determination to effectuate a test-ban treaty is a living example.

He was his own profile in courage. His unrelenting devotion to equality and civil rights attests that fact.

He was devoted to our system of constitutional government. His attitude toward the separation of church and state looms like a shining example.

He had the great virtue of spiritual grace. If at any moment he may have seemed frustrated over a proposition, it was so transitory. If he showed any sign of petulance, it was so fleeting. There were no souring acids in his spirit. If at any moment he may have seemed overeager, it was but the reflection of a zealous crusader and missioner who knew where he was going.

If, at any moment, he seemed to depart from the covenant which he and his party made with the people, it was only because he believed that accelerated events and circumstances did not always heed the clock and the calendar. If his course sometimes seemed at variance with his own party leaders or with the opposition, it was only because a deep conviction dictated his course.

On the tablets of memory, we who knew him well as a friend and colleague can well inscribe this sentiment:

Senator John Fitzgerald Kennedy, who became the 35th President of the United States—young, vigorous, aggressive and scholarly—one who estimated the needs of his country and the world and sought to fulfill that need—one who was wedded to peace and vigorously sought this greatest of all goals of mankind—one who sensed how catastrophic nuclear conflict could be and sought a realistic course to avert it—one who sensed the danger that lurked in a continuing inequality in our land and sought a rational and durable solution—one to whom the phrase "the national interest" was more than a string of words—one who could disagree without vindictiveness—one who believed that the expansion of the enjoyment of living by all people was an achievable goal—one who believed that each generation must contribute its best to the fulfillment of the American dream.

The *Te Deums* which will be sung this day may be wafted away by the evening breeze which caresses the last resting place of those who served the Republic, but here in this chamber where he served and prepared for higher responsibility, the memory of John Fitzgerald Kennedy will long linger to nourish the faith of all who serve that same great land.

Commencement Address
American University
Washington, D.C.

June 10, 1963

President Anderson, members of the faculty, board of trustees, distinguished guests, my old colleague Senator Bob Byrd, who has earned his degree through many years of attending night law school, while I am earning mine in the next 30 minutes, ladies and gentlemen:

. . . "There are few earthly things more beautiful than a university," wrote John Masefield, in his tribute to English universities —and his words are equally true today. He did not refer to spires and towers, to campus greens and ivied walls. He admired the splendid beauty of the university, he said, because it was "a place where those who hate ignorance may strive to know, where those who perceive truth may strive to make others see."

I have, therefore, chosen this time and this place to discuss a topic on which ignorance too often abounds and the truth is too rarely perceived—yet it is the most important topic on earth: world peace.

What kind of peace do I mean? What kind of peace do we seek? Not a Pax Americana enforced on the world by American weapons of war. Not the peace of the grave or the security of the slave. I am talking about genuine peace, the kind of peace that makes life on earth worth living, the kind that enables men and nations to grow and to hope and to build a better life for their children— not merely peace for Americans but peace for all men and women —not merely peace in our time but peace for all time.

I speak of peace because of the new face of war. Total war makes no sense in an age when great powers can maintain large and relatively invulnerable nuclear forces and refuse to surrender without resort to those forces. It makes no sense in an age when a single nuclear weapon contains almost ten times the explosive force delivered by all of the allied air forces in the Second World War. It makes no sense in an age when the deadly poisons produced by a nuclear exchange would be carried by wind and water and soil and seed to the far corners of the globe and to generations yet unborn.

Today the expenditure of billions of dollars every year on weapons acquired for the purpose of making sure we never need to use them is essential to keeping the peace. But surely the acquisition of such idle stockpiles—which can only destroy and never create—is not the only, much less the most efficient, means of assuring peace.

I speak of peace, therefore, as the necessary rational end of rational men. I realize that the pursuit of peace is not as dramatic as the pursuit of war—and frequently the words of the pursuer fall on deaf ears. But we have no more urgent task.

Some say that it is useless to speak of world peace or world law or world disarmament—and that it will be useless until the leaders of the Soviet Union adopt a more enlightened attitude.

I hope they do. I believe we can help them do it. But I also believe that we must reexamine our own attitude—as individuals and as a Nation—for our attitude is as essential as theirs. And every graduate of this school, every thoughtful citizen who despairs of war and wishes to bring peace, should begin by looking inward—by examining his own attitude toward the possibilities of peace, toward the Soviet Union, toward the course of the cold war and toward freedom and peace here at home.

First: Let us examine our attitude toward peace itself. Too many of us think it is impossible. Too many think it is unreal. But that is a dangerous, defeatist belief. It leads to the conclusion that war is inevitable—that mankind is doomed—that we are gripped by forces we cannot control.

We need not accept that view. Our problems are manmade—therefore, they can be solved by man. And man can be as big as he wants. No problem of human destiny is beyond human beings. Man's reason and spirit have often solved the seemingly unsolvable —and we believe they can do it again.

I am not referring to the absolute, infinite concept of universal peace and good will of which some fantasies and fanatics dream. I do not deny the value of hopes and dreams, but we merely invite discouragement and incredulity by making that our only and immediate goal.

Let us focus instead on a more practical, more attainable peace —based not on a sudden revolution in human nature but on a gradual evolution in human institutions—on a series of concrete actions and effective agreements which are in the interest of all concerned. There is no single, simple key to this peace—no grand or magic formula to be adopted by one or two powers. Genuine peace must be the product of many nations, the sum of many acts. It must be dynamic, not static, changing to meet the challenge of each new generation. For peace is a process—a way of solving problems.

With such a peace, there will still be quarrels and conflicting interests, as there are within families and nations. World peace, like community peace, does not require that each man love his neighbor—it requires only that they live together in mutual tolerance, submitting their disputes to a just and peaceful settlement. And history teaches us that enemies between nations, as between individuals, do not last forever. However fixed our likes and dislikes may seem, the tide of time and events will often bring surprising changes in the relations between nations and neighbors.

So let us persevere. Peace need not be the impracticable, and war need not be inevitable. By defining our goal more clearly, by making it seem more manageable and less remote, we can help all peoples to see it, to draw hope from it, and to move irresistibly toward it.

Second: Let us reexamine our attitude toward the Soviet Union. It is discouraging to think that their leaders may actually believe what their propagandists write. It is discouraging to read a recent authoritative Soviet text on *Military Strategy* and find, on page after page, wholly baseless and incredible claims—such as the allegation that "American imperialist circles are preparing to unleash different types of wars . . . that there is a very real threat of a preventive war being unleashed by American imperialists against the Soviet Union . . . [and that] the political aims of the American imperialists are to enslave economically and politically the European and other capitalist countries . . . [and] to achieve world domination . . . by means of aggressive wars."

Truly as it was written long ago: "The wicked flee when no man pursueth." Yet it is sad to read these Soviet statements—to realize the extent of the gulf between us. But it is also a warning—a warning to the American people not to fall into the same trap as the Soviets, not to see only a distorted and desperate view of the other side, not to see conflict as inevitable, accommodation as impossible, and communication as nothing more than an exchange of threats.

No government or social system is so evil that its people must be considered as lacking in virtue. As Americans, we find communism profoundly repugnant as a negation of personal freedom and dignity. But we can still hail the Russian people for their economic and industrial growth, in culture and in acts of courage.

Among the many traits the peoples of our two countries have in common, none is stronger than our mutual abhorrence of war. Almost unique among the major world powers, we have never been at war with each other. And no nation in the history of battle ever suffered more than the Soviet Union suffered in the course of the Second World War. At least 20 million lost their lives. Countless millions of homes and farms were burned or sacked. A third of the Nation's territory, including nearly two thirds of its industrial base, was turned into a wasteland—a loss equivalent to the devastation of this country east of Chicago.

Today, should total war ever break out again—no matter how—our two countries woud become the primary targets. It is an ironic but accurate fact that the two strongest powers are the two in the most danger of devastation. All we have built, all we have worked for, would be destroyed in the first 24 hours. And even in the cold war, which brings burdens and dangers to so many countries, including this Nation's closest allies—our two countries bear the heaviest burdens. For we are both devoting massive sums of money to weapons that could be better devoted to combating ignorance, poverty, and disease. We are both caught up in a vicious and dangerous cycle in which suspicion on one side breeds suspicion on the other, and new weapons beget counterweapons.

In short, both the United States and its allies, and the Soviet Union and its allies, have a mutually deep interest in a just and genuine peace and in halting the arms race. Agreements to this end are in the interests of the Soviet Union as well as ours—and even the most hostile nations can be relied upon to accept and keep those treaty obligations, and only those treaty obligations, which are in their own interest.

So, let us not be blind to our differences—but let us also direct attention to our common interests and to the means by which those differences can be resolved. And if we cannot end now our differences, at least we can help make the world safe for diversity. For, in the final analysis, our most basic common link is that we all inhabit this small planet. We all breathe the same air. We all cherish our children's future. And we are all mortal.

Third: Let us reexamine our attitude toward the cold war, remembering that we are not engaged in a debate, seeking to pile up debating points. We are not here distributing blame or pointing the finger of judgment. We must deal with the world as it is, and not as it might have been had the history of the last 18 years been different.

We must, therefore, persevere in the search for peace in the hope that constructive changes within the Communist bloc might bring within reach solutions which now seem beyond us. We must conduct our affairs in such a way that it becomes in the Communists' interest to agree on a genuine peace. Above all, while defending our own vital interests, nuclear powers must avert those confrontations which bring an adversary to a choice of either a humiliating retreat or a nuclear war. To adopt that kind of course in the nuclear age would be evidence only of the bankruptcy of our policy—or of a collective death-wish for the world.

To secure these ends, America's weapons are non-provocative, carefully controlled, designed to deter, and capable of selective use. Our military forces are committed to peace and disciplined self-restraint. Our diplomats are instructed to avoid unnecessary irritants and purely rhetorical hostility.

For we can seek a relaxation of tensions without relaxing our guard. And, for our part, we do not need to use threats to prove that we are resolute. We do not need to jam foreign broadcasts out of fear our faith will be eroded. We are unwilling to impose our system on any unwilling people—but we are willing and able to engage in peaceful competition with any people on the earth.

Meanwhile, we seek to strengthen the United Nations, to help solve its financial problems, to make it a more effective instrument for peace, to develop it into a genuine world security system—a system capable of resolving disputes on the basis of law, of insuring the security of the large and the small, and of creating conditions under which arms can finally be abolished.

At the same time we seek to keep peace inside the non-Communist world, where many nations, all of them our friends, are divided over issues which weaken Western unity, which invite Communist intervention or which threaten to erupt into war. Our efforts in West New Guinea, in the Congo, in the Middle East, and in the Indian subcontinent have been persistent and patient despite criticism from both sides. We have also tried to set an example for others—by seeking to adjust small but significant differences with our own closest neighbors in Mexico and Canada.

Speaking of other nations, I wish to make one point clear. We are bound to many nations by alliances. Those alliances exist because our concern and theirs substantially overlap. Our commitment to defend Western Europe and West Berlin, for example, stands undiminished because of the identity of our vital interests. The United States will make no deal with the Soviet Union at the expense of other nations and other peoples, not merely because they are our partners, but also because their interests and ours converge.

Our interests converge, however, not only in defending the frontiers of freedom, but in pursuing the paths of peace. It is our hope—and the purpose of allied policies—to convince the Soviet Union that she, too, should let each nation choose its own future, so long as that choice does not interfere with the choices of others. The Communist drive to impose their political and economic system on others is the primary cause of world tension today. For there can be no doubt that, if all nations could refrain from interfering in the self-determination of others, the peace would be much more assured.

This will require a new effort to achieve world law—a new context for world discussions. It will require increased understanding between the Soviets and ourselves. And increased understanding will require increased contact and communications. One step in this direction is the proposed arrangement for a direct line between Moscow and Washington, to avoid on each side the dangerous delays, misunderstandings, and misreadings of the other's actions which might occur at a time of crisis.

We have also been talking in Geneva about other first-step

measures of arms control, designed to limit the intensity of the arms race and to reduce the risks of accidental war. Our primary long-range interest in Geneva, however, is general and complete disarmament—designed to take place by stages, permitting parallel political developments to build the new institutions of peace which would take the place of arms. The pursuit of disarmament has been an effort of this Government since the 1920's. It has been urgently sought by the past three administrations. And however dim the prospects may be today, we intend to continue this effort—to continue it in order that all countries, including our own, can better grasp what the problems and possibilities of disarmament are.

The one major area of these negotiations where the end is in sight, yet where a fresh start is badly needed, is in a treaty to outlaw nuclear tests. The conclusions of such a treaty, so near and yet so far, would check the spiraling arms race in one of its most dangerous areas. It would place the nuclear powers in a position to deal more effectively with one of the greatest hazards which man faces in 1963, the further spread of nuclear arms. It would increase our security —it would decrease the prospects of war. Surely this goal is sufficiently important to require our steady pursuit, yielding neither to the temptation to give up the whole effort nor the temptation to give up our insistence on vital and responsible safeguards.

I am taking this opportunity, therefore, to announce two important decisions in this regard.

First: Chairman Khrushchev, Prime Minister Macmillan, and I have agreed that high-level discussions will shortly begin in Moscow, looking toward early agreement on a comprehensive test-ban treaty. Our hopes must be tempered with the caution of history— but with our hopes go the hopes of all mankind.

Second: To make clear our good faith and solemn convictions on the matter, I now declare that the United States does not propose to conduct nuclear tests in the atmosphere so long as other states do not do so. We will not be the first to resume. Such a declaration is no substitute for a formal binding treaty, but I hope it will help us achieve one. Nor would such a treaty be a substitute for disarmament, but I hope it will help us achieve it.

Finally, my fellow Americans, let us examine our attitude toward peace, and freedom here at home. The quality and spirit of our own society must justify and support our efforts abroad. We must show it in the dedication of our own lives—as many of you who are graduating today will have a unique opportunity to do, by serving without pay in the Peace Corps abroad or in the proposed National Service Corps here at home.

But wherever we are, we must all, in our daily lives, live up to the age-old faith that peace and freedom walk together. In too many of our cities today, the peace is not secure because freedom is incomplete.

It is the responsibility of the executive branch at all levels of government—local, State, and National—to provide and protect that freedom for all of our citizens by all means within their authority. It is the responsibility of the legislative branch at all levels, wherever that authority is not now adequate, to make it adequate. And it is the responsibility of all citizens in all sections of this country to respect the law of the land.

All this is not unrelated to world peace. "When a man's ways please the Lord," the Scriptures tell us, "he maketh even his enemies to be at peace with him." And is not peace, in the last analysis, basically a matter of human rights—the right to live out our lives without fear of devastation—the right to breathe air as nature provided it—the right of future generations to a healthy existence?

While we proceed to safeguard our national interests, let us also safeguard human interests. And the elimination of war and arms is clearly in the interest of both. No treaty, however much it may be to the advantage of all, however tightly it may be worded, can provide absolute security against the risks of deception and evasion. But it can—if it is sufficiently effective in its enforcement and if it is sufficiently in the interests of its signers—offer far more security and far fewer risks than an unabated, uncontrolled, unpredictable arms race.

The United States, as the world knows, will never start a war. We do not want a war. We do not now expect a war. This generation of Americans has already had enough—more than enough—of war and hate and oppression. We shall be prepared if others wish it. We shall be alert to try to stop it. But we shall also do our part to build a world of peace where the weak are safe and the strong are just. We are not helpless before that task or hopeless of its success. Confident and unafraid, we labor on—not toward a strategy of annihilation but toward a strategy of peace.

from The Kennedy Wit

by Bill Adler

During the hard-fought and crucial West Virginia primary, President Kennedy's youngest brother, Ted, had just finished giving an enthusiastic speech in which he said, "Do you want a man who will give the country leadership? Do you want a man who has vigor and vision?" When candidate Jack Kennedy took the microphone from his younger brother, he opened his remarks by saying:

I would like to tell my brother that you cannot be elected President until you are thirty-five years of age.

from

My Twelve Years
with John F. Kennedy

by Evelyn Lincoln

Chapter 28

The Kennedy Touch

*As personal secretary to John F. Kennedy for twelve years,
Mrs. Evelyn Lincoln got to know the President as few
others could. In addition to performing her many and demanding
White House functions, she accompanied him on many national
and international trips, and even attended some of the
splendid and gracious social events which marked the Kennedy
years. Her book records not only the major events and decisions of
John Kennedy's Presidency, but also the smaller, more intimate
and equally revealing events, offering new insights into
a rich personality.*

President and Mrs. Kennedy had not been in the White House
twenty-four hours before they were discussing changes they would

like to make. They were concerned not only with their own comfort and convenience and acute sense of beauty; they also wanted to make the White House a national shrine of historical interest to all Americans.

At the end of their first year in the Executive Mansion, it bore the Kennedy touch inside and out. The interest they had created in the White House was reflected in the number of tourists who lined up daily for a tour of the state rooms.

Mrs. Kennedy felt the key to what the White House should represent to the nation was the historical nature of the Mansion, which had come a long way since Abigail Adams, the first President's wife to live there, had complained about its barn-like, unfurnished vastness.

Mrs. Kennedy wanted to remove everything that was second-rate and replace it with genuine antiques that either had belonged to the Presidents or were of their periods.

"Everything that is here," she said, "should have a reason for being here." And she began her expeditions into the dark cellar storerooms of the White House, coming up with all sorts of forgotten treasures, including "some old junk" that turned out to be President Monroe's gold and silver flatware, made to his order in France in 1817.

It was immediately obvious to Mrs. Kennedy that it would not be possible for her to do the restoration alone. A White House Historical Association was formed to help locate antique furniture of historic value and raise donations to purchase the pieces, if necessary. She persuaded Congress to pass a law making donations to the White House collection tax-deductible, and soon lovely things began to arrive.

Secretary of the Treasury and Mrs. C. Douglas Dillon gave a whole room full of American Empire furniture, including a sofa that once belonged to Dolly Madison. A rare portrait of Benjamin Franklin worth $165,000 was given by Walter Annenberg, a Philadelphia publisher, and was hung over the mantel in the Green Room. Eighteenth-century French furniture valued at

$100,000 was donated by Mr. and Mrs. John Loeb of New York. People all over the country sent things large and small, authentic and phony, valuable and worthless. Each gift was carefully screened by experts, and accepted or returned. Mrs. John N. Pearce was employed as full-time curator for the White House. Gradually the Presidential Mansion took on a new, more historic look.

The Green Room, to the rear of the first floor of the Mansion, was the first one completely refurnished by Mrs. Kennedy's White House Historical Association. It soon became a fashionable, Federal parlor in which President Jefferson or John Adams would have been right at home. Abigail Adams, I am sure, would have loved Mrs. Kennedy's choice of the "Adams style" Axminster carpet, the moss-green watered silk walls with matching draperies, the Empire mantelpiece, the early American Sheraton, Chippendale, and Hepplewhite furnishings.

Her own favorite, I was told, was the Red Room, which she furnished as an Empire parlor of the period around 1820. Situated on the opposite side of the south portico from the Green Room, this room has a bright fuchsia silk wall covering with a gold-scroll border, and the furnishings used the same color and design. In this room the furniture donated by the Dillons was placed. The Blue Room reflected the President Monroe period, and to the Diplomatic Reception Room, on the ground floor beneath the Blue Room, which had been partly restored by the Eisenhowers, Mrs. Kennedy added a lovely, bright panoramic wallpaper made in Alsace in 1830.

Another room that greatly benefited from Mrs. Kennedy's touch was the state dining room, which was decorated in white and gold instead of the previous somber green.

Although the restoration was Mrs. Kennedy's project, the President himself was keenly interested in every step. Many times when Mrs. Kennedy or Mrs. Pearce, the curator, came across something they thought would interest the President, they would rush it over to my office, or call and tell me about it, and ask me to check with the President to see what he thought.

The President and Mrs. Kennedy spent many, many hours at

night going over the various plans and acquisitions, and he was particularly pleased with her television presentation of a Tour of the White House, which was telecast on February 14, 1962. The next morning he was as anxious to learn what everyone thought of her presentation as he was to get the responses to his own television appearances. The actual filming of the tour took place on January 15th, and the President made a final statement in the Treaty Room, which was restored as a conference room with furnishings of the Ulysses S. Grant period and with framed treaties on the walls.

One day the President received a letter from columnist David Lawrence concerning a typewriter that had been in the White House during President Wilson's administration—the typewriter on which President Wilson had typed his Fourteen Points and other important statements. It had recently been at the American Red Cross, but because of its historical significance, Mr. Lawrence thought it would be a valuable asset to the collection of articles in the White House, and he presented it in a ceremony in the President's office. In accepting it, the President drew laughs when he commented, "My wife has collected everything and this is my— this is the only thing I have produced. . . ."

He was proud of it, and after the donors left, I put it in my office until he could decide where he wanted to keep it. One day he said, "Why don't we put it in the Fish Room?" And there it remained—displayed for its visitors to see.

The President had his own project for the beautification of the White House: the garden just outside his office in the West Wing. Morning after morning, as he walked along the portico on his way from the Mansion to his office, he passed the barren plot of ground commonly called the Rose Garden. Only a few rose trees and some rows of hedge were planted there.

One morning he came into my office and wanted to know if the gardeners could consider planting flowers along the walkway. He asked me to have one of the gardeners come over to talk to him about it, and then he learned there was no money available for the type of garden in which he was interested. Mrs. Paul Mellon of Upperville, Virginia, a good friend of the Kennedys, learned of the President's dream for a flower garden and offered to supply trees, shrubs, and flowers necessary to make this garden a beautiful one. The blueprints were drawn and accepted.

Before the actual planting was begun, the President designed the new steps that led from the top of the walk down to the garden. The top step was built as a platform from which he could talk to groups gathered at the west end of the garden. There was also a place to set up microphones on the top step.

It was early in the spring of 1962 that the garden renovation began. First the area was cleared of all vegetation. Then four full-grown magnolia trees were brought in to be planted in the corners of the rectangular garden. After they were planted, it seemed as if they had always been there. The President watched each develop-ment with interest.

"What I want is blooming flowers on the three sides, and especially along the portico where I receive groups," he said. "And I would like to look at these flowers as I walk from the Mansion to my office. And I would like them changed from season to season."

Sometimes Mrs. Mellon was in the garden supervising the planting. When the President saw her, he would hurry out to talk with her. He was eager for the blossoms to appear, although he had no preferences among flowers. He liked them all. He asked only that as soon as one kind of flower faded away, another kind be planted in its place so there would always be an array of color and profusion of blooms.

After the flowers had been put in the border of the new geo-metric pattern of Speaker Sam rose bushes, rows of grass were planted in the center of the rectangle. At the east end, on a patio of Pennsylvania flagstone, was an arrangement of chairs. Sometimes the President would take his callers there for their conferences.

At first it took the grass a little while to take hold, and the President became impatient. It was not uncommon for him to come into my office in the mornings and say, "Mrs. Lincoln, do you see that brown spot out there on the lawn? Will you tell them to have that fixed?" Sometimes when there was to be a meeting in the garden, the gardeners would spray the grass with a green substance to make sure that none of the brown spots showed.

The President loved this garden so much that he would take guests, even heads of state, for walks out on the grass. I would watch him coming around the corner from the Mansion, enjoying every minute of the walk as he surveyed his garden.

Several times he called from his office, "Mrs. Lincoln, get Macaroni out of my garden." I would rush out and chase Caroline's pony out of his garden. It was not long before Macaroni was forbidden the freedom of the White House lawn.

Oftentimes when Caroline and John were playing on the lawn, he would walk out on the portico and into the garden and clap his hands twice. Caroline, more fleet of foot, would arrive first, running as fast as she could, excited and out of breath. Little John would follow, in the care of Miss Shaw.

Right after the Cuban missile crisis, the President dictated a letter to Mrs. Mellon to let her know how much he appreciated the garden she had made possible. "I need not tell you that your garden has been our brightest spot in the somber surroundings of the last few days," he said.

The Kennedy touch soon became evident in yet another area: the entertaining in the White House. The most celebrated social event in the Kennedy Administration was the dinner President and Mrs. Kennedy gave to honor the forty-nine Nobel Prize winners. Many of America's greatest intellectuals gathered for an event that culminated in the first public reading of an unpublished work by the late Ernest Hemingway. The President was very grateful to Fredric March for the reading, and dictated a letter to him the next morning. He also had copies of pictures taken at the dinner sent to each winner with a letter he signed personally.

In addition to the Nobel winners, one hundred and twenty-four other scientists, writers, editors, and educators were invited. The guest list included seven Pulitzer Prize-winning writers, including the President himself, and two politically controversial scientists, Dr. Linus C. Pauling and Dr. J. Robert Oppenheimer. The President described the dinner to his guests as "probably the greatest concentration of talent and genius in this house, except for those times when Jefferson ate alone."

Being a scholar himself, he sincerely appreciated the companionship and the challenge of such outstanding minds. The event proved so enjoyable to all the notables that the dinner lasted longer than had been planned.

The Kennedys introduced theater in the royal tradition to the White House. Early in October of their second year in residence there, scenes from *Macbeth* and four other Shakespearean plays were presented on a specially built stage in the East Room following a state dinner in honor of President Ibrahim Abboud of the Sudan.

A month later Pablo Casals, who had last appeared at the White House for Theodore Roosevelt and had sworn never to perform in any country that recognized Spain's Franco, gave a much-celebrated concert in the East Room following a state dinner. In inviting the famed cellist to appear, the President had written, "We feel that your performance as one of the world's greatest artists would lend distinction to the entertainment of our invited guests."

Another evening, following a state dinner for the Grand Duchess Charlotte of Luxembourg, the poetry and music of Elizabethan England echoed from a three-tiered platform with a red velvet backdrop. In time the stage, which could be dismantled and stored when not in use, was used for presenting ballerinas and bassos, sopranos and symphonies.

The Kennedys also had a platform erected on the south lawn, where various groups performed. One chilly spring day in 1962, the Greater Boston Youth Symphony Orchestra played there for an audience of children. President and Mrs. Kennedy went out to meet the children and to listen to some of the concert. The President returned to his office before the concert was over, but he told them he was going to leave his office door open so that he could hear the music. Although it became quite cold in both his office and mine, he would not let me close the door as long as the orchestra played.

Remarks at Amherst College Upon Receiving an Honorary Degree

October 26, 1963

Mr. [John J.] McCloy, President [Calvin H.] Plimpton, Mr. Mac-Leish, distinguished guests, ladies and gentlemen:

I am very honored to be here with you on this occasion which means so much to this college and also means so much to art and the progress of the United States. . . .

This day devoted to the memory of Robert Frost offers an opportunity for reflection which is prized by politicians as well as by others, and even by poets, for Robert Frost was one of the granite figures of our time in America. He was supremely two things: an artist and an American. A nation reveals itself not only by the men it produces but also by the men it honors, the men it remembers.

In America, our heroes have customarily run to men of large accomplishments. But today this college and country honor a man whose contribution was not to our size but to our spirit, not to our political beliefs but to our insight, not to our self-esteem, but to our self-comprehension. In honoring Robert Frost, we therefore can pay honor to the deepest sources of our national strength. That strength takes many forms, and the most obvious forms are not always the most significant. The men who create power make an indispensable contribution to the Nation's greatness, but the men who question power make a contribution just as indispensable, especially when that questioning is disinterested, for they determine whether we use power or power uses us.

Our national strength matters, but the spirit which informs and controls our strength matters just as much. This was the special significance of Robert Frost. He brought an unsparing instinct for reality to bear on the platitudes and pieties of society. His sense of the human tragedy fortified him against self-deception and easy consolation. "I have been," he wrote, "one acquainted with the night." And because he knew the midnight as well as the high noon, because he understood the ordeal as well as the triumph of the human spirit, he gave his age strength with which to overcome despair. At bottom, he held a deep faith in the spirit of man, and it is hardly an accident that Robert Frost coupled poetry and power, for he saw poetry as a means of saving power from itself. When power leads man toward arrogance, poetry reminds him of his limitations. When power narrows the areas of man's concern, poetry reminds him of the rightness and diversity of his existence. When power corrupts, poetry cleanses. For art establishes the basic human truth which must serve as the touchstone of our judgment.

The artist, however faithful to his personal vision of reality, becomes the last champion of the individual mind and sensibility against an intrusive society and an officious state. The great artist is thus a solitary figure. He has, as Frost said, a lover's quarrel with the world. In pursuing his perceptions of reality, he must often sail against the currents of his time. This is not a popular role. If Robert

Frost was much honored during his lifetime, it was because a good many preferred to ignore his darker truths. Yet in retrospect we see how the artist's fidelity has strengthened the fibre of our national life.

If sometimes our great artists have been the most critical of our society, it is because their sensitivity and their concern for justice, which must motivate any true artist, make them aware that our Nation falls short of its highest potential. I see little of more importance to the future of our country and our civilization than full recognition of the place of the artist.

If art is to nourish the roots of our culture, society must set the artist free to follow his vision wherever it takes him. We must never forget that art is not a form of propaganda; it is a form of truth. And as Mr. MacLeish once remarked of poets, there is nothing worse for our trade than to be in style. In free society art is not a weapon and it does not belong to the sphere of polemics and ideology. Artists are not engineers of the soul. It may be different elsewhere. But democratic society—in it, the highest duty of the writer, the composer, the artist is to remain true to himself and let the chips fall where they may. In serving his vision of the truth, the artist best serves his nation. And the nation which disdains the mission of art invites the fate of Robert Frost's hired man, the fate of having "nothing to look backward to with pride, and nothing to look forward to with hope."

I look forward to a great future for America, a future in which our country will match its military strength with our moral restraint, its wealth with our wisdom, its power with our purpose. I look forward to an America which will not be afraid of grace and beauty, which will protect the beauty of our natural environment, which will preserve the great old American houses and squares and parks of our national past, and which will build handsome and balanced cities for our future.

I look forward to an America which will reward achievement in the arts as we reward achievement in business or statecraft. I look forward to an America which will steadily raise the standards of artistic accomplishment and which will steadily enlarge cultural opportunities for all of our citizens. And I look forward to an America which commands respect throughout the world not only for its strength but for its civilization as well. And I look forward to a world which will be safe not only for democracy and diversity but also for personal distinction.

Robert Frost was often skeptical about prospects for human improvement, yet I do not think he would disdain this hope. As he wrote during the uncertain days of the Second War:

> Take human nature altogether since time began . . .
> And it must be a little more in favor of man,
> Say a fraction of one percent at the very least . . .
> Our hold on the planet wouldn't have so increased.

Because of Mr. Frost's life and work, because of the life and work of this college, our hold on this planet has increased.

John F. Kennedy loved poetry, and was beloved by many poets because he seemed to incarnate, in his every word and act, a great and optimistic joy in living. His death, its manner and its meaning, occasioned an enormous body of poetry. In their collection Of Poetry and Power, *editors Erwin A. Glikes and Paul Schwaber have gathered the best poems by seventy-nine of the poets who submitted works for publication. Three of these poems, varying widely in theme and style, are included in this volume.*

from

Of Poetry and Power

*Poems Occasioned by the Presidency and
by the Death of John F. Kennedy*

Edited by
Erwin A. Glikes and Paul Schwaber

November 22, 1963

By Lewis Turco

Weeping, I write this. You are dead. The dark
animal of the heart, the beast that bides
stilly in its web of flesh, has stolen
flight again out of the air. What is there
to say? That I wish we were gods? That the
mind of man were equal to his lusts? It
is not—not yet. You were a man, but more:
you were an idea dreamt in a sweet

hour while the spider slept. We make our
web: its habitant makes greatness of its
prey. We are ourselves victim and victor.
You were and are ourselves. In killing you
we murder an emblem of what we strive
to be: not men, but Man. In mourning you,
good Man, we grieve for what we are, not what
we may become.
    Sleep, my heart. We will try
Once more. Sleep, sleep, John. We will try again.

Elegy for the New Year

By Jack Marshall

1.

Dulled by the news, all day I keep behind
The curtains of my room. They will have to do
In keeping my dried-out-self
From falling through the air like a leaf
As the year tapers to a close.
This is the legendary season
When the young die sooner than the old.

2.

Calm as a hurricane's eye,
My T.V. set in black and white
Stares unblinking at Washington—
Pearly, spacious, dazzled with shock—
Where under a sky of cold
Lingering Confederate grey,
A stallion, Black Jack, tosses
And snorts, spirited as your soul
Gone from this world, ours by default.

3.

America stops turning over her conscience,
Halved these hundred years like Hamlet's
And clutches her flag's reopened wound
Running red through the bandages.
In a sky swept clean of cherry blossoms,
She seems to see a future drained
Of all color but black and white, alternatives.
White Christmas come,
The Union will twinkle
Like a child, her arms full of gifts,
Pretending all is well.

4.

Someone who has dreamed his father dear,
And stepped away from the dream, holding
His breath like a shoe in each hand,
Comes to himself, a honeycomb of fear,
Each cell a nursery weeping for home;
Hears the wind tiptoe from door to door and whisper,
"There is no place to be homesick for. You're free."
A soul winging like a gunshot
Through the ether's paper bag,
Beyond sight, beyond recognition . . . breaking apart,
Wrings an old restlessness from me,
Heart all aflutter for the take-off.

In Arlington Cemetery

By Stanley Koehler

In the city of memorials,
among tombstones and small

headstones, I look through the cold
not for a monument
but for a grave with ferns
and evergreens lent
from the season past. A flame burns
in the air, not a leaf
to shelter it, blown like our grief,
variable and new, endless and old.

Uphill, over open ground,
on the wind's edge are coming
echoes of drummers drumming
on tight-stretched skin,
tattooing the stillness
to the funeral sound
of hoofs at the hobble,
unharnessed, held in
to the ritual pace;
and of wheels on the cobble.

The carriage circles a green park
with its temple, the dark
porch where the Form in his chair
sheds a marble tear
for what is fated like him:
statues for whom
there are robes of stone.
Love waves in her car
while Hate takes aim
through a lens from far

off, and History bleeds, an old charade,
and Madmen fly
the line of parade
down empty walks, and from the shocked

stage the Actor's shout
is driven out.
Still, in those marble eyes
deepgrained as memory,
the barns are burning, the streets are blocked,
while motorcade and obsequies

through iron gates
to somber guns and the horn's last notes
continually come.
For this to end, for the drum
to be stilled at last,
more than this green bough
will be cut and cast.

The flame leaps up. Fresh as our vow,
it makes a gentle monument at night
with the simplicity of light.

from The Kennedy Wit

by Bill Adler

Question: Senator, you were promised military intelligence briefing from the President. Have you received that?
Mr. Kennedy: Yes. I talked on Thursday morning to General Wheeler from the Defense Department.
Question: What was his first name?
Mr. Kennedy: He didn't brief me on that.

Press Conference
Anchorage, Alaska
September 4, 1960

I appreciate your welcome. As the cow said to the Maine farmer, "Thank you for a warm hand on a cold morning."

Los Angeles, California
November 2, 1960

from

Profiles in Courage

by John F. Kennedy

Chapter VI
Edmund G. Ross

"I . . . looked down into my open grave."

In a lonely grave, forgotten and unknown, lies "the man who saved a President," and who as a result may well have preserved for ourselves and posterity constitutional government in the United States —the man who performed in 1868 what one historian has called "the most heroic act in American history, incomparably more difficult than any deed of valor upon the field of battle"—but a United States Senator whose name no one recalls: Edmund G. Ross of Kansas.

The impeachment of President Andrew Johnson, the event in which the obscure Ross was to play such a dramatic role, was the sensational climax to the bitter struggle between the President, determined to carry out Abraham Lincoln's policies of reconciliation with the defeated South, and the more radical Republican leaders in Congress, who sought to administer the downtrodden Southern states as conquered provinces which had forfeited their rights under the Constitution. It was, moreover, a struggle between Executive and Legislative authority. Andrew Johnson, the courageous if untactful Tennesseean who had been the only Southern member of Congress to refuse to secede with his state, had committed himself to the policies of the Great Emancipator to whose high station he had succeeded only by the course of an assassin's bullet. He knew that Lincoln prior to his death had already clashed with the extremists in Congress who had opposed his approach to reconstruction in a constitutional and charitable manner and sought to make the Legislative Branch of the government supreme. And his own belligerent temperament soon destroyed any hope that Congress might now join hands in carrying out Lincoln's policies of permitting the South to resume its place in the Union with as little delay and controversy as possible.

By 1866, when Edmund Ross first came to the Senate, the two branches of the government were already at each other's throats, snarling and bristling with anger. Bill after bill was vetoed by the President on the grounds that they were unconstitutional, too harsh in their treatment of the South, an unnecessary prolongation of military rule in peacetime or undue interference with the authority of the Executive Branch. And for the first time in our nation's history, important public measures were passed over a President's veto and became law without his support.

But not all of Andrew Johnson's vetoes were overturned; and the "Radical" Republicans of the Congress promptly realized that one final step was necessary before they could crush their despised foe (and in the heat of political battle their vengeance was turned upon their President far more than their former military enemies of the South). That one remaining step was the assurance of a two-thirds majority in the Senate—for under the Constitution, such a majority was necessary to override a Presidential veto. And more important, such a majority was constitutionally required to accomplish their major ambition, now an ill-kept secret: conviction of the President under an impeachment and his dismissal from office!

The temporary and unstable two-thirds majority which had enabled the Senate Radical Republicans on several occasions to enact legislation over the President's veto was, they knew, insufficiently reliable for an impeachment conviction. To solidify this bloc became the paramount goal of Congress, expressly or impliedly governing its decisions on other issues—particularly the admission of new states, the readmission of Southern states, and the determination of senatorial credentials. By extremely dubious methods a pro-Johnson Senator was denied his seat. Over the President's veto Nebraska was admitted to the Union, seating two more anti-administration Senators. Although last minute maneuvers failed to admit Colorado over the President's veto (sparsely populated Colorado had rejected statehood in a referendum), an unexpected tragedy brought false tears and fresh hopes for a new vote, in Kansas.

Senator Jim Lane of Kansas had been a "conservative" Republican sympathetic to Johnson's plans to carry out Lincoln's reconstruction policies. But his frontier state was one of the most "radical" in the Union. When Lane voted to uphold Johnson's veto of the Civil Rights Bill of 1866 and introduced the administration's bill for recognition of the new state government of Arkansas, Kansas had arisen in outraged heat. A mass meeting at Lawrence had vilified the Senator and speedily reported resolutions sharply condemning his position. Humiliated, mentally ailing, broken in health and laboring under charges of financial irregularities, Jim Lane took his own life on July 1, 1866.

With this thorn in their side removed, the Radical Republicans in Washington looked anxiously toward Kansas and the selection of Lane's successor. Their fondest hopes were realized, for the new Senator from Kansas turned out to be Edmund G. Ross, the very man who had introduced the resolutions attacking Lane at Lawrence.

There could be no doubt as to where Ross's sympathies lay, for his entire career was one of determined opposition to the slave states of the South, their practices and their friends. In 1854, when only twenty-eight, he had taken part in the mob rescue of a fugitive slave in Milwaukee. In 1856, he had joined that flood of antislavery immigrants to "bleeding" Kansas who intended to keep it a free territory. Disgusted with the Democratic party of his youth he had left that party, and volunteered in the Kansas Free State Army to drive back a force of proslavery men invading the territory. In 1862, he had given up his newspaper work to enlist in the Union Army, from which he emerged a Major. His leading role in the condemnation of Lane at Lawrence convinced the Radical Republican leaders in Congress that in Edmund G. Ross they had a solid member of that vital two-thirds.

The stage was now set for the final scene—the removal of Johnson. Early in 1867, Congress enacted over the President's veto the Tenure-of-Office Bill which prevented the President from removing without the consent of the Senate all new officeholders whose appointment required confirmation by that body. At the time nothing more than the cry for more patronage was involved, Cabinet members having originally been specifically exempt.

On August 5, 1867, President Johnson—convinced that the Secretary of War whom he had inherited from Lincoln, Edwin M. Stanton, was the surreptitious tool of the Radical Republicans and was seeking to become the almighty dictator of the conquered South—asked for his immediate resignation; and Stanton arrogantly fired back the reply that he declined to resign before the next meeting of Congress. Not one to cower before this kind of effrontery, the President one week later suspended Stanton, and appointed in his place the one man whom Stanton did not dare resist, General Grant. On January 13, 1868, an angry Senate notified the President and Grant that it did not concur in the suspension of Stanton, and Grant vacated the office upon Stanton's return. But the situation was intolerable. The Secretary of War was unable to attend Cabinet meetings or associate with his colleagues in the administration; and on February 21, President Johnson, anxious to obtain a court test of the act he believed obviously unconstitutional, again notified

Stanton that he had been summarily removed from the office of Secretary of War.

While Stanton, refusing to yield possession, barricaded himself in his office, public opinion in the nation ran heavily against the President. He had intentionally broken the law and dictatorially thwarted the will of Congress! Although previous resolutions of impeachment had been defeated in the House, both in committee and on the floor, a new resolution was swiftly reported and adopted on February 24 by a tremendous vote. Every single Republican voted in the affirmative, and Thaddeus Stevens of Pennsylvania—the crippled, fanatical personification of the extremes of the Radical Republican movement, master of the House of Representatives, with a mouth like the thin edge of an ax—warned both Houses of the Congress coldly: "Let me see the recreant who would vote to let such a criminal escape. Point me to one who will dare do it and I will show you one who will dare the infamy of posterity."

With the President impeached—in effect, indicted—by the House, the frenzied trial for his conviction or acquittal under the Articles of Impeachment began on March 5 in the Senate, presided over by the Chief Justice. It was a trial to rank with all of the great trials of history—Charles I before the High Court of Justice, Louis XVI before the French Convention, and Warren Hastings before the House of Lords. Two great elements of drama were missing: the actual cause for which the President was being tried was not fundamental to the welfare of the nation; and the defendant himself was at all times absent.

But every other element of the highest courtroom drama was present. To each Senator the Chief Justice administered an oath "to do impartial justice" (including even the hotheaded Radical Senator from Ohio, Benjamin Wade, who as President Pro Tempore of the Senate was next in line for the Presidency). The chief prosecutor for the House was General Benjamin F. Butler, the "butcher of New Orleans," a talented but coarse and demagogic Congressman from Massachusetts. (When he lost his seat in 1874, he was so hated by his own party as well as his opponents that one Republican wired concerning the Democratic sweep, "Butler defeated, everything else lost.") Some one thousand tickets were printed for admission to the Senate galleries during the trial, and every conceivable device was used to obtain one of the four tickets allotted each Senator.

From the fifth of March to the sixteenth of May, the drama continued. Of the eleven Articles of Impeachment adopted by the House, the first eight were based upon the removal of Stanton and the appointment of a new Secretary of War in violation of the Tenure-of-Office Act; the ninth related to Johnson's conversation with a general which was said to induce violations of the Army Appropriations Act; the tenth recited that Johnson had delivered "intemperate, inflammatory and scandalous harangues . . . as well against Congress as the laws of the United States"; and the eleventh was a deliberately obscure conglomeration of all the charges in the preceding articles, which had been designed by Thaddeus Stevens to furnish a common ground for those who favored conviction but were unwilling to identify themselves on basic issues. In opposition to Butler's inflammatory arguments in support of this hastily drawn indictment, Johnson's able and learned counsel replied with considerable effectiveness. They insisted that the Tenure-of-Office Act was null and void as a clear violation of the Constitution; that even if it were valid, it would not apply to Stanton, for the reasons previously mentioned; and that the only way that a judicial test of the law could be obtained was for Stanton to be dismissed and sue for his rights in the courts.

But as the trial progressed, it became increasingly apparent that the impatient Republicans did not intend to give the President a fair trial on the formal issues upon which the impeachment was drawn, but intended instead to depose him from the White House on any grounds, real or imagined, for refusing to accept their policies. Telling evidence in the President's favor was arbitrarily excluded. Prejudgment on the part of most Senators was brazenly announced. Attempted bribery and other forms of pressure were rampant. The chief interest was not in the trial or the evidence, but in the tallying of votes necessary for conviction.

Twenty-seven states (excluding the unrecognized Southern states) in the Union meant fifty-four members of the Senate, and thirty-six votes were required to constitute the two-thirds majority for conviction. All twelve Democratic votes were obviously lost, and the forty-two Republicans knew that they could afford to lose only six of their own members if Johnson were to be ousted. To their dismay, at a preliminary Republican caucus, six courageous Republicans indicated that the evidence so far introduced was not in their opinion sufficient to convict Johnson under the Articles of Impeachment. "Infamy!" cried the Philadelphia Press. The Republic had "been betrayed in the house of its friends!"

But if the remaining thirty-six Republicans would hold, there would be no doubt as to the outcome. All must stand together! But one Republican would not announce his verdict in the preliminary poll—Edmund G. Ross of Kansas. The Radicals were outraged that a Senator from such an anti-Johnson stronghold as Kansas could be doubtful. "It was a very clear case," Senator Sumner of Massachusetts fumed, "especially for a Kansas man. I did not think that a Kansas man could quibble against his country."

From the very time Ross had taken his seat, the Radical leaders had been confident of his vote. His entire background, as already indicated, was one of firm support of their cause. One of his first acts in the Senate had been to read a declaration of his adherence to Radical Republican policy, and he had silently voted for all of their measures. He had made it clear that he was not in sympathy with Andrew Johnson personally or politically; and after the removal of Stanton, he had voted with the majority in adopting a resolution declaring such removal unlawful. His colleague from Kansas, Senator Pomeroy, was one of the most Radical leaders of the anti-Johnson group. The Republicans insisted that Ross's crucial vote was rightfully theirs, and they were determined to get it by whatever means available. As stated by De Witt in his memorable *Impeachment of Andrew Johnson*, "The full brunt of the struggle turned at last on the one remaining doubtful Senator, Edmund G. Ross."

When the impeachment resolution had passed the House, Senator Ross had casually remarked to Senator Sprague of Rhode

Island, "Well, Sprague, the thing is here; and, so far as I am concerned, though a Republican and opposed to Mr. Johnson and his policy, he shall have as fair a trial as an accused man ever had on this earth." Immediately the word spread that "Ross was shaky." "From that hour," he later wrote, "not a day passed that did not bring me, by mail and telegraph and in personal intercourse, appeals to stand fast for impeachment, and not a few were admonitions of condign visitations upon any indication even of lukewarmness."

Throughout the country, and in all walks of life, as indicated by the correspondence of Members of the Senate, the condition of the public mind was not unlike that preceding a great battle. The dominant party of the nation seemed to occupy the position of public prosecutor, and it was scarcely in the mood to brook delay for the trial or to hear defense. Washington had become during the trial the central point of the politically dissatisfied and swarmed with representatives of every state of the Union, demanding in a practically united voice the deposition of the President. The footsteps of anti-impeaching Republicans were dogged from the day's beginning, to its end and far into the night, with entreaties, considerations and threats. The newspapers came daily filled with not a few threats of violence upon their return to their constituents.

Ross and his fellow Republicans were daily pestered, spied upon and subjected to every form of pressure. Their residences were carefully watched, their social circles suspiciously scrutinized, and their every move and companion secretly marked in special notebooks. They were warned in the party press, harangued by their constituents, and sent dire warnings threatening political ostracism and even assassination. Stanton, himself, from his barricaded headquarters in the War Department, worked day and night to bring to bear upon the doubtful Senators all the weight of his impressive military associations. The Philadelphia *Press* reported "a fearful avalanche of telegrams from every section of the country," a great surge of public opinion from the "common people" who had given their money and lives to the country and would not "willingly or unavenged see their great sacrifice made naught."

The New York *Tribune* reported that Edmund Ross in particular was "mercilessly dragged this way and that by both sides, hunted like a fox night and day and badgered by his own colleagues, like the bridge at Arcola now trod upon by one army and now trampled by the other." His background and life were investigated from top to bottom, and his constituents and colleagues pursued him throughout Washington to gain some inkling of his opinion. He was the target of every eye, his name was on every mouth and his intentions were discussed in every newspaper. Although there is evidence that he gave some hint of agreement to each side, and each attempted to claim him publicly, he actually kept both sides in a state of complete suspense by his judicial silence.

But with no experience in political turmoil, no reputation in the Senate, no independent income and the most radical state in the Union to deal with, Ross was judged to be the most sensitive to criticism and the most certain to be swayed by expert tactics. A committee of Congressmen and Senators sent to Kansas, and to the states of the other doubtful Republicans, this telegram: "Great danger to the peace of the country and the Republican cause if impeachment fails. Send to your Senators public opinion by resolutions, letters, and delegations." A member of the Kansas Legislature called upon Ross at the Capitol. A general urged on by Stanton remained at his lodge until four o'clock in the morning determined to see him. His brother received a letter offering $20,000 for revelation of the Senator's intentions. Gruff Ben Butler exclaimed of Ross, "There is a bushel of money! How much does that damned scoundrel want?" The night before the Senate was to take its first vote for the conviction or acquittal of Johnson, Ross received this telegram from home:

> Kansas has heard the evidence and demands the conviction of the President.
>
> > (signed) D. R. Anthony and 1,000 Others

And on that fateful morning of May 16 Ross replied:

> To D. R. Anthony and 1,000 Others: I do not recognize your right to demand that I vote for or against conviction. I have taken

an oath to do impartial justice according to the Constitution and laws, and trust that I shall have the courage to vote according to the dictates of my judgment and for the highest good of the country.

(signed) E. G. Ross

That morning spies traced Ross to his breakfast; and ten minutes before the vote was taken his Kansas colleague warned him in the presence of Thaddeus Stevens that a vote for acquittal would mean trumped-up charges and his political death.

But now the fateful hour was at hand. Neither escape, delay nor indecision was possible. As Ross himself later described it: "The galleries were packed. Tickets of admission were at an enormous premium. The House had adjourned and all of its members were in the Senate chamber. Every chair on the Senate floor was filled with a Senator, a Cabinet Officer, a member of the President's counsel or a member of the House." Every Senator was in his seat, the desperately ill Grimes of Iowa being literally carried in.

It had been decided to take the first vote under that broad Eleventh Article of Impeachment, believed to command the widest support. As the Chief Justice announced the voting would begin, he reminded "the citizens and strangers in the galleries that absolute silence and perfect order are required." But already a deathlike stillness enveloped the Senate chamber. A Congressman later recalled that "Some of the members of the House near me grew pale and sick under the burden and suspense"; and Ross noted that there was even "a subsidence of the shuffling of feet, the rustling of silks, the fluttering of fans, and of conversation."

The voting tensely commenced. By the time the Chief Justice reached the name of Edmund Ross twenty-four "guilties" had been pronounced. Ten more were certain. Only Ross's vote was needed to obtain the thirty-six votes necessary to convict the President. But not a single person in the room knew how this young Kansan would vote. Unable to conceal the suspense and emotion in his voice, the Chief Justice put the question to him: "Mr. Senator Ross, how say you? Is the respondent Andrew Johnson guilty or not guilty of a high misdemeanor as charged in this Article?" Every voice was still; every eye was upon the freshman Senator from Kansas. The hopes and fears, the hatred and bitterness of past decades were centered upon this °one man.

As Ross himself later described it, his "powers of hearing and seeing seemed developed in an abnormal degree."

> Every individual in that great audience seemed distinctly visible, some with lips apart and bending forward in anxious expectancy, others with hand uplifted as if to ward off an apprehended blow . . . and each peering with an intensity that was almost tragic upon the face of him who was about to cast the fateful vote. . . . Every fan was folded, not a foot moved, not the rustle of a garment, not a whisper was heard. . . . Hope and fear seemed blended in every face, instantaneously alternating, some with revengeful hate . . . others lighted with hope. . . . The Senators in their seats leaned over their desks, many with hand to ear. . . . It was a tremendous responsibility, and it was not strange that he upon whom it had been imposed by a fateful combination of conditions should have sought to avoid it, to put it away from him as one shuns, or tries to fight off, a nightmare . . . I almost literally looked down into my open grave. Friendships, position, fortune, everything that makes life desirable to an ambitious man were about to be swept away by the breath of my mouth, perhaps forever. It is not strange that my answer was carried waveringly over the air and failed to reach the limits of the audience, or that repetition was called for by distant Senators on the opposition side of the Chamber.

Then came the answer again in a voice that could not be mis-understood—full, final, definite, unhesitating and unmistakable: "Not guilty." The deed was done, the President saved, the trial as good as over and the conviction lost. The remainder of the roll call was unimportant; conviction had failed by the margin of a single vote, and a general rumbling filled the Chamber until the Chief Justice proclaimed that "on this Article thirty-five Senators have voted guilty and nineteen not guilty, a two-thirds majority not having voted for conviction, the President is, therefore, acquitted under this Article."

A ten-day recess followed, ten turbulent days to change votes on the remaining Articles. An attempt was made to rush through bills to readmit six Southern states whose twelve Senators were guaranteed to vote for conviction. But they could not be accomplished in time. Again Ross was the only one uncommitted on the other Articles, the only one whose vote could not be predicted in advance. And again he was subjected to terrible pressure. From "D. R. Anthony and Others," he received a wire informing him that "Kansas repudiates you as she does all perjurers and skunks." Every incident in his life was examined and distorted. Professional witnesses were found by Senator Pomeroy to testify before a special House committee that Ross had indicated a willingness to change his vote for a consideration. (Unfortunately this witness was so delighted in his exciting role that he also swore that Senator Pomeroy had made an offer to produce three votes for acquittal for $40,000.) When Ross, in his capacity as a Committee Chairman, took several bills to the President, James G. Blaine remarked: "There goes the rascal to get his pay." (Long afterward Blaine was to admit: "In the exaggerated denunciation caused by the anger and chagrin of the moment, great injustice was done to statesmen of spotless character.")

Again the wild rumors spread that Ross had been won over on the remaining Articles of Impeachment. As the Senate reassembled, he was the only one of the seven "renegade" Republicans to vote with the majority on preliminary procedural matters. But when the second and third Articles of Impeachment were read, and the name of Ross was reached again with the same intense suspense of ten days earlier, again came the calm answer "Not guilty."

Why did Ross, whose dislike for Johnson continued, vote "Not guilty"? His motives appear clearly from his own writings on the subject years later in articles contributed to *Scribner's* and *Forum* magazines:

In a large sense, the independence of the executive office as a coordinate branch of the government was on trial. . . . If . . . the President must step down . . . a disgraced man and a political outcast . . . upon insufficient proofs and from partisan considerations, the office of President would be degraded, cease to be a coordinate branch of the government, and ever after subordinated to the legislative will. It would practically have revolutionized our splendid political fabric into partisan Congressional autocracy. . . . This government had never faced so insidious a danger . . . control by the worst elements of American politics. . . . If Andrew Johnson were acquitted by a nonpartisan vote . . . America would pass the danger point of partisan rule and that intolerance which so often characterizes the sway of great majorities and makes them dangerous.

The "open grave" which Edmund Ross had foreseen was hardly an exaggeration. A Justice of the Kansas Supreme Court telegraphed him that "the rope with which Judas Iscariot hanged himself is lost, but Jim Lane's pistol is at your service." An editorial in a Kansas newspaper screamed:

On Saturday last Edmund G. Ross, United States Senator from Kansas, sold himself, and betrayed his constituents; stultified his own record, basely lied to his friends, shamefully violated his solemn pledge . . . and to the utmost of his poor ability signed the death warrant of this country's liberty. The act was done deliberately, because the traitor, like Benedict Arnold, loved money better than he did principle, friends, honor and his country, all combined. Poor, pitiful, shriveled wretch, with a soul so small that a little pelf would outweigh all things else that dignify or ennoble manhood.

Ross's political career was ended. To the New York *Tribune,* he was nothing but a "miserable poltroon and traitor." The Philadelphia *Press* said that in Ross "littleness" had "simply borne its legitimate fruit," and that he and his fellow recalcitrant Republicans had "plunged from a precipice of fame into the groveling depths of infamy and death." The Philadelphia *Inquirer* said that "They have tried, convicted and sentenced themselves." From them there could be "no allowance, no clemency."

Comparative peace returned to Washington as Stanton relinquished his office and Johnson served out the rest of his term, later —unlike his Republican defenders—to return triumphantly to the Senate as Senator from Tennessee. But no one paid attention when Ross tried unsuccessfully to explain his vote and denounce the falsehoods of Ben Butler's investigating committee, recalling that the General's "well known groveling instincts and proneness to slime and uncleanness" had led "the public to insult the brute creation by dubbing him 'the beast'!" He clung unhappily to his seat in the Senate until the expiration of his term, frequently referred to as "the traitor Ross," and complaining that his fellow Congressmen, as well as citizens on the street, considered association with him "disreputable and scandalous," and passed him by as if he were "a leper, with averted face and every indication of hatred and disgust."

Neither Ross nor any other Republican who had voted for the acquittal of Johnson was ever re-elected to the Senate, nor a one of them retaining the support of their party's organization. When he returned to Kansas in 1871, he and his family suffered social ostracism, physical attack, and near poverty.

Who was Edmund G. Ross? Practically nobody. Not a single public law bears his name, not a single history book includes his picture, not a single list of Senate "greats" mentions his service. His one heroic deed has been all but forgotten. But who might Edmund G. Ross have been? That is the question—for Ross, a man with an excellent command of words, an excellent background for politics and an excellent future in the Senate, might well have outstripped his colleagues in prestige and power throughout a long Senate career. Instead, he chose to throw all of this away for one act of conscience.

But the twisting course of human events eventually upheld the faith he expressed to his wife shortly after the trial: "Millions of men cursing me today will bless me tomorrow for having saved the country from the greatest peril through which it has ever passed, though none but God can ever know the struggle it has cost me." For twenty years later Congress repealed the Tenure-of-Office Act, to which every President after Johnson, regardless of party, had objected; and still later the Supreme Court, referring to "the extremes of that episode in our government," held it to be unconstitutional. Ross moved to New Mexico, where in his later years he was to be appointed Territorial Governor. Just prior to his death when he was awarded a special pension by Congress for his service in the Civil War, the press and the country took the opportunity to pay tribute to his fidelity to principle in a trying hour and his courage in saving his government from a devastating reign of terror. They now agreed with Ross's earlier judgment that his vote had "saved the country from . . . a strain that would have wrecked any other form of government." Those Kansas newspapers and political leaders who had bitterly denounced him in earlier years praised Ross for his stand against legislative mob rule: "By the firmness and courage of Senator Ross," it was said, "the country was saved from calamity greater than war, while it consigned him to political martyrdom, the most cruel in our history. . . . Ross was the victim of a wild flame of intolerance which swept everything before it. He did his duty knowing that it meant his political death. . . . It was a brave thing for Ross to do, but Ross did it. He acted for his conscience and with a lofty patriotism, regardless of what he knew must be the ruinous consequences to himself. He acted right." . . .

Men of Courage and Conscience in Politics

by Edwin D. Canham

Book Review of
Profiles in Courage
by John F. Kennedy

THE CHRISTIAN SCIENCE MONITOR
January 5, 1956

The Junior Senator from Massachusetts has recently had to spend a lot of time in convalescence. He has spent it well. For he has made a particular study of political courage—the kind of courage which requires a man (and in almost all cases of this book, a Senator) to break with his friends, his party, his constituents, in the interest of his conscience.

In concentrating on courageous independence from party and special interest, Senator Kennedy inevitably invites attention to his own political career. I can think of three particular instances (there have been others) in which he has been tested. In one of them, he refused to make a defamatory speech against his opponent in 1952, then Senator Henry Cabot Lodge, though he was under close and influential pressure to do so. He won the election anyway, though narrowly and against many expectations, and the speech could hardly have done him much good. But I always felt he deserved real credit for not making it.

In the second instance, Senator Kennedy voted against the general assumption of Boston and Massachusetts interest in supporting the St. Lawrence Seaway legislation. He suffered no visible political harm, and he explained himself well at the time.

In the third instance, Senator Kennedy neither voted nor was paired when the Senate took its crucial votes on the "censure" of Senator McCarthy.

On the whole, the Senator stacks up well, and he must watch his step in the future, for he has set up high standards of political integrity for comparison. The men he writes about include some titans of American history, and a nobody—Senator Edmund G. Ross, of Kansas, whose vote was one of the seven any one of which may be credited with preventing the impeachment of President Andrew Johnson. Senator Kennedy justifies selecting Senator Ross on the ground that the six other Republicans who refused to vote for impeachment had made their positions known earlier, and that Ross was under pressure to the end. All of them, as he adds rather as an afterthought, deserve very great credit, and certainly Senator Ross—who was punished for many years by his stand—merits discussion.

In these days, any study of political independence and courage is to be welcomed. But that a United States Senator, a young man of independent means with a gallant and thoughtful background, should have produced this study is as remarkable as it is hopeful. It is a splendid flag that Senator Kennedy has nailed to his mast. May he keep it there.

Men Who Dared to
Stand Alone

by Cabell Phillips

Book Review of
John F. Kennedy's
Profiles in Courage

One of the reasons that the profession of politics suffers from such low public esteem is that it is constantly being run down by politicians themselves. No one can make such an epithet of the expression "Politics!" as a self-righteous politician, who seems to be striving thereby to elevate himself above his calling.

In this unfortunate state of affairs, it is refreshing and enlightening to have a first-rate politician write a thoughtful and persuasive book about political integrity. This is the burden of *Profiles in Courage*, by John F. Kennedy, Democratic Senator from Massachusetts. His subjects are John Quincy Adams, Daniel Webster, Thomas Hart Benton, Sam Houston, Edmund G. Ross, Lucius Quintus Cincinnatus Lamar, George Norris and Robert A.

Taft, each of whom at some moment of crisis staked his principles against the massed furies of bigotry, sectionalism and conformity.

Conspicuous courage is difficult to come by under most circumstances, but it is weighted with extra penalties in the political world, and particularly in Congress. The reason is that elective officials have far less mastery over their destiny than other men: the best can be destroyed as quickly by the inscrutable caprice of their constituents as the worst by some deliberate malfeasance in office. And further complicating their lives is the fact that the way of duty lies in a murky, uncharted line between the Scylla of constituent interest and the Charybdis of national welfare. The conscientious legislator must forever be weighing and compromising between these often antagonistic imperatives, and with the hot breath of the voters back home forever blowing on his neck.

"The way of getting along," Senator Kennedy says he was told early in his Congressional career, "is to go along." This certainly is the counsel of prudence, and a great many of his colleagues, dead and living, have assiduously followed it into a peaceful oblivion.

For himself, he rejects the view that "the people of Massachusetts sent me to Washington to serve merely as a seismograph to record shifts in popular opinion. . . . The voters selected us because they had confidence in our judgment and our ability to exercise that judgment [in] their own best interests as a part of the nation's interests. This may mean that we on occasion lead, inform, correct and sometimes even ignore constituent opinion."

It was this doctrine, too, as he clearly shows, that animated the heroes of his book, costing some their political heads but endowing each with the nimbus of immortality. These are stirring tales, packed with drama, suspense, high purpose, reward and retribution. Each character took a stand—some fearlessly, others in frank trepidation—on some critical issue of his day that was unpopular with his constituents or his party but which his conscience would not let him evade. . . .

Senator Kennedy writes from the dual eminence of a perceptive and reflective mind and of practical, first-hand political experience.

Like many able younger members of Congress, he has brooded over the role of the Legislature and the legislator, their weaknesses and unrealized potentials, and whether, indeed, the days of giants are gone forever. He crystallized these meditations during the course of a long convalescence last spring. What made the subject so appealing to him was that, as a politician, he is peculiarly attuned to the challenges and the sacrifices that the conscientious practitioner encounters. . . . He is no dilettante at his trade, but a solid journeyman full of ideals, but few illusions. His book is the sort to restore respect for a venerable and much abused profession.

from The Kennedy Wit

by Bill Adler

When we got into office, the thing that surprised me most was to find that things were just as bad as we'd been saying they were.

> *Washington, D.C. dinner honoring*
> *President Kennedy's 44th birthday*
> May 27, 1961

In September, 1963, at the Salt Lake City, Utah, airport, President Kennedy pulled the switch to activate generators at the Green River in the Colorado River basin 150 miles away.

I never know when I press these whether I am going to blow up Massachusetts or start the project.

An Intelligent Courageous Presidency

Editorial, LIFE Magazine

November 29, 1963

Next to the incredulous shock and sorrow, perhaps the commonest emotion after President Kennedy's assassination was fury. It was the kind of helpless fury rational people feel at an irrational act. As Theodore Roosevelt wrote about the last assassination of a President, that of McKinley: "It was in the most naked way an assault not on power, nor on wealth, but simply and solely upon free government, government by the common people, because it was government and because it yet stood for order as well as for liberty."

. . . Assassination cannot undermine the republic though it can martyr a leader. The crime of November 22, 1963, removed from the White House one of the most intelligent and attractive of our 35 Presidents, John F. Kennedy, to whom may God give rest.

Intelligence was the keynote of Kennedy's short presidency, and with it came a style, flair and excitement which had not been seen in the office for many years. Whatever you thought of John Kennedy's solutions, he grasped problems quickly, the great and little, and with the help of his high-caliber team was a master of their detail. He was beautifully equipped for the presidency. He had sought it hard and he liked it fine. "We learned from the Kennedy men that they play politics with a hard ball in the east," said a western governor after the 1960 convention. Kennedy sought it hard for the simple reason that the presidency meant power. He liked it fine because the power meant he could do something about "all the problems which if I was not the President, I would be concerned about as a father or citizen." He did not make the White House seem a prison or "the loneliest job in the world." He was at home there and made it a brighter place.

Nevertheless he soon found that the powers of the presidency are not what they had looked like from his seat in the Senate. Too much of the power was nuclear and not to be brandished; the rest, especially his power with Congress, proved elusive and hard to bring to bear. No experience, he admitted, "can possibly prepare you adequately for the presidency"; the responsibilities were greater, the decisions harder, and the limitations stricter "than I had imagined them to be." He suffered frustration in his legislative program; yet before his death, instead of making new enemies, he was making it harder for his old enemies to say just why they opposed him. He leaves the nation prosperous. He had even begun to lead it toward a clear confrontation with our greatest moral and social problem, Negro equality. Hearing the news of the President's death while driving a couple across the Brooklyn Bridge, a Negro cab driver said, "It was the first time I cried with white people."

Abroad, the shock disclosed more love and regard for President Kennedy than most Americans had known was there. "It seems as though all the presidents of all the Latin American countries have died," said a man in Bogotá. French leaders spoke of his "spiritual and intellectual aura"; the British Prime Minister called him "the best of allies"; and 60,000 Berliners thronged a great square to mourn the man who, two years ago, erased the deadline from Khrushchev's threat to their city. And Moscow too was grief-stricken because, said one citizen, "We Russians honored this man, and trusted him, like no other American before."

The world changed fast in Kennedy's three years. Whether or not he controlled these changes, he was never put off balance by them; and his courage in the Cuban missile showdown may have changed the history of the world. Authough his détente with Khrushchev and his Alliance for Progress are precarious, and NATO is in trouble, he set some things in motion that time may give wings to; and nobody ever doubted the nobility of his aims. His inaugural called for "a new world of law, where the strong are just and the weak secure and the peace preserved. . . . In your hands, my fellow citizens, more than mine, will rest the final success or failure of our course." He died before he could be judged a great President by his contemporaries. He could have become one.

One thing he left us beyond question: a high personal example of intelligence and grace in action. The rewards he found in his job, he said this month, were those of the Greek definition of happiness: "the full use of your powers along lines of excellence." His excellence was many sided. At Amherst, last month, he discussed the unpresidential subject of poetry. "When power leads man toward arrogance, poetry reminds him of his limitations. When power narrows the areas of man's concern, poetry reminds him of the richness and diversity of his existence. When power corrupts, poetry cleanses. . . . I look forward to an America which will not be afraid of grace and beauty . . . which will steadily enlarge cultural opportunities for all of our citizens . . . which commands respect not only for its strength but for its civilization as well. And I look forward to a world which will be safe not only for democracy and diversity but also for personal distinction." John F. Kennedy had personal distinction, and his country and the world are the richer for it. . . .

Upon Education Rests
The Fate of the Nation

by Sen. John F. Kennedy

NEA JOURNAL
January, 1958

*This article was written by Senator John F. Kennedy
in January, 1958. In it the future President expresses his belief
in the great value of education and the urgent need to take
measures to ensure adequate teaching facilities for the impending
explosion in school enrollment.*

Crucial questions confront America today: Will we provide world
leadership or display fatal weakness? Will we succeed or fail in
the struggle for survival during the years to come?

The answers, I sincerely believe, depend on whether our educational system is capable of meeting the challenge of today or
whether a shortage of teachers, classrooms, and money—with a
consequent lack of high-quality education—will prove in the long
run to be the undoing of our nation.

That public education is in a state of crisis today is well known. There is less agreement on the cause and the cure. I only hope that those who recognize the urgent need of improving public education in this country will not exhaust their efforts in looking for a scapegoat but will join in attacking the problem at its very roots.

The responsibility for ending this crisis, in my opinion, must be shared at three levels—federal, state and local.

First, the federal government, which has far greater, as well as more effective, means for raising public revenues, has an unavoidable responsibility to enact promptly a bold and imaginative program of federal assistance to the states and to local school districts for the construction of public schools, leaving all direction of academic content and standards, of course, in local hands.

Our teachers cannot be expected to fulfill their critical responsibilities when nearly a million boys and girls are deprived by the classroom shortage of full-time schooling, and when hundreds of thousands more are held back in unwieldy classes of 40 or more. We need this year additional classrooms to meet the requirements of several million more pupils than we presently have adequate room for in our elementary and secondary schools.

The valiant efforts of state and local authorities, which spent over $2.5 billion in school construction during the last school year, must be supplemented by federal action to meet this nation-wide crisis.

But more and better classrooms are not enough. More and better teachers are also needed—better trained, better paid, better utilized. Here the state and local authorities share responsibility.

Our state governments must provide teachers' colleges that attract the best students and provide the best education. Some states still have too many teachers' colleges, which are, as a result, too small, too poorly financed and staffed, and too ill equipped in terms of physical plant, libraries, laboratories and other facilities.

Authorities on the state level could also take steps to improve teacher certification, re-examining outmoded statutory requirements, maintaining standards, and providing for those who become certificated a sense of accomplishment and prestige comparable to that felt by candidates admitted to the legal and medical professions.

Finally, a large measure of responsibility for improving the quality of teaching in our schools rests with local school boards and school administrators.

Not as a United States Senator, but as an interested citizen, I would respectfully suggest that present methods for recruiting teachers be improved in order to attract the best students, to select the best graduates, and to compete in the labor market with the expertly developed recruitment methods of American business.

Although the figure is too staggering to comprehend fully, the fact is that our schools must recruit in the next three years alone almost three-quarters of a million new teachers—more than our entire school system contained not too long ago.

Once teachers are recruited and hired, more can be done to improve the methods of teacher promotion. We must find better means for providing better rewards for our better teachers, we must make actual use of probationary periods to retain only those with satisfactory performance records, and we must demonstrate concretely to young beginners in the field that real opportunities for advancement await those whose contribution is of the highest caliber.

More can be done, in terms of better teacher utilization—by removing burdensome administrative details and paper work that might better be done by electronic computers or by parent volunteers.

And perhaps most important, school boards, school patrons, and all of our citizens must cooperate in the effort to achieve better teachers' salaries. No profession of such importance in the United States today is so poorly paid. No other occupational group in the country is asked to do so much for so little.

No amount of new classrooms, television, training, and recruitment techniques can attract and retain good teachers as long as their salaries are beneath the responsibility and dignity of their position. We pay the average railway conductor nearly twice as much as we pay the teacher who conducts our elementary classes. Plumbers, plasterers, and steamfitters are paid more for improving our homes than we pay teachers for improving our children.

Help from the federal level for more and better classrooms; help from the state level for better teachers' colleges and better teacher certification; help from the local level for better salaries and for better recruitment, promotion, and utilization of teachers— those are the goals toward which must move all who recognize that upon education rests the fate of the nation.

"Knowledge is power," said Francis Bacon. It is also light. In the dark and despairing days ahead, our youth shall need all the light the teaching profession can bring to bear upon the future.

In his book, *One Man's America,* Alistair Cooke tells a story which illustrates my point. On May 19, 1780, as he describes it, in Hartford, Connecticut, the skies at noon turned from blue to gray, "and by midafternoon had blackened over so densely that, in that religious age, men fell on their knees and begged a final blessing before the end came.

"The Connecticut House of Representatives was in session. And as some men fell down [in the darkened chamber] and others clamored for an immediate adjournment, the Speaker of the House, one Colonel Davenport, came to his feet. And he silenced the din with these words: 'The day of Judgement is either approaching or it is not. If it is not, there is no cause for adjournment. If it is, I choose to be found doing my duty. I wish, therefore, that candles may be brought.' "

Today, all of us who hope for future peace and security must look to the teachers of America as we ask that "candles may be brought" to light the way ahead.

On Civil Rights

Special Message to the Congress

February 28, 1963

To the Congress of the United States:

"Our Constitution is color blind," wrote Mr. Justice Harlan before the turn of the century, "and neither knows nor tolerates classes among citizens." But the practices of the country do not always conform to the principles of the Constitution. And this Message is intended to examine how far we have come in achieving first-class citizenship for all citizens regardless of color, how far we have yet to go, and what further tasks remain to be carried out—by the Executive and Legislative Branches of the Federal Government, as well as by state and local governments and private citizens and organizations.

One hundred years ago the Emancipation Proclamation was

signed by a President who believed in the equal worth and opportunity of every human being. That Proclamation was only a first step—a step which its author unhappily did not live to follow up, a step which some of its critics dismissed as an action which "frees the slave but ignores the Negro." Through these long one hundred years, while slavery has vanished, progress for the Negro has been too often blocked and delayed. Equality before the law has not always meant equal treatment and opportunity. And the harmful, wasteful and wrongful results of racial discrimination and segregation still appear in virtually every aspect of national life, in virtually every part of the Nation.

The Negro baby born in America today—regardless of the section or state in which he is born—has about one-half as much chance of completing high school as a white baby born in the same place on the same day—one-third as much chance of becoming a professional man—twice as much chance of becoming unemployed —about one-seventh as much chance of earning $10,000 per year —and the prospects of earning only half as much.

No American who believes in the basic truth that "all men are created equal, that they are endowed by their Creator with certain unalienable Rights," can fully excuse, explain or defend the picture these statistics portray. Race discrimination hampers our economic growth by preventing the maximum development and utilization of our manpower. It hampers our world leadership by contradicting at home the message we preach abroad. It mars the atmosphere of a united and classless society in which this Nation rose to greatness. It increases the costs of public welfare, crime, delinquency and disorder. Above all, it is wrong.

Therefore, let it be clear, in our own hearts and minds, that it is not merely because of the Cold War, and not merely because of the economic waste of discrimination, that we are committed to achieving true equality of opportunity. The basic reason is because it is right.

The cruel disease of discrimination knows no sectional or state boundaries. The continuing attack on this problem must be equally broad. It must be both private and public—it must be conducted at national, state and local levels—and it must include both legislative and executive action.

In the last two years, more progress has been made in securing the civil rights of all Americans than in any comparable period in our history. Progress has been made—through executive action, litigation, persuasion and private initiative—in achieving and protecting equality of opportunity in education, voting, transportation, employment, housing, government, and the enjoyment of public accommodations.

But pride in our progress must not give way to relaxation of our effort. Nor does progress in the Executive Branch enable the Legislative Branch to escape its own obligations. On the contrary, it is in the light of this nationwide progress, and in the belief that Congress will wish once again to meet its responsibilities in this matter, that I stress in the following agenda of existing and prospective action important legislative as well as administrative measures.

I. THE RIGHT TO VOTE

The right to vote in a Free American election is the most powerful and precious right in the world—and it must not be denied on the grounds of race or color. It is a potent key to achieving other rights of citizenship. For American history—both recent and past —clearly reveals that the power of the ballot has enabled those who achieve it to win other achievements as well, to gain a full voice in the affairs of their state and nation, and to see their interests represented in the governmental bodies which affect their future. In a free society, those with the power to govern are necessarily responsive to those with the right to vote.

In enacting the 1957 and 1960 Civil Rights Acts, Congress provided the Department of Justice with basic tools for protecting the right to vote—and this Administration has not hesitated to use those tools. . . . As a result, thousands of Negro citizens are registering and voting for the first time—many of them in counties where no Negro has ever voted before. The Department of Justice will continue to take whatever action is required to secure the right to vote for all Americans.

Experience has shown, however, that these highly useful Acts of the 85th and 86th Congresses suffer from two major defects. One is the usual long and difficult delay which occurs between the filing of a lawsuit and its ultimate conclusion. . . .

Too often those who attempt to assert their constitutional rights are intimidated. Prospective registrants are fired. Registration workers are arrested. In some instances, churches in which registration meetings are held have been burned. In one case where Negro tenant farmers chose to exercise their right to vote, it was necessary for the Justice Department to seek injunctions to halt their eviction and for the Department of Agriculture to help feed them from surplus stocks. Under these circumstances, continued delay in the granting of the franchise—particularly in counties where there is mass racial disfranchisement—permits the intent of the Congress to be openly flouted.

Federal executive action in such cases—no matter how speedy and how drastic—can never fully correct such abuses of power. It is necessary to free the forces of our democratic system within these areas by promptly insuring the franchise to all citizens, making it possible for their elected officials to be truly responsive to all their constituents.

The second and somewhat overlapping gap in these statutes is their failure to deal specifically with the most common forms of abuse of discretion on the part of local election officials who do not treat all applicants uniformly. . . .

An indication of the magnitude of the overall problem, as well as the need for speedy action, is a recent five-state survey disclosing over 200 counties in which fewer than 15 per cent of the Negroes of voting age are registered to vote. This cannot continue. I am therefore recommending legislation to deal with this problem of judicial delay and administrative abuse. . . .

II. EDUCATION

Nearly nine years have elapsed since the Supreme Court ruled that state laws requiring or permitting segregated schools violate the Constitution. That decision represented both good law and good judgment—it was both legally and morally right. Since that time it has become increasingly clear that neither violence nor legalistic evasions will be tolerated as a means of thwarting court-ordered desegregation, that closed schools are not an answer, and that responsible communities are able to handle the desegregation process in a calm and sensible manner. This is as it should be—for, as I stated to the Nation at the time of the Mississippi violence last September:

". . . Our Nation is founded on the principle that observance of the law is the eternal safeguard of liberty, and defiance of the law is the surest road to tyranny. The law which we obey includes the final rulings of the courts, as well as the enactments of our legislative bodies. Even among law-abiding men, few laws are universally loved—but they are uniformly respected and not resisted.

"Americans are free to disagree with the law but not to disobey it. For in a government of laws and not of men, no man, however prominent or powerful, and no mob, however unruly or boisterous, is entitled to defy a court of law. If this country should ever reach the point where any man or group of men, by force or threat of force, could long defy the commands of our court and our Constitution, then no law would stand free from doubt, no judge would be sure of his writ, and no citizen would be safe from his neighbors."

The shameful violence which accompanied but did not prevent the end of segregation at the University of Mississippi was an exception. State supported universities in Georgia and South Carolina met this test in recent years with calm and maturity, as did the state supported universities of Virginia, North Carolina, Florida, Texas, Louisiana, Tennessee, Arkansas, and Kentucky in earlier years. In addition, progress toward the desegregation of education at all levels has made other notable and peaceful strides. . . .

Despite these efforts, however, progress toward primary and

secondary school desegregation has still been too slow, often painfully so. Those children who are being denied their constitutional rights are suffering a loss which can never be regained, and which will leave scars which can never be fully healed. I have in the past expressed my belief that the full authority of the Federal government should be placed behind the achievement of school desegregation, in accordance with the command of the Constitution. One obvious area of Federal action is to help facilitate the transition to desegregation in those areas which are conforming or wish to conform their practices to the law.

Many of these communities lack the resources necessary to eliminate segregation in their public schools while at the same time assuring that educational standards will be maintained and improved. The problem has been compounded by the fact that the climate of mistrust in many communities has left many school officials with no qualified source to turn to for information and advice. . . .

I recommend, therefore, a program of Federal technical and financial assistance to aid school districts in the process of desegregation in compliance with the Constitution.

Finally, it is obvious that the unconstitutional and outmoded concept of "separate but equal" does not belong in the Federal statute books. This is particularly true with respect to higher education, where peaceful desegregation has been underway in practically every state for some time. I repeat, therefore, this Administration's recommendation of last year that this phrase be eliminated from the Morrill Land Grant College Act.

III. EXTENSION AND EXPANSION OF THE COMMISSION ON CIVIL RIGHTS

The Commission on Civil Rights, established by the Civil Rights Act of 1957, has been in operation for more than five years and is scheduled to expire on November 30, 1963. During this time it has fulfilled its statutory mandate by investigating deprivations of the right to vote and denials of equal protection of the laws in education, employment, housing, and the administration of justice. The Commission's reports and recommendations have provided the basis for remedial action by both Congress and the Executive Branch.

There are, of course, many areas of denials of rights yet to be fully investigated. But the Commission is now in a position to provide even more useful service to the Nation. As more communities evidence a willingness to face frankly their problems of racial discrimination, there is an increasing need for expert guidance and assistance in devising workable programs for civil rights progress. Agencies of state and local government, industry, labor and community organizations, when faced with problems of segregation and racial tensions, all can benefit from information about how these problems have been solved in the past. The opportunity to seek an experienced and sympathetic forum on a voluntary basis can often open channels of communication between contending parties and help bring about the conditions necessary for orderly progress. And the use of public hearings—to contribute to public knowledge of the requirements of the Constitution and national policy—can create in these communities the atmosphere of understanding which is indispensable to peaceful and permanent solutions to racial problems.

The Federal Civil Rights Commission has the experience and capability to make a significant contribution toward achieving these objectives. It has advised the Executive branch not only about desirable policy changes but also the administrative techniques needed to make these changes effective. If, however, the Commission is to perform these additional services effectively, changes in its authorizing statute are necessary and it should be placed on a more stable and permanent basis. A proposal that the Commission be made a permanent body would be a pessimistic prediction that our problems will never be solved. On the other hand, to let the experience and knowledge gathered by the Commission go to waste by allowing it to expire, or by extending its life only for another two years with no changes in responsibility, would ignore the very real contribution this agency can make toward meeting our racial problems. I recommend, therefore, that the Congress authorize the Civil Rights Commission to serve as a national civil rights clearing house providing information, advice, and technical assistance to any requesting agency, private or public; that in order to fulfill these new responsibilities, the Commission be authorized to concentrate its activities upon those problems within the scope of its statute which most need attention; and that the life of the Commission be extended for a term of at least four more years.

IV. EMPLOYMENT

Racial discrimination in employment is especially injurious both to its victims and to the national economy. It results in a great waste of human resources and creates serious community problems. It is, moreover, inconsistent with the democratic principle that no man should be denied employment commensurate with his abilities because of his race or creed or ancestry.

The President's Committee on Equal Employment Opportunity, reconstituted by Executive Order in early 1961, has under the leadership of the Vice President taken significant steps to eliminate racial discrimination by those who do business with the Government. Hundreds of companies—covering 17 million jobs—have agreed to stringent non-discriminatory provisions now standard in all Government contracts—including most of the Nation's major employers—and have in addition signed agreements calling for an affirmative attack on discrimination in employment; and 117 labor unions, representing about 85 per cent of the membership of the AFL-CIO, have signed similar agreements with the Committee. . . .

In addition, the Federal Government, as an employer, has continued to pursue a policy of non-discrimination in its employment and promotion programs. Negro high school and college graduates are now being intensively sought out and recruited. A policy of not distinguishing on grounds of race is not limited to the appointment of distinguished Negroes—although they have in fact been appointed to a record number of high policy-making judicial and administrative posts. There has also been a significant increase in the number of Negroes employed in the middle and upper grades of the career Federal service. . . .

This Government has also adopted a new Executive policy with respect to the organization of its employees. As part of this policy, only those Federal employee labor organizations that do not discriminate on grounds of race or color will be recognized. . . .

V. PUBLIC ACCOMMODATIONS

No act is more contrary to the spirit of our democracy and Constitution—or more rightfully resented by a Negro citizen who seeks only equal treatment—than the barring of that citizen from restaurants, hotels, theatres, recreational areas and other public accommodations and facilities.

Wherever possible, this Administration has dealt sternly with such acts. In 1961, the Justice Department and the Interstate Commerce Commission successfully took action to bring an end to discrimination in rail and bus facilities. In 1962, the fifteen airports still maintaining segregated facilities were persuaded to change their practices, thirteen voluntary and two others after the Department of Justice brought legal action. As a result of these steps, systematic segregation in interstate transportation terminals, restaurants, rest rooms and other facilities will continue to crop up, but any such discrimination will be dealt with promptly.

In addition, restaurants and public facilities in buildings leased by the Federal Government have been opened to all Federal employees in areas where previously they had been segregated. The General Services Administration no longer contracts for the lease of space in office buildings unless such facilities are available to all Federal employees without regard to race. This move has taken place without fanfare and practically without incident; and full equality of facilities will continue to be made available to all Federal employees in every state.

National parks, forests and other recreation areas—and the District of Columbia Stadium—are open to all without regard to race. Meetings sponsored by the Federal Government or addressed by Federal appointees are held in hotels and halls which do not practice discrimination or segregation. The Department of Justice has asked the Supreme Court to reverse the convictions of Negroes arrested for seeking to use public accommodations; and took action both through the Courts and the use of Federal marshals to protect those who were testing the desegregation of transportation facilities.

In these and other ways, the Federal Government will continue to encourage and support action by state and local communities and by private entrepreneurs, to assure all members of the public equal access to all public accommodations. A country with a "color blind" Constitution, and with no castes or classes among its citizens, cannot afford to do less.

VI. OTHER USES OF FEDERAL FUNDS

The basic standard of non-discrimination—which I earlier stated has now been applied by the Executive Branch to every area of its activity—affects other programs not listed above:

—Although President Truman ordered the armed services of this country desegregated in 1948, it was necessary in 1962 to bar segregation formally and specifically in the Army and Air Force Reserves and in the training of all civil defense workers.

—A new Executive Order on housing, as unanimously recommended by the Civil Rights Commission in 1959, prohibits discrimination in the sale, lease or use of housing owned or constructed in the future by the Federal Government or guaranteed under the FHA, VA, and Farmers Home Administration program. . . .

—The Department of Justice has increased its prosecution of police brutality cases, many of them in Northern states—and is assisting state and local police departments in meeting this problem.

—State employee merit systems operating programs financed with Federal funds are now prohibited from discriminating on the basis of race or color.

—The Justice Department is challenging the constitutionality of the "separate but equal" provisions which permit hospitals constructed with Federal funds to discriminate in the location of patients and the acceptance of doctors.

In short, the Executive Branch of the Federal Government, under this Administration and in all of its activities, now stands squarely behind the principle of equal opportunity, without segregation or discrimination, in the employment of Federal funds, facilities and personnel. All officials at every level are charged with the responsibility of implementing this principle—and a formal interdepartmental action group, under White House chairmanship, oversees this effort and follows through on each directive. For the first time, the full force of Federal Executive authority is being exerted in the battle against race discrimination.

CONCLUSION

The various steps which have been undertaken or which are proposed in this Message do not constitute a final answer to the problems of race discrimination in this country. They do constitute a list of priorities—steps which can be taken by the Executive Branch and measures which can be enacted by the 88th Congress. Other measures directed toward these same goals will be favorably commented on and supported, as they have in the past—and they will be signed, if enacted into law.

In addition, it is my hope that this message will lend encouragement to those state and local governments—and to private organizations, corporations, and individuals—who share my concern over the gap between our precepts and our practices. This is an effort in which every individual who asks what he can do for his country should be able and willing to take part. It is important, for example, for private citizens and local governments to support the State Department's effort to end the discriminatory treatment suffered by too many foreign diplomats, students and visitors to this country. But it is not enough to treat those from other lands with equality and dignity—the same treatment must be afforded to every American citizen.

The program outlined in this message should not provide the occasion for sectional bitterness. No state or section of this Nation can pretend a self-righteous role, for every area has its own civil rights problems.

Nor should the basic elements of this program be imperiled by partisanship. The proposals put forth are consistent with the platforms of both parties and with the positions of their leaders. Inevitably there will be disagreement about means and strategy. But I would hope that on issues of constitutional rights and freedom, as in matters affecting our national security, there is a fundamental unity among us that will survive partisan debate over particular issues.

The centennial of the issuance of the Emancipation Proclamation is an occasion for celebration, for a sober assessment of our failures, and for rededication to the goals of freedom. Surely there could be no more meaningful observance of the centennial than the enactment of effective civil rights legislation and the continuation of effective executive action.

from

Mr. Kennedy and
the Negroes

by Harry Golden

Chapter Six

"Get the Road Maps—and Go"

Harry Golden is a man of extraordinary literary
background, with numerous books, including the popular
Only in America, *to his credit. Publisher of the*
Carolina Israelite, *he is a public prosecutor of injustice*
in all its forms; Mr. Kennedy and the Negroes *is a natural*
outgrowth of that interest. The chapter included herein is a
history of John F. Kennedy's involvement with the cause of
civil rights during his Presidency.

Whooping rebel yells, the twenty delegates from Mississippi gave
their votes for the Vice-Presidential nomination to John Fitzgerald
Kennedy, the junior Senator from the Commonwealth of Massa-

chusetts. It was Friday, August 17, 1956, and the Democratic National Convention was drawing to an exciting close. Its nominee for President, Adlai E. Stevenson, had urged the delegates to select by open balloting his running mate. The choice narrowed between two candidates—Senators Kennedy and Estes Kefauver.

The Southerners made Kennedy their favorite. Throughout the balloting, the South Carolina delegation kept up a steady, rhythmic chant, "We want Kennedy! We want Kennedy!" Senator Sam J. Ervin of North Carolina reported that his delegation, led by Governor Luther H. Hodges, cast seventeen and one-half votes for Kennedy. The delegates from Alabama, Georgia, Texas, and Virginia waved Confederate flags and cheered at this news. North Carolina, the most "regular" Democratic state in the Union, had given this young Massachusetts politican two thirds of its votes and this meant he might conceivably win the number two spot on the ticket.

The Southerners were cheering wildly for a graduate of Harvard University, a Roman Catholic, and an intellectual; they were cheering a New Englander who just the month before, in the pages of *Atlantic Monthly,* had deplored the flight of the textile industry from Massachusetts to the South. And the Southerners could not have been unaware of the civil rights speech the young Senator had delivered on February 7, 1956, before the New York Democratic Club, in which he said, "The Democratic party must not weasel on the issue. . . . President Truman was returned to the White House in 1948 despite a firm stand on civil rights that led even to a third party effort in the South. . . . We might alienate Southern support but the Supreme Court decision is the law of the land."[1]

The Southern delegates wanted Senator Kennedy as Vice-President not because he was for the racial status quo, but because his opponent for the nomination was the late Senator Estes Kefauver from Tennessee, a Southerner who, because of his own outspoken views on civil rights for the Negroes, was therefore a renegade. Of

---

[1] *The New York Times,* February 8, 1956, p. 1.

Kefauver, Senator Sam J. Ervin of North Carolina remarked, "I have never known him to stand with Southern Senators on any problem concerning the South."[2]

But the Northern and Midwestern states carried the day for Mr. Kefauver. Senator John F. Kennedy conceded. Perhaps the wild enthusiasm of the Southern delegates as he made his way to the platform signaled the rise of the Kennedy star. Certainly it signaled one for the more erratic patterns in racial politics and the attempt of the Southerners to maintain legally enforced segregation.

The test came during the Senate debate on the Civil Rights Act of 1957. Senator Kennedy took some hard knocks from friends and enemies of civil rights. James M. Burns, in *John Kennedy, a Political Profile,* says:

> Unluckily for Kennedy, the very first vote on the bill threatened to throw him into a political embrace with Senator James Eastland, of Mississippi, the hated symbol of Southern racism. Under the regular procedure, the civil rights bill passed by the House would go to the Senate Judiciary Committee, chaired by Eastland, before coming to the Senate floor. Knowing of the Mississippian's dexterity in blotting up such measures, liberals sought to invoke a little-used Senate rule that would let the bill bypass the committee.
>
> Kennedy would have none of it. The temporary advantage to be gained by bypassing Eastland's committee, he felt, was not worth a dangerous precedent that might come back to haunt liberals. He argued, too, that a discharge petition could be used to pry the bill out of Eastland's pocket, and he promised to vote for such a petition if one was needed. Morse strongly supported this view, but most liberal Democrats, including Humphrey and Symington, favored the bypass, which barely carried the Senate.
>
> "The most dangerous news I have read in a long time," a Long Island Negro wrote Kennedy on hearing of his position. . . .
>
> When it came to the substance of the bill, however, Kennedy was all militancy. The acid test was section 3, which authorized the

---

[2] Charlotte *Observer,* Aug. 18, 1956, p. 1.

attorney general to use injunctive power to enforce school desegregation and other civil rights, hence allowing greater use of civil sanc-
tions instead of cumbersome criminal prosecution. The implications
of section 3 were enormous; it might become the device by which a
liberal President could push school integration, as well as voting
rights, throughout the South. Well aware of these possibilities, the
Southerners were seething, and the White House itself had misgiv-
ings. One might expect, then, that the "moderate" Kennedy would
shy from it. But no—Kennedy not only backed section 3 but took
the floor to make his views clear.[3]

A year later Senator Kennedy began to lose his Southern support. He addressed a meeting in Jackson, Mississippi, in the fall of
1957, and told Southerners, "I accept the Supreme Court decision
as the supreme law of the land. . . . We must all agree on the necessity
to uphold law and order in every part of the land." Doris Fleeson
wrote in the St. Petersburg *Times,* October 24, 1957: "Sen. John
F. Kennedy's romance with the South, one of the most provocative
features of the 1956 Democratic convention, is the latest victim of
Little Rock. . . . Since his return to Washington [from Mississippi]
his mail, a part of it written more in sorrow than in anger, has indicated that he cannot expect from the South in 1960 the same support which in coalition with big state delegations almost put him
over for the vice presidential nomination last year. . . ."

On June 23, 1960, the romance was shattered once and for all.
Mr. Kennedy addressed the Liberal party of New York and said
that he hoped to win the Democratic nomination for President without a single Southern vote in the convention. He also told his audience he regarded the civil rights issue as a moral question. . . .

*

The hatred for John F. Kennedy among Southern politicians
was not universal, but it was nevertheless intense and widespread
and confined almost wholly to the race problem. It was at a desperate
intensity just before he was assassinated.

---

[3] James M. Burns, *John Kennedy, a Political Profile* (New York, Harcourt Brace
& Co., 1960), p. 201.

Early in December, 1963, Samuel Lubell, political analyst, wrote from the deep South:

> Only nine days before President Kennedy's death I sampled a workers' precinct in Birmingham, Alabama, which in 1960 had given him a clear majority. In a day's ringing of doorbells I found just one Kennedy supporter left.
>
> All the other voters interviewed vowed they would go Republican or for an independent party in 1964—"Anyone as long as it isn't Kennedy." The bitter anger that saturated the precinct burst forth in comments such as, "He's cramming the nigger down our throats" or "if he's re-elected it will be the end of America."
>
> A construction manager from Baton Rouge, Louisiana, confessed, "I'd be satisfied to let them pass anything if they indicated they wouldn't be tough in enforcing it."
>
> Others said hopefully, "If Bobby Kennedy was out of there that would do it."[5]

And on November 17, the South's only "New Frontier" governor, Terry Sanford of North Carolina, sadly admitted that if the election were held at that moment Mr. Kennedy would probably lose the state. And North Carolina, remember, had gone twice for Adlai Stevenson.

Nor was the hatred simple political hatred. Indeed, the hatred was pervasive. Schoolteachers in Mississippi, Alabama, Louisiana, and Georgia must have been of one mind, judging from the tone of letters sent to the White House and to the Attorney General's office. Whole classrooms of children sent off letters in identical phraseology: "We had such a good relationship with the Negroes. They were so happy until you forced integration. Now there is only suspicion, hate, and fear. . . ."

The Attorney General answered the letters directed to him:

> . . . What the Federal Government has done in your state is to see that the orders of the Federal Courts are followed. Is that what

---

[5] Charlotte *Observer*, Dec. 10, 1963, p.3B.

upsets you? Do you think everybody in the United States should make his or her own determination as to what laws they are going to follow? . . . Are you aware that only about five per cent of the Negroes in your state are registered and can vote for Governor or even in national elections? . . . Do you and your fellow teenagers feel that this is the way you want your state run? . . .

It is instructive that in all the telephone conversations the President, the Attorney General, and Assistant Attorney General Burke Marshall made during the racial crisis at the state universities, the governors and officials of Mississippi and Alabama raised the same arguments as the children.

President Kennedy was aware of the swelling resentment throughout the South. He and his aides were concerned lest it spread to the North, especially to the "Oh, no! Not next door!" moderates in suburbia. Undoubtedly he knew that this resentment endangered his chances for reelection. He admitted as much to A. Philip Randolph: "I know this whole thing could cost me the election but I have no intention of turning back now or ever."

This serious criticism came not from political enemies or segregationists whom the New Frontier had written off, but from Democratic liberals and Negroes who complained that President Kennedy had wasted two years before he ended housing segregation in government-financed units; and that when the President did end it by his celebrated promise of "a stroke of the pen" it was not half as strong as they hoped it would be. Northern liberals taunted Robert Kennedy with the fact that he let federal officials in Albany, Georgia, put Negroes on trial for conspiracy while Southern whites went about blowing up Negro homes with impunity. . . .

But the people not fooled by the liberal and Negro critics of the President were those who had devoted their adult lives to keeping the Negro "in his place"—the Southern segregationists. They were not put off by the prospects of a slow passage of a watered-down Kennedy Civil Rights Bill. The segregationist politicians knew what was going on and it alarmed them. The Kennedy Administration alarmed them to a greater degree than the Roosevelt,

Harry Golden

Truman, or Eisenhower administrations ever had. President John
F. Kennedy, the Attorney General and his civil rights staff were
slowly but surely cutting the heart out of the racial status quo of
the South. And they were doing it with the "watered-down" Civil
Rights Act of 1957 and the equally compromised Civil Rights Act
of 1960.

President Kennedy had accepted the challenge of the segregationists to fight the battle, county by county, school by school, and
Negro by Negro. He was using laws which were there all the time
—for two and a half years of President Eisenhower's second term—
but they were laws which had not been made into effective legal
weapons.

When Robert F. Kennedy was confirmed as Attorney General,
the chairman of the Senate Judiciary Committee, Senator James
Eastland of Mississippi, congratulated him and with a wink said,
"Your predecessor never brought a civil rights case in Mississippi."
But the next day Robert Kennedy and the Civil Rights Division of
the Department of Justice received their standing orders from the
President: *"Get the road maps—and go."* . . .

*

"Keep pushing the cases" was having its effect in hundreds of
Southern counties not yet visited by Burke Marshall, John Doar
and the other lawyers and investigators with the road maps.

By December 1, 1961, virtually every bus station, every railroad
station, and every airport in the South had been desegregated. For
the first time the Attorney General's office entered a brief seeking to
forbid hospitals built with federal funds to discriminate racially
against doctors or patients. The Department of Justice also brought
suit to require the desegregation of a school district financed with
federal impacted area funds. Robert Kennedy said it made no sense
for the United States to ask its citizens to serve their country in the
armed forces and then put them in a place where their children
would be discriminated against because of their race.[19]

---

[19] Speech by Robert F. Kennedy, October 28, 1962, to the American Jewish
Congress.

On July 24, 1962, the Attorney General instituted the first proceeding of its kind under the Civil Rights Act of 1960, with the result that twenty-six Negroes of East Carroll Parish in northeast Louisiana were registered as voters by Federal Judge Erwin F. Hunter, Jr.[20]

On August 28, 1962, the Department of Justice filed a complaint in the United States District Court in Jackson, Mississippi. It asked the court to declare unconstitutional two sections of the Mississippi Constitution which require interpretation tests and "good moral character" requirements and made a similar request concerning seven state laws which set up other devices allegedly used to discriminate against prospective Negro voters.[21]

Not every Negro was aware of the way the President, the Attorney General, and Burke Marshall were proceeding, for not every Negro voted nor was every colored school child free from segregation. But it is safe to say that every segregationist knew. The segregationists remembered Dr. Martin Luther King saying to his followers: "The Negro elected Kennedy. We must not hesitate to remind him of that." By 1963 segregationists had more than enough evidence to convince them that Kennedy never needed reminding. For if the Negroes thought of the 1960's as their crucible, John Fitzgerald Kennedy thought of the 1960's as America's.

On his inauguration day, when the campaign was over and the next campaign promises four years off, John F. Kennedy, joyfully watching the parade, turned at one point and told the then Vice-President, Lyndon B. Johnson, "Did you notice there were no Negroes marching with the Coast Guard unit?"

Actually, Negro students were not excluded from the Coast Guard Academy. But after Mr. Kennedy's memorandum of January 23, 1961, two days after his inauguration, the Coast Guard began an all-out recruiting drive to enroll Negroes. During 1963 two Negro officers, Lieutenant Bobby Wilks and Lieutenant Andrew

---

[20] New Orleans *Times-Picayune*, July 25, 1962, p. 11. See also *United States v. Manning*, 206 F. Supp. 632—W. D. La. 1962.

[21] *United States v. Mississippi*, F. Supp. S.D. Miss. 1962.

Holleman, toured the country, visiting 199 schools, talking to 11,000 students and personally interviewing 561 Negro boys through the NAACP and the United League in an attempt to enroll them in the Academy.[22]

Watching the inaugural parade that cold afternoon, John F. Kennedy must have been turning over in his mind the meeting he would have with Premier Nikita Khrushchev of the Soviet Union, the unprecedented trade bill he would ask enacted, the possibilities of a rapprochement with President Charles De Gaulle of France, and the plans he was making for America's entry into the Space Age. Yet in the front of his consciousness was the absence of Negro cadets in the Coast Guard Academy contingent. Civil rights for the American Negro would be the big problem with which he would wrestle every day during the less than three years he would live.

At the first Cabinet meeting in January, 1961, President Kennedy issued orders that positive action be taken immediately to promote equal opportunity for all persons employed by the federal government. Mr. Kennedy said that it is up to Congress, the people themselves, to legislate change but that he intended to do everything possible to enforce the laws already on the books. One of the first things the President noted was that out of nine hundred lawyers employed by the government in Washington, only ten were Negroes. The situation was changed within six months when there were seven times that many. For the first time Negroes were serving as district judges in continental United States, and the NAACP lawyer Thurgood Marshall, who had won the big case of the century, was appointed by Mr. Kennedy to the United States Court of Appeals for the Second Circuit.

It has been said that John F. Kennedy tried to find an answer, not to force a solution. His aim was to find the ways and means of granting every American the same fundamental and basic rights

---

[22] Mr. Kennedy's Inauguration Day comment and subsequent action were provided by Lee C. White, Assistant Special Counsel to the President; Recruiting information, Capt. W. K. Thompson, Jr., Chief Public Information, U.S. Coast Guard, Treasury Department.

without producing a national convulsion. As soon as he had formulated his policies, he found he had also formulated his opposition. As the Department of Justice began its activities, the feeling against the President and his brother, the Attorney General, began to rise. For the President it was a meta-political opposition welling from those who somehow sensed that *this was it,* that they would soon be deprived of certain privileges and honors they had always enjoyed without any individual effort or struggle. It was a resentment, as close as I can gauge it, greater than the resentment the South mustered against President Harry Truman after he accepted the Civil Rights plank in the Democratic party platform in 1948.

Senator Strom Thurmond of South Carolina and other Dixiecrats were so outraged by the Truman platform they subtracted four Southern states from the Democratic column. But many segregationists still suspected Harry Truman of campaigning on a civil rights platform simply to get elected. Underneath they thought (wrongly, it turned out) that he was one of them.

But John F. Kennedy and the Justice Department challenged the notion of the caste system itself. Had he lived to make the campaign in 1964, it would probably have been far more acrimonious and bitter than Truman's in 1948. I remember then hearing a Democratic County Committee leader in my state urge his membership, "To hell with the head of the ticket, let's just make sure we send our Representative back to Congress." . . .

*

The South hated Kennedy because even as a candidate he understood the proportions of the problem. In Minneapolis, a month before election, in answer to the question "What legislation do you propose for the civil rights issue?" Kennedy replied,

First, there is a good deal that can be done by the Executive branch without legislation. For example, the President could sign an executive order ending discrimination in housing tomorrow. Second, the President could compel all companies which do business with the Government, and after all, that is nearly every American company, to practice open, fair hiring of personnel without regard to race, creed or color. . . . In addition, the Department of Justice can pursue the right to vote with far more vigor. The Vice-President's Commission on Contracts has been completely ineffective. It has not instituted one suit outside of the District of Columbia. So I would say that the greater opportunity is in the Executive branch without Congressional action [a point on which the late President was to change his mind]. The things I would ask the Congress to do are really twofold. First, to pass Title 3, which gives the Attorney General additional powers to institute suits to provide for constitutional rights. Secondly . . . provide technical assistance to school districts that are trying to desegregate.

Yet it was two years before Mr. Kennedy issued an Executive directive against discrimination in government housing. Political considerations stayed him. He had been a member of both the House and the Senate and he appreciated the *quid pro quo* of politics. He had other bills he wanted passed and could not afford to alienate Southern Democrats, and the bipartisan Republican support which would make them law.

This reasoning is explained by Helen Fuller in *Year of Trial*. Miss Fuller is not only an experienced journalist, but also a lawyer who served with the Department of Justice. She tells of the President's deep concern for the passage of the Trade Bill and his worry that any new civil rights proposals would have angered Southerners to the point where they would have deliberately stalled Administration policies in foreign affairs. The Housing Sub-Committees in both House and Senate were headed by Alabamans, Representative Alfred Rains and Senator John Sparkman, respectively. Both vehemently opposed an executive order on housing. Kennedy counted on Rains and Sparkman for support for the Trade Bill which indeed they gave, at the same time threatening to surrender their committee chairmanships in the event of a housing order from the White House.[24]

---

[24] Helen Fuller, *Year of Trial* (New York, Harcourt, Brace & World, 1962), pp. 37-42.

These were mild reactions compared to those, say, of Senator Richard Russell of Georgia or Senator John Stennis of Mississippi who voted against the Nuclear Test Ban Treaty, a gesture their apologists futilely said had nothing to do with their anger at President Kennedy's new civil rights proposals. . . .

*

It is important to concentrate on these political decisions of the late President because we are a political society, and all the decisions which have made this society great and powerful have been political decisions. John F. Kennedy dealt with the race problem both politically and morally, but he dealt with it politically first.

In October, 1961, President Kennedy sent Congress a proposal for the establishment of a new Cabinet post, Secretary of the Department of Urban Affairs and Housing. Surprisingly, he told a press conference he intended to appoint Robert Weaver, a Negro and administrator of the Housing and Home Finance Agency, as his first Secretary.

In January, 1962, the House Rules Committee, composed of five Republicans, two anti-Administration Southerners, five non-Southern Democrats, and three pro-Administration Southerners, voted 9 to 6 to let the bill die in committee. Kennedy next tried establishing the new agency under the powers conferred upon him by the Reorganization Act whereby the Chief Executive can send a "plan" for the creation of a new Department to the Congress and if neither house votes to reject it within sixty days, the agency is automatically established. Thus did Dwight D. Eisenhower create the Department of Health, Education and Welfare. The House of Representatives by the unexpected margin of 264 to 150 votes defeated the President's proposal.

Many were disappointed. Urban political leaders in particular blamed the bill's defeat on Kennedy's public announcement of wanting to appoint a Negro to the Cabinet. Everyone critical of Mr. Kennedy said he was playing politics.

Certainly this was true. That he played politics is one of his claims to greatness. He was playing politics in an attempt to get as much mileage out of his fight to end racial segregation as possible. Mr. Kennedy was aware that the House of Representatives is controlled to a dismaying degree by rural and small town legislators, although two thirds of our population live in cities. He was aware that his proposal for a Department of Urban Affairs and Housing would have rough going because of the disproportionate representation. But the President wanted to make a defeat for his proposal as costly as possible to the opposition. If they beat down a Department of Urban Affairs, they would have to vote against the Negro too.

Afterward, Republican leaders suggested Mr. Kennedy appoint Robert Weaver to the post of Secretary of Health, Education and Welfare when Senator Abraham Ribicoff resigned. They promised to give Mr. Weaver a vote of confirmation to show they did not mean to oppose Mr. Weaver when they voted against the Department of Urban Affairs. To which Mr. Kennedy replied at his next news conference, "I see now that various people who opposed the Urban Department are ready to support Mr. Weaver for any Cabinet position he wishes, Defense, State, Treasury, or anything else. While I'm sure he's grateful for those good wishes for a Cabinet position where there is no vacancy, I think he would have been, that this country would have been, better served to have voted for an Urban Department and permitted him to continue his service in that capacity."

Had Mr. Kennedy succeeded in establishing this Department, he planned to swear in Mr. Weaver as the first Negro Cabinet officer in an unprecedented ceremony, a ceremony televised and photographed for every corner of the world.

The several Negro leaders who expressed their skepticism concerning Mr. Kennedy's designation of a Negro for a Cabinet post not yet created proved only that Mr. Kennedy was far ahead of them. He was "using" the problem in hopes of advancing more than one solution.

Nothing impressed Negro leaders more, however, than their visit with the President after the protest March on Washington on

August 28, 1963. Even such knowledgeable men as A. Philip Randolph and Roy Wilkins came to realize how much they had underestimated John F. Kennedy. After the March, Negro leaders, bubbling with excitement, came to the White House and posed for the photographers with the President. It had been an awe-inspiring demonstration. Not only had two hundred and ten thousand people converged on Washington for a single day, but the demonstration had gone off without incident. A great mass of Negroes and whites had protested an evil, and had protested in "the inspiration of Christ and the method of Gandhi," as Dr. Martin Luther King would have it.

Mr. Kennedy shook hands with these happy, excited men, but he did not show any particular enthusiasm. He did not pat them on the back and tell them they had done a great job. Instead, when they assembled around a table filled with sandwiches, coffee, and milk, the President told them about the Civil Rights Bill he had before the Congress and that the people "on the hill" were the only ones who could really help now. He told the Negro leaders they faced hard work in their districts, cities and states, and with pencil and paper Mr. Kennedy spelled it out for each man how to use his influence with labor unions, state political leaders, and even down to the local precinct officials. He gave each of them an assignment, warning them this was but a beginning. Negro leaders left the White House subdued in their realization that they were dealing not only with a President who was on their side but with a President who was determined that their side win.

Mr. Kennedy followed this same procedure with all the professional, religious, business, and labor groups he met in the White House. He never gave a pep talk about the evils of segregation; he always directed his attention to what could be done to end racial segregation, discrimination, and exploitation in the United States.

To the college presidents and educators, Mr. Kennedy said it was not enough that they disapproved of segregation. They had to do something about it. He suggested an exchange of white college professors with Negro college professors and an exchange of students. . . .

Following is a list of the groups to whom Mr. Kennedy talked civil rights in a forty-day period:

Leadership Group	Date	No. Attending
Governors	May 29, 1963	9
Hotel, Restaurant, and Theater Owners	June 4	120
Labor Leaders	June 13	215
Religious Leaders	June 17	215
Governors	June 18	8
Educators	June 19	250
Lawyers	June 21	250
Civil Rights Leaders	June 22	30
Women's Meeting	July 9	350
Business Council	July 11	70
Governors	July 12	6

Both the President and the Attorney General spoke at these meetings. The President said nothing could be done in Washington as effectively as what could be done community by community throughout the country. He warned that the schedule of civil rights would not be set by the Congress, by the President, by the public, but by the Negro community, and that it was the job of the clergy, business, labor and professional leaders to insure that the transition from second-class citizenship to full-privileged citizenship would be as orderly as possible.

When a Southern clergyman asked the dramatic question about intermarriage, the President replied that the question before the country was not one of intermarriage but one of voting rights, jobs, and equal opportunities in education. He told the clergymen he had not asked them to desegregate their churches but to desegregate the public domain. He closed with the remark that they were a most fortunate group, that it was not often that people had had such a role to play in history.[26]

These informal conversations were influential. When Mr.

---

[26] Conversation with Rabbi Philip S. Bernstein of Rochester, New York, who attended the President's meeting with the clergy.

Kennedy met with the top trade unionists, Walter Reuther, vice-president of the AFL-CIO, cut through the rhetoric with the crisp declaration: "If we really wanted to do something about it, the men gathered in the room right now could do more for civil rights in one month than the whole Government could in five years." Reuther, in fact, spearheaded the drive for $160,000 to post the bail for Negroes arrested in the Birmingham, Alabama, demonstrations.[27]

Up to a certain point, John F. Kennedy thought the power and prestige of the Presidency was enough to resolve the race issue if coupled with the support of the courts. He was to sign three executive orders on civil rights: (1) Executive Order 10925, on March 7, 1961, establishing the President's Committee on Equal Employment Opportunity; (2) Executive Order 11063, on November 20, 1962, creating equal opportunity in housing; and (3) Executive Order 11114, on June 22, 1963, extending the authority of the President's Committee on Equal Employment Opportunity. But Mr. Kennedy was perhaps the first to realize that the Presidency was not enough for the simple reason that the courts themselves were not enough. The revolution which surges about us is waged for human dignity and equal opportunity and justice and the right to exercise free opinion. Down deep, however, this revolution has one focus: it is a war fought to see whether all of us will obey the law or only some of us. Revolutions are won only when everyone fights, when everyone becomes a participant.

The essential corruption of racial segregation is not that it is supported by lies but that people believe the lies. The segregationists will be disabused of their illusions not when the President says such beliefs are unworthy of Americans, but when the Congress and the whole force of public opinion say these lies transgress not only reasonable decency but the law itself.

Several months after the inauguration of President Kennedy, I

[27] A. H. Raskin, "Walter Reuther's Great Big Union," *Atlantic Monthly,* October 1963, p. 92.

discussed with Edward R. Murrow, then the director of the United States Information Agency, the advisability of submitting an idea for a "Second Emancipation Proclamation" declaring an end to segregation on every level of American life on which the United States Government touched—property, contracts, installations, subsidies, grants, and loans. Mr. Murrow agreed to suggest it to Mr. Kennedy, who said, "Let's see what you fellows can come up with."

It was a pithy "declaration," not at all detailed, but something the folks could frame and put up on the wall. By the time Mr. Kennedy received it, however, he had come to the conclusion that the Congress and the people, as well as the President, must play appropriate roles in the civil rights struggle. It was a wise decision. While the folks might have had something for the wall, this did not open up the avenues of freedom.

I never heard directly from the President about the "declaration," but one of the President's friends might have been expressing Mr. Kennedy's own thoughts on the matter. When I asked him about it, he said: "Remember that even Abraham Lincoln found it necessary to add in his Emancipation Proclamation that it was an act of justice, warranted by the Constitution, *upon military necessity.*" (My italics are on the words the President's friend had emphasized.)

Mr. Kennedy readily admitted that he was controlled by events. To a Negro leader he said that the Negroes owed their heaviest debt to the dogs of Birmingham, Alabama, and to those who unleashed them, provoking a national crisis. Other events had been the assassination of Medgar Evers, an official of the Mississippi NAACP; the sniper murder of Willie Moore, the postman who thought he could bring good will to the deep South; the bombing of the Sixteenth Street Baptist Church in Birmingham, which claimed the lives of four little girls; and, earlier, the open defiance of federal court orders by Governor Ross Barnett of Mississippi and Governor George C. Wallace of Alabama.

The order of events, each augmenting the terror of the preceding event and promising an even more virulent succession, decided Mr. Kennedy's comprehensive policy. He resolved to make the Congress and the people participate in the struggle.

We Americans are violent before we are moral, and much of our expressed morality is a sexual morality. Pushed to the moral act, we can respond if that act is war against a foreign enemy, but we are liable to lethargy if it is not.

Zeus chained Prometheus to the rock because Prometheus gave fire to man. Zeus was right and Prometheus wrong. Zeus wanted men strong enough not to need fire, and Prometheus, in the tragic view, made man weak. We Americans have a Prometheus complex. We want Prometheus off the rock but we will not give up the comfort of fire. If the President cannot solve the race problem, we want it to go away and stop annoying us.

But the constant pressures of the Negro made this a continuing public issue. Negroes took their causes to the streets before the general populace. They advanced. One of the reasons they advanced is because the late President John F. Kennedy focused the country's attention on the moral stakes for which the Negroes played.

Very early in his Presidential career, Mr. Kennedy outlined the moral possibilities of the race question. In return for his rights, the Negro offered no barter. This was the unusual truth the President had to tell the people. Speaking in Los Angeles on September 9, 1960, Mr. Kennedy said:

> When our next President takes office in January, he must be prepared to move forward in the field of human rights in three general areas: as a legislative leader, as Chief Executive, and as the center of the moral power of the United States. . . . As a moral leader, the next President must play his role in interpreting the great moral and educational forces which are involved in our crusade for human rights. He must exert the great moral and educational facilities from churches to lunch counters, and to support the right of every American to stand up for his rights, even if on occasion he must sit down for them. For only the President, not the Senate and not the House and not the Supreme Court, in a real sense, only the President

can create the understanding and tolerance necessary as the spokes-man for all the American people, as the symbol of the moral impera-tive upon which any free society is based.

By June of 1963, Mr. Kennedy had realized that the moral imperative belonged not to him alone. Because it was a moral issue it had permeated every level of society. To the nation over the television networks, Mr. Kennedy said:

This is not a legal or legislative issue alone. . . . We are con-fronted with a moral issue. It is as old as the Scriptures and is as clear as the American Constitution. The heart of the question is whether all Americans are to be afforded equal rights and equal op-portunities, whether we are going to treat our fellow Americans as we want to be treated. . . . This nation, for all its hopes and all its boasts, will not be fully free until all its citizens are free. . . . We face, therefore, a moral crisis as a country and as a people. It cannot be met by repressive police action. It cannot be left to increased demonstrations in the streets. It cannot be quieted by token moves. . . . It is time to act in the Congress, in your state and local legislative body, and above all, in all of our daily lives.

Eight days later, on June 19, 1963, the President concluded his message to Congress by asking for new civil rights legislation with:

I ask you to look into your hearts—not in search of charity, for the Negro neither wants nor needs condescension—but for one plain, proud, and priceless quality that unites us all as Americans: a sense of justice. In this year of the Emancipation Centennial, justice re-quires us to insure the blessings of liberty for all Americans and their posterity—not merely for reasons of economic efficiency, world diplomacy and domestic tranquillity—but above all, because it is right.

It was in these ways that Mr. Kennedy lent the weight and prestige of his office to the Negro revolution. He acted decisively whenever the power of his office was challenged. Though he did not issue his Housing Directive until he was two years in office, he was barely in office when he found the solid ground he and the New Frontier needed to pursue to resolve inequities: "Get the road maps and go," he said about the Civil Rights Acts of 1957 and 1960; and after the first report on voting rights by the Department of Justice, he wrote confidently, "Keep pushing the cases."

Burke Marshall and his men were tramping the back roads and the back counties knocking on the doors of Negro share-croppers asking, "Did you ever vote? Did you ever try to vote? Did you ever try to register? What happened?" They also asked about schools. In those cases where Mr. Marshall's men have challenged registration tests and standards, they wanted to be in a position to prove further racial discrimination. Such tests and standards are inherently unfair to Negroes because they had been afforded inferior educational opportunities. Thus the Attorney General's office was primarily interested in the kind of school the voter went to, which gave them the additional insight into the kind of school the voter's children go to.

But the job is not quite that simple. The challenge to Mr. Kennedy to implement the Constitution "Negro by Negro" is a complicated process. For every Negro interviewed, it was necessary to analyze the registration records of the white voters. In preparing their voting cases, the civil rights people in the Department of Justice might prove discrimination. They must show the registration card of a Negro who had been rejected and compare it with the registration card of a white citizen who had been allowed to vote. . . .

*

If the segregationists of the South said it was a fight, Negro by Negro, school board by school board, voting registrar by voting registrar, so be it. Mr. Kennedy said the United States of America had met greater challenges in its history and had overcome them. The fight shifted from lawyers in morning coats before the Supreme Court to lawyers with prod sticks and dogs. It is a slow process. But it is an inexorable one. A political man, Mr. Kennedy thought in terms of voting rights. While the Negro needed additional legislation in housing, employment, and public accommodations, Mr. Kennedy felt voting rights was the key to the issue. The late President told Martin Luther King, "Once you get the ballot and the Negroes are educated to its use, all other things will fall in proper place." Medgar Evers, the murdered NAACP official of Mississippi, had said the same thing a year before: "If we could get the ballot we could weed out many of the injustices that Negroes suffer."[29]

When Mr. Kennedy was campaigning for the Presidency, he could have been expected to say as his opponent said and as most of the liberals said, that while in favor of civil rights he was opposed to "extremists," a phrase which, if it means anything, means let nature take its course lest the actions of men disturb it. But Mr. Kennedy did not resort to the hollow safety of sane but insipid phrases, even in the heat of a bitter campaign. He said he favored Freedom Riders and sit-in protests and he said this when no other national leaders said it.

Mr. Kennedy inspired a moral tone which washed over the entire country. It influenced everyone, particularly those close to him. Three years later, Mr. Kennedy's Secretary of State Dean Rusk, a Southerner born in Georgia, made his point wholly understood before a Senate Commerce Committee during the hearings on the Civil Rights Bill: "If I were denied what our Negro citizens are denied, I would demonstrate also." At this same hearing, Mr. Rusk said that foreign policy considerations were "secondary" to the fact that racial bias was wrong, but he added that failure to enact the President's Civil Rights Bill would evoke world-wide questioning of "the real convictions of the American people."[30]

Mr. Kennedy's whole life gave him an understanding of discrimination and bigotry, because he came from a religion and a

---

[29] James Graham Cook, *The Segregationists* (New York, Appleton-Century-Crofts, 1962), pp. 95-96.
[30] *Facts on File,* Vol. XXIII, no. 1187, July 25, 1963, p. 269.

nationality which had known persecution. In a pamphlet on immigration written for the Anti-Defamation League of the B'nai B'rith, Mr. Kennedy wrote:

> By 1830 there were 150,000 Irish Catholics in New York City. Feeling against them was very strong and erupted from time to time in riots, the burning of churches and considerable bloodshed. The first appearance of this sentiment in national politics was the Presidential election of 1836, when Martin Van Buren was accused by his enemies of being a Catholic.
>
> The hatred of Irish and Catholic immigrants, and, more particularly, of the Catholic Church, led to the founding of the Native-American or Know-Nothing Party in 1845. This party, whose whole platform consisted of three planks—vote only for native-born candidates, a long period of naturalization, and opposition to the Catholic Church—had the swiftest rise and the swiftest fall of any major party in American history. . . .
>
> Yet it is a remarkable fact that in spite of . . . this agitation there was no official government response. . . . The sense of America as a refuge for oppressed and down-trodden people was never far from the consciousness of Americans.[31]

In private conversation the President expressed wonder at the vitality of the Negro civil rights movement. We may relate this wonder to the ideas he expressed in his little book on immigration. Mr. Kennedy was worried about America's future, this much we know. He was worried about the hard decisions yet to be made in our struggle with the Communist world. And he was also worried that a more relaxed and affluent society may have lost much of its drive. The immigrant, on the other hand, has no choice. He must make good or remain forever alien.

When Mr. Kennedy publicly applauded the unorganized street demonstrations and approved the March on Washington, he may have related this vitality of the American Negro to the determina-

---

[31] John F. Kennedy, *A Nation of Immigrants* (New York, The Anti-Defamation League, 1963), p. 2.

tion with which the Irish immigrant went about the task of making a better world for his children. . . .

*

It is probably to the everlasting good fortune of America that after a whole generation of restricted immigration, we have been suddenly confronted with some nineteen millions of our very own people with that same intense drive to enter the open society of America and participate fully in all its assorted wonders. Like the immigrant, the American Negro is determined at all costs to succeed, and indeed, if he does not, like the immigrant, he, too, will regard himself as irrevocably lost. (The Negro population of the United States is 19,300,000, according to the latest reliable estimate. Knowledgeable Negro leaders, however, put the figure at closer to 23,000,000, which includes, they say, from 3 to 4 million Negroes who have passed into the white society.)

The Negroes say, "No white man can think black." They say this even of their closest white allies and they may be right. In his total commitment, Mr. Kennedy saw the social revolution of the American Negro as something more than a white man thinking "black." When Mr. Kennedy refused to frown publicly on the street demonstrations, and actually applauded the March on Washington, he saw in the Negro a charismatic symbol of a renewed vitality of the American civilization.

In his meeting with labor leaders on June 13, 1963, Mr. Kennedy said that he did not agree with Negro leaders who urge "preferential" or "quota" employment for Negroes to help "close the gap." But the President acknowledged that something will have to be done for the Negro and in order to "reach" him, said Mr. Kennedy, the American 1960s will have to do it for all: for the poor, the unemployed, and the displaced, without regard to color, race, or creed. Mr. Kennedy said that we owe a debt of gratitude to the Negro "in the streets" for calling attention to the American Dream.[33]

---

[33] Author's conversation with Walter Reuther, Vice-President, AFL-CIO, Washington, D.C., August 28, 1963.

from The Kennedy Wit

by Bill Adler

I want to express my appreciation to the Governor. Every time he introduces me as the potentially greatest President in the history of the United States, I always think perhaps he is overstating it one or two degrees. George Washington wasn't a bad President and I do want to say a word for Thomas Jefferson. But, otherwise, I will accept the compliment.

Muskegon, Michigan
September 5, 1960

Question: Senator, when does the moratorium end on Nixon's hospitalization and your ability to attack him?
Mr. Kennedy: Well, I said I would not mention him unless I could praise him until he got out of the hospital, and I have not mentioned him.

Burbank, California
September 9, 1960

Jim Bishop, currently a columnist for New York's new World-Journal-Tribune, *is the author of* The Day Lincoln Was Shot, *and "A Day in the Life of Eisenhower." He gathered the material for* A Day in the Life of President Kennedy *in a period of four days in 1963, during which he was allowed to observe the President's entire daily routine. The manuscript was delivered to the White House on November 18, and on November 22 Pierre Salinger was reading it in Honolulu when the news of the assassination reached him. "To my eternal sorrow," says Bishop in his introduction, "I was the last writer to work with President Kennedy on an exclusive story. Therefore I asked to have it published as it was written, without anything added or changed, when the world was bright for him and the future held the warm promise of goodness and victory. What you will read in this book is a portrait of the Kennedy family as it looked then—with no premonition that, for him, time had run out."*

from

A Day in the Life of
President Kennedy

by Jim Bishop

7:00 A.M.

The sun, like almost everyone in Washington, is on time. It comes up from a hummock of tall pin oaks and poplars on Capitol Hill, throws a pink spangle at the statue of Freedom atop the Capitol, and paints the granite shaft of the Washington Monument from top down. The streets are in blue shadow. The flowers in the little formal gardens of Georgetown hang their heads heavily and plots of grass have aged overnight with the silver of hoarfrost.

The cardinals and bluejays are awake first, and they curve and bank the shuttle service between trees, always eager to assert their rights over the majority—the sparrows. The early busses snort and sigh from corner to corner; sugar-cube milk trucks complete their rounds and tinkle with the music of empty bottles; the statue of a general in Lafayette Park throws a longer shadow than he did in life; the mist in the Tidal Basin lies lightly on the bosom of the water; on the White House lawn a gray squirrel sits transfixed, aching to be friendly but forever afraid.

It is a good morning, a morning of cool loveliness and exalted promise; a morning on which the breeze from the south is so slight, so lazy, that it spins the leaves of the poplars in slow motion, like a magician turning his hands to show that he has nothing up his sleeve; a morning when a far-off plane appears to be pinned to the cobalt-blue; a morning when parents sit at breakfast with their children, smiling behind their authoritative masks at the chatter of their own magpies.

The good feeling pervades the being of George Edward Thomas, who steps out of Room 324 in the east hall of the White House and closes the door softly behind him. He pats his black bow tie once more, then hefts the newspapers under his arm. George Thomas is fifty-five. He comes down the hall with the stumpy walk of a man who has spent a lot of time on his feet. He is a cherubic-looking Negro, with roundnesses in successive sizes, starting with the eyes and working toward the face and then the figure. He has been the President's valet since 1947, when John F. Kennedy was a freshman member of the House of Representatives.

Mr. Thomas pauses at the private elevator, looks up at the indicator, and decides not to wait for it. He walks down the curving marble steps to the second floor, through the dining-room door, and into the kitchen. Nick, a cook, looks up. He too has a good-morning smile. Nick is a Filipino who learned to cook when he was in the United States Navy. He and George Thomas have coffee and exchange the small talk of men who walk the same beat. Nick always marvels that George never needs an alarm clock. The valet can go to sleep at one A.M. or two, and still awaken at precisely six-thirty. But now that George is awake, he keeps looking at the clock. He talks awhile longer, sipping coffee and watching the big hand sneak imperceptibly toward six.

In the east wing of the White House, Floyd Boring looks up and sees that the time is almost seven-thirty. Normally he takes the eight-to-four shift of the Secret Service. Last night he assumed the late shift. In the west wing, a police sergeant sits back in a swivel chair, in the soft somnolence of a man who is awake, but not truly. On the second floor, Maud Shaw, the children's nurse, supervises the washing and dressing of the gleefully shouting Miss Caroline Kennedy, six, and Master John F. Kennedy, Jr., three.

On the ground floor of this long, bar-bell-shaped building, the first shaft of sunlight pierces the security of the President's office. It has slanted across the south lawn, passed the old rose garden, and entered the oval-shaped room through the tall French doors.

The high-backed leather chair is imposing. The big mahogany desk, with the Great Seal of the United States on its face, was given to President McKinley by Queen Victoria. The oval rug matches the contours of the room. It is pale green but it looks deeper in color now because the sun has not yet reached it. The top of the desk is neat—a blotter, a desk set, a photograph frame which holds a list of the President's appointments for yesterday, and some ivory mementoes; opposite the desk there is a fireplace, flanked by two beige-covered sofas, a rocking chair presented by the crew of the carrier *Kitty Hawk,* and some wall paintings of naval battles of the War of 1812.

At seven-thirty two Secret Service men enter the office. They are about to undertake a task which is done frequently, but not every day. One crouches along the perimeter of the wall and moves slowly around the office. In his hand is a Geiger counter. He will test every object in the room for radioactivity. Later, and unobtrusively, he will pass the counter over the President's wristwatch.

The man does not expect to find anything alarming. Nor does his confrere, who unscrews the transmitter of both presidential telephones. He is looking for a transistor radio—the size of a girl's fingernail—which can be hidden in a telephone. Both phones have attached "scramblers" which render all presidential conversation unintelligible except at the recipient's end of the line—but a tiny transistor could pick the words up before they are scrambled and broadcast them a short distance, where they could be relayed to anyone who is interested.

American intelligence of all branches—C.I.A., F.B.I., and U.S. Army—are aware that the newest method of subtle assassination is to plant a minuscule amount of radioactive material on the person of the victim, or close to him. Abroad, some political figures who have died of so-called natural causes have been found to have their rings and watches pierced with tiny holes. Inside was uranium; in all cases the death was slow and nauseous, similar to pernicious anemia or leukemia.

On the second floor, George Thomas taps his mouth with a napkin, looks at the wall clock once more, and says: "About twenty or twenty-five minutes, Nick," meaning the President will be ready for breakfast then. George leaves the little kitchen and walks into the private quarters of the Kennedy family in the west wing of the mansion. He has the newspapers—*The New York Times,* the *Washington Post,* the *St. Louis Post-Dispatch,* the *Wall Street Journal*—and he strides through the sitting room, across the soft rugs, and into a door on the left. Mr. Thomas places the newspapers on the bed of the small bedroom, which is empty. He walks softly into the bathroom, and taps lightly on another bedroom door at the far side.

"Mr. President," he whispers hoarsely. "It's close to seven-thirty."

The time is closer to seven-forty. Mr. Thomas listens, and hears a clearing of the throat. The President of the United States is awake. Unlike some of his predecessors, he requires no time for collecting his wits, yawning, or a second rap on the door. He is out of bed at once, quickly and quietly. The metamorphosis from deep slumber to keen alertness is about ten seconds.

He walks through a foyer to the empty bedroom. "Good morning, George," the President says. George is busy pulling the drapes back and closing the windows. "Morning, Mr. President," he says. Mr. Kennedy props the pillows on the bed. He puts a robe over his nightshirt (George calls it a topcoat) and lies on the bed with his newspapers. Few persons can read with the speed and absorption of this man. As his hazel eyes traverse staggering mountains of eight-point type, it seems as though he is reading vertically, rather than from left to right. Within fifteen minutes he can read four newspapers and be prepared to discuss every story of consequence in any of them.

He devours thoughts, ideas and reports. The President reads a story with care, even though it is based on a statement made by him—or rather, more especially if it originated with him. Newspapers have been the sounding board of presidents for over a hundred years, but no other president has listened so hard to find out if what he has said includes the echo of warm applause or cold mockery.

Most presidents assume office with hopeful solicitude toward the press. In time, the criticisms of the newspapers, even those who espouse a president's cause, raise welts on the sensibilities of the chief of state; and like Harry Truman and Dwight D. Eisenhower, Mr. Kennedy tended to skip reading the columns and editorials of those he felt had betrayed him. Once he announced that the New York *Herald-Tribune* would no longer be delivered at the White House, but this helped neither himself nor his program, and so the paper was reinstated.

John F. Kennedy is no happier with the press than his predecessors, but he now reads his critics as assiduously as those who attest his greatness.

George Thomas has finished drawing the President's bath. He goes to the wardrobe closet and begins to lay out the attire for today. It consists of a blue suit, a white shirt, black shoes, a plain dark tie and socks. It is wrong in the case of President Kennedy to refer to any suit of clothes as the "attire for today," because the President redresses from the skin out at least twice a day, even on a day such as this one when no public functions are scheduled. He averages three, and sometimes four shirts each day. (The President has between fifteen and eighteen suits of clothes and about eight pairs of shoes.)

The President prefers a tub to a shower. He bathes as he does everything else: purposefully and forthrightly. He treats time as though he has been told he has a week to live. From the first waking moment until the last, the President moves at flank speed. He comes out of the bathroom, bathed and shaved and brushed, in a terry-cloth robe, and he moves toward his breakfast tray as though this too is a task to be accomplished in stride.

8:00 A.M.

Mr. Kennedy's associates refer to him as a meat-and-potatoes man. This implies that his taste for food is simple. It is. He finds little time for savoring food, or for educating his palate to the subtleties of flavor. His breakfast, for example, is almost always the same: large glass of orange juice, toast and jelly, two four-and-a-half minute eggs, broiled bacon, and coffee with cream and sugar.

The President sits in a wing chair, eating and making his phone calls. Usually the calls are to presidential assistants, and they are largely inspired by what he has read in the morning newspapers. He phones Kenneth O'Donnell, his appointments secretary—and it is a minor source of irritation to O'Donnell, as it is to all other assistants, that the President sees stories which have escaped their notice.

"Ken," he says, "have you seen the corn-surplus story on page fourteen of the *Times?* No? Well, read it and ask Freeman to stop in and see me around ten." Or he may call Theodore Sorensen, foreign affairs advisor, speech writer, member of the National Security Council. "Ted, have you read the Gromyko speech in Leningrad? Well, it's on page four of the *Washington Post* and I wish you would check it out with Rusk [Secretary of State] and Kohler [U.S. Ambassador to the Soviet Union] and find out if it represents a change of view on Cuba."

Only rarely does he receive calls. No one disturbs the President at breakfast unless the matter is too important to wait until he arrives at the office. Since the close of World War II, the most powerful political adversary of the United States—and the potential military one—has remained the Union of Soviet Socialist Republics, and the time zone in Moscow is eight hours ahead of the time in Washington. In a conflict of chronic tensions, Russia has the advantage, because whatever Moscow wants to say in the matter of explosive utterances can be said at ten A.M. Moscow time, which is two A.M. Washington time. Whatever the matter may be, it is often difficult to decide whether the President should be awakened to deal with it at once.

The phone calls stop when the children come in to see their father. At a few minutes past eight they run pell-mell through the second-floor hall from their rooms to his. It is impossible to assess which side draws more joy from these wild and noisy sessions, but it is a certainty that Caroline, John-John, and Mrs. Kennedy are the only people who cause the President to forget the clock.

They arrive at top speed, banking the turns in their robes and slippers, and the President of the United States makes haste to drop his toast, his knife, pat his mouth, move the breakfast tray aside, and brace himself for the hugs, the kisses, the high excitement of childish conversation, a cascade of words which tumble and intermingle so that only they know what they are talking about.

Caroline has more reserve than little John. She shows her father a paper on which she has printed her first name twenty times in large block letters. The President studies it and leans back, obviously overcome and a little awed at the accomplishment. "Caroline!" he says, spending each word separately. "Did . . . you . . . do . . . this?" She nods her head, almost shy with pride, and this calls for a congratulatory kiss.

Both children have almost honey-blond hair. Both are active and energetic types, like their parents. Little John swoops around the bedroom carrying a red-plush box. "Look at my due-ry box," he says. His father looks at it. It is empty, but he is impelled to react as though it were the wonder of the age. The President does not want his son to be called "Jack" or "Johnny." To emphasize the point, he addresses the boy as John-John.

"Next Saturday," he says, pointing a finger over the top of

Caroline, "we're going to ride the helicopter again." John-John drops the jewelry box and jumps with glee. He loves aircraft. "We're going to Camp David," the President says to Caroline, "and you can ride the horses."

They talk about Caroline's schoolwork, about an imaginary character called Floppy-Ears, and about their five dogs. These range in size from a big lean Irish wolfhound named Wolf, to a German shepherd called Clipper whose monotonous ambition is to chase a thrown piece of wood, down to a slightly ruffled cocker spaniel, Shannon, who asserts himself against the larger dogs. They sleep in a room on the south side of the ground floor, between the flower room and the swimming pool.

Mr. Kennedy is conscious of the importance of full-time parenthood; so conscious, in fact, that he often interrupts meetings of state to be with the children. Only recently he began to arrange his evening swim so that Caroline and John-John could join him, and now this event is established practice. When Mrs. Kennedy is away, he arranges his schedule so that he can spend extra time with the children.

For a time both parents worried about the effect on the youngsters of life in the White House, which is a hurlyburly of splendor, sycophancy, and security. But Mrs. Kennedy has succeeded in keeping a private, normal family life, with time for conversation, time for reading, time for personal friends, time for private recreation in a park, on a farm, on the water. Perhaps because of her efforts, the worries of the Kennedys about the effect of public adulation on the children proved groundless. Both children understand that their father is President of the United States, but they do not appreciate what it means. If there is a difference between their lives and the lives of other children, it is that no matter where they go, one or two Secret Service men walk behind them. However, as neither child understands the meaning of Secret Service, they think of these men as helpful friends of Daddy and Mummy.

Miss Shaw, the children's nurse, stands outside the President's bedroom and calls the children. They run out as swiftly as they arrived. The President finishes his breakfast, and begins to dress. Sometimes George Thomas hands the clothes to Mr. Kennedy. At other times—if the President's back is paining him—he assists with donning socks and shoes and trousers.

The presidential back has received much attention in the world press, but it is not a serious medical matter. Below the lumbar region, in the sacroiliac area, tendons and nerve areas are chronically irritated. Heat treatment, massage, and infrared radiation do little more than ameliorate pain. The President masks this pain well, and is reconciled to the fact that it is something which will come and go and might be with him for the rest of his life.

This morning he dresses by himself. Then he picks up a folder of "homework"—mostly problems of state, speeches, and written briefings and recommendations which he has digested and annotated between dinnertime last night and bedtime—and steps out of the bedroom into the sitting room. If Mrs. Kennedy is up, he spends some time with her. Usually they discuss the predictable events of the day. If she is still sleeping, he cautions the children against making undue noise and sits on a couch near the big west window, his legs crossed, and studies the folder of work once more.

In the west wing a dark slender woman walks through the maze of offices and corridors toward the President's office. She is Mrs. Evelyn Lincoln, private secretary to the President. She wears glasses and looks vaguely like a brunette Bette Davis. She has a slight, shy sense of humor which dies when some politician says heartily: "Well, it's good to have a Lincoln back in the White House."

Mrs. Lincoln arrives a few minutes after eight, and goes directly to her bright pleasant office. Most of the time she keeps the door between her office and the President's ajar, so that if he calls her she can hear him. She has worked for Mr. Kennedy for over ten years, and with his phenomenal rise to power, her work has increased. The presidential mail is an example. It amounts, on the average, to 30,000 pieces each week, or about 5,000 each mail-delivery day.

It is sorted in the offices of the old State Department Building, across the street from the White House. Out of the pile about a hundred letters reach the desk of Mrs. Lincoln each morning. These are considered important enough to warrant her attention. Of the remainder, every fiftieth unsolicited letter is taken from the pile at random and placed in a folder. The President reads these to get a good cross section of public opinion.

The total of private and random mail is two hundred letters. Mrs. Lincoln gives these her personal screening when she arrives, and can usually cut the total in half by redirecting inquiries to the proper government departments. All phone calls to the President go through her desk. She is subject to the unremitting pressures of all—from the Vice-President down to the newest stenographer in the press secretary's office. Mrs. Lincoln is one of three direct avenues to Mr. Kennedy. The others are Kenneth O'Donnell, his appointments secretary, and Pierre Salinger, his press secretary. However, most of the four hundred employees within the White House, who "must" see the President "at once," ask Mrs. Lincoln to intercede for them. Anyone from the pantry boy on up, who, for example, wants an autographed photo of the President, will usually consult Mrs. Lincoln. Thus, as Mr. Kennedy sits at his desk he faces three doors—the one at the left belongs to O'Donnell; the one at the center is used occasionally by Salinger; the one at the right, slightly ajar, is Mrs. Lincoln's.

The President places the folder under his arm, and leaves his quarters. At the elevator two Secret Service men are waiting. They fall into step with him after an exchange of morning greetings. They ride to the ground floor, and as they step off, they turn left in a corridor, then right to get to the west wing. They pass a White House policeman, on station in the red-carpeted hall, who salutes. The President nods, smiles briefly, and steps briskly toward the greenhouse and the colonnades which lead past the rose garden to his office.

It is eight-twenty and the White House has been coming alive with cumulative speed. Kenneth O'Donnell is already in his office, and the presidential appointment list for the day has been typed and inserted in the picture frame on Mr. Kennedy's desk; copies have been passed around to other offices. O'Donnell's assistants and secretaries are at work on the day's plans.

A round-faced young lady arrives on the Pennsylvania Avenue side of the White House and is escorted up to the third floor. She is Alice Grimes, who teaches the private first-grade elementary school in the White House. On the top floor she walks past George Thomas's room and then turns right and walks up an incline behind the coping of the roof. On top is a medium-sized squarish room with a good view of the lawn, stretching a third of a mile down to the south. There is a small pond and a huge effervescent fountain within her view as she removes her hat and makes her classroom ready.

At the west gate, newspaper reporters and television photographers begin to move in. Each is challenged or accorded a good morning by the White House policemen in sentry boxes; each carries White House Correspondent credentials. A man with an elegant smile comes through the gate. He is J. Bernard West, chief usher of the White House. He is, in effect, master of the household. Very little ever happens within the main part of the mansion which has not survived his scrutiny and approbation.

Two minutes behind him is a good-looking woman with mahogany skin. She wears an amiable regality and a barely repressed sense of humor on a handsome face. She is Mrs. Providencia Paredes, personal maid to Mrs. Kennedy. She was born in San Pedro Macoris, Santo Domingo, thirty-seven years ago. Mrs. Paredes supports her mother and two growing sons. She goes to the third floor, where she has a room near the private school. There she picks up a phone and asks the White House operators if they have awakened Mrs. Kennedy yet. She is told yes. Mrs. Paredes hangs up, then walks down to the private quarters on the second floor.

A minute ahead of her, McGeorge Bundy, the President's assistant in charge of foreign affairs, arrives in the west wing. He is youngish, broad-faced, wears glasses and is balding. He has already concluded a half hour of volley tennis, and he walks quickly down to the back offices he uses—with his staff—for national security. Major General C. V. Clifton, tall, ramrod-straight even when at his ease, waits for him. Clifton is the President's military aide, and he works closely with Bundy and the Department of Defense.

One hundred and fifty yards away on the east side of the White House, the eight-to-four shift of the Secret Service arrives and is checked out for duty. Down the hall from their office, Nancy Tuckerman, social secretary to the First Lady, arrives at her desk. She is young and gracious and alert, and to her falls the responsibility of carrying out the explicit directions of Mrs. Kennedy in matters ranging all the way from who sits where at a state dinner, to why the lighting is dim in the East Room.

Miss Tuckerman has two stenographers to assist with correspondence, which is of such magnitude that Mrs. Kennedy too gets a folder of "homework" to pore over in the late hours. Pamela Turnure, a brunette pixyish girl, arrives. She is Mrs. Kennedy's press secretary, possibly the first of her kind.

In the press office, Christine Camp is now at her desk. She assists Pierre Salinger. Helen Ganns, who has worked in the press department since President Truman's time, adjusts her snowy hair to its fluffiest, and shares some coffee with the newest worker, a stenographer with a Miss America figure, Nancy Larson. David Powers walks into O'Donnell's office. He is a bald second-generation Irishman from Boston, the President's crony. Powers has the wonderment of a priest in his eyes, and the tickle of blarney on his tongue. He is not only the best raconteur in the White House, but he has the sharpest memory for detail.

The main White House kitchen is filling with chefs, cooks, waiters, and dishwashers. Captain Seckel of the White House police sits like a Latin Buddha behind his desk in the press reception room. Samuel Mitchell, the Negro major-domo of the reception room, stands behind his desk with fingertips barely touching the wood, watching through his glasses as two assistants jump to their morning work of distributing newspapers and messages, and escorting visitors to the proper offices.

On the south lawn, four men push blowing machines across the grass. They pile the fallen leaves into isolated mounds, to be swept up and carried away later in the day. It is eight forty-five and the official day is beginning. A policeman at the southwest gate checks a small truck bringing delicacies for the official table. The vehicle, the driver, and all packages are examined, unless the policeman knows the truck as a "regular."

Mrs. Paredes, called "Provey" by everyone, opens the drapes in Mrs. Kennedy's room and pulls back the curtains facing south and west. The First Lady is not only stunningly handsome; she has the distressing habit of looking cheerful and attractive even when she first awakens. Provey has been Jacqueline Kennedy's maid for ten years, and cannot remember one morning in which her presence did not evoke a big smile, a lazy good morning, and the solicitous conversation of two women who understand each other. Mrs. Paredes has a slight Spanish accent, and her brand of English is sometimes an improvement over the correct word. The President considers Provey one of the most intelligent persons in the White House.

Mrs. Kennedy slips into a dressing robe and has breakfast in bed. The breakfast is appetizing: scrambled eggs, two strips of bacon, toast, orange juice, honey, a glass of skim milk—sometimes tea, sometimes coffee. Provey makes no comment on what Mrs. Kennedy does with breakfast, but she feels that her mistress does not eat enough. The bath is drawn while the food is aggravated from one side of the plate to the other, and little of it is consumed. This hurts Provey, who, at home, often says to her mother: "How she keep alive dat way?" John often has breakfast with his mother and usually eats all her honey and bacon.

Sometimes Mrs. Kennedy wears tortoise-shell glasses at night to read. In the morning she reads without them. Her personal secretary, Mary Gallagher, is outside in the sitting room waiting for the morning dictation to begin. When the bath is ready, Mrs. Kennedy is ready. Like the President, she plans ahead, parcels her time carefully, and somehow manages to be wife, mother, household manager, and First Lady. Provey lays out casual clothes for the morning—beige slacks, beige orlon sweater, and dark-brown flat shoes, gleaming. No adornments, no jewelry.

Miss Shaw permits Caroline to run in and kiss her mother good-bye before attending school. John-John dashes in and wants to know, "Where we going to go?" He always wants to know, and it doesn't matter how often he gets a reply, he wants to know anew. Mrs. Kennedy has a wonderful way with children. She has more than love, she has understanding. In the bedlam around her, she can continue a conversation with Provey, not hearing and yet sensitive to the play screams of her children; but if there is a scream of another pitch, she is alert to it by reflex and is on her feet hurrying toward the sound before she knows the cause. If there is a crash, she jumps too, but when she finds that it is not a child who fell, just an expensive painting knocked down, she smiles with relief. She is attuned to children; not merely her own, but all children.

She talks to Caroline with an arm around the child, smiling archly at the little girlish triumphs, frowning and almost mirroring her daughter's expression if matters are not going right. There is a farewell kiss, and Miss Shaw escorts Caroline to the third floor class.

In the main lobby of the White House, her classmates start to arrive. There are seven little girls, four boys. They are not the progeny of government people *per se;* in the main, they are the sons and daughters of old friends of the Kennedys from their Georgetown days. The idea of a small school started in 1962, when Mrs. Kennedy and her friends brought the children to a different house one day each week, and had Elizabeth Boyd, a kindergarten teacher, organize them into a play group.

The Kennedys do not pay for the little private school on the third floor. The cost of teacher, desks, and small open lockers is shared by the parents of all students. The ten children who do not

live in the White House arrive each morning in a car-pool arrangement. They stand in the main lobby until the last one arrives; then
they are taken upstairs. Each brings his lunchbox.

At eight forty-five the class is called to order. The sun is now
fairly high, and it slants in off the back of the room. Hair is tidy,
little frocks and suits are neat, and hands are clasped on the edge
of desks. Sweaters are hung on pegs in the plywood lockers. Miss
Grimes begins by discussing what day this is, and what date.

She seldom sits, perferring to walk around the small class as
she talks. Sometimes she sits in the back of the room, still talking,
or asking questions. If there is a presidential reception on the south
lawn for a visiting chief of state, with its twenty-one gun salute of
cannon, the barking orders to the military, the strains of the national
anthems coming from the red-coated U.S. Marine Band, the teacher
will recess class for a few moments so that the children can press
their noses to the windows and see the excitement.

At other, duller times, Miss Grimes discusses the projects of
the first grade for the day. Then she will begin to read a story, and
ask each child in turn to pick up the thread of it and read on a little
further. She is patient with her charges, but firm in the discipline
of learning. She insists that on arrival, each child shake hands with
her and say: "Good morning, Miss Grimes." She also makes certain
that each student studies French at least four days each week. During this period the teacher does not permit the children to speak in
English.

On the first floor, the President runs through his mail. Sometimes, when he is ready to dictate replies, he will not call Mrs.
Lincoln to him. He will go to her desk, and stand there, calling
upon his extensive vocabulary quickly and easily, making his answers succinct. Sometimes he will say: "I just heard that Joe
———— is in the hospital. Take a letter to him." On other occasions
he uses an electric dictating machine, but he does not do so well in
marshaling his thoughts as when he is facing Mrs. Lincoln.

Doubt is a rare condition for Mr. Kennedy's mind. Almost
always he knows what he wants to say, or do, and he makes it plain

that he wants to say or do it at once. His assistants rate him as a good assessor of situations. Sometimes, to their surprise, he can see something bad in good news. In an action by the Soviet Union, he not only sees what is being done, but relates it to past performance, the policy of countries friendly to Russia, and the propaganda effect on world opinion. He encourages disagreement among his close assistants; in fact, anyone in the small group around him is expected to disagree, and disagree loudly, if he feels so disposed. However, after all the discussion it is John F. Kennedy who will make the decision, and once he makes it, all hands abide by it whether they find it palatable or not.

Pierre Salinger is in his office. He leans back, puffs on a long cigar, and places his heels on the desk. He is dark and sturdy, almost chubby, and gives the appearance of total relaxation, but his reflexes betray tension. For a heavy man, he can come to his feet faster than most men can sit.

In Mrs. Lincoln's office, the President concludes the immediate mail. Other letters are on his desk, but the urgent ones are taken care of. Mrs. Lincoln gives the President a sheaf of mail sent to Cabinet officers and ranking members of his official family—mail which they hesitate to answer without presidential direction. This adds to his daily workload, but he takes it back to his office with him.

On a small table near Mrs. Lincoln's desk, there are square chunks of milk chocolate on a plate. They are there to tempt any visitor, but Mr. Kennedy has never eaten one. He does not eat candy at any time, and he is averse to between-meal snacks. As he turns to leave, he says softly: "Tell Ken I want to see him."

Four Days

by Bruce Catton
Senior Editor of
AMERICAN HERITAGE Magazine

from the Introduction

Four Days, *a pictorial and textual history of the assassination
of President Kennedy and its aftermath, was compiled by United
Press International and* American Heritage *Magazine.
The "Introduction" which follows was written by Bruce Catton,
senior editor of* American Heritage *and eminent historian.
It is one of the most thoughtful and eloquent
of all the eulogies.*

What John F. Kennedy left us most of all was an attitude. To put
it in the simplest terms, he looked ahead. He knew no more than
anyone else what the future was going to be like, but he did know
that that was where he ought to be looking. Only to a limited extent

are we prisoners of the past. The future sets us free. It is our escape hatch. We can shape it to our liking, and we had better start thinking about how we would like it.

It was time for us to take that attitude, because we thought we were growing old. We had lived through hard experiences and we were tired, and out of our weariness came caution, suspicion, and the crippling desire to play it safe. We became so worried about what we had to lose that we never began to think about what was still to be gained, and sometimes it looked as if we were becoming a nation of fuddy-duddies. The world was moving faster than ever before and we were beginning to regret that it was moving at all because we were afraid where it might take us.

But President Kennedy personified youth and vigor—and perhaps it was symbolic that both his friends and his foes picked up his Boston accent and began to say "vigah." He went about hatless, he liked to mingle with crowds and shake the hands of all and sundry, for recreation he played touch football, and for the rest he sat in an old-fashioned rocking chair as if in sly mockery of his own exuberance. He seemed to think that things like music and painting and literature were essential parts of American life and that it was worthwhile to know what the musicians and artists and writers were doing. Whatever he did was done with zest, as if youth were for the first time touching life and finding it exciting.

With all of this there was a cool maturity of outlook. By itself, vigor is not enough. Courage is needed also, and when youth has courage it acquires composure. In the most perilous moments President Kennedy kept his poise. He challenged the power of darkness at least once, and during the hours when his hand had to stay close to the fateful trigger he was composed and unafraid. Once in a great while a nation, like a man, has to be ready to spend itself utterly for some value that means more than survival itself means. President Kennedy led us through such a time, and we began to see that the power of darkness is perhaps not as strong as we had supposed—and that even if it were, there is something else that matters much more.

It was his attitude that made the difference. Performance can be adjudged in various ways, and we have plenty of time to appraise the value or the lack of value of the concrete achievements of the Kennedy Administration. The President who called on us to stop thinking about what our country could do for us and to think instead about what we could do for our country may or may not have given us specific programs that would embody that ideal in actual practice; the point is that he wrenched us out of ourselves and compelled us to meditate about the whole that is greater than the sum of its parts. From the beginning, the whole of our American experiment has been made up of an infinite number of aspirations and unremembered bits of heroism, devotion, and hope, lodged in the hearts of innumerable separate Americans. When all of these are brought together, the nation goes forward.

That, in the last analysis, is the faith America has wanted to live by. We are always uneasy when we find ourselves keeping our noblest ideals in mothballs, carefully shielded from contact with the workaday world; deep in our hearts we know that we are supposed to take them out and work for them even if contact with harsh reality occasionally knocks chips off them here and there. Whether this man knew the best ways to put our ideals into practical use is a secondary consideration now. He did think we ought to try our best to do something about them, and that belief his death did not take away from us, because we came to share in it.

We turned some sort of corner in the last few years. Almost without our knowing it, one era came to an end and a new one began. The change had little to do with formal acts of government— with specific programs, bits of legislation, or exercises of presidential power. It reflected a change in the times themselves. For a whole generation we had had to face terrible immediate problems—depression, war, cold war, the infinite destructive power of the nuclear mystery that we knew how to release but did not quite know how to control. Then came a breathing spell, a faint but definite easing of the tensions. Almost for the first moment in our lifetimes we began to look ahead once more and to realize that it was not only possible but imperative to think about the limitless future rather than about the mere problem of warding off disaster.

President Kennedy came to symbolize that moment of change, not because he caused it but because he fitted into it; not because of what he did but simply because of what he was. He might almost have been speaking from Shakespeare's text, telling us that being ready is what really matters—being ready to meet any challenge, to assume any responsibility, to lose fear for ourselves in an abiding concern for the common good. The four harrowing days that began on November 22, 1963, brought us face to face with the future. What happens next is up to us. *The readiness is all.*

That is why those four days are worth re-examining. We relive that time of tragedy less to commemorate a departed President than to dedicate ourselves. When the army bugler sent the haunting notes of "Taps" across that grave in Arlington Cemetery he sounded a long goodbye and a commitment to eternal rest for John F. Kennedy. For all the rest of us, that was the trumpet of dawn itself.

from The Kennedy Wit

by Bill Adler

Barry Goldwater is an excellent photographer. He once took a good picture of President Kennedy and sent it to him for an autograph. The picture came back with this inscription:

> For Barry Goldwater, whom I urge to follow the career for which he has shown so much talent—photography. From his friend, John Kennedy.

On a return visit to the White House, former President Truman entertained President Kennedy and the assembled dinner guests with a few selections on the piano. President Kennedy was quoted as having made this comment after Mr. Truman finished his piano recital:

> Don't say there is no justice in the world. Stalin has been kicked out of Lenin's tomb and President Truman is back in the White House.
>
> November 5, 1961

from

John F. Kennedy, President

By Hugh Sidey

A Way of Life

Four generations of family journalists are the heritage of Hugh Sidey, who is currently upholding the tradition as White House correspondent and Washington deputy bureau chief for Time *magazine.* John F. Kennedy, President *is his first book, an interesting description and analysis of the new President and the early part of his administration. In the excerpt reprinted here, Sidey turns his attention to that most heralded aspect of the Kennedy Administration, "The New Frontier."*

The New Frontier grew to be more than government. It became a way of life, it became Washington's new society, it became sensitivity to the arts, no better illustrated than through Jackie's broad program of restoration for the White House. It was a vigorous outdoor life of riding, swimming, golf, tennis, boating and touch football, not to mention skiing and hiking and softball. And, in fact, it all became so vigorous sometimes that it was overdone, a step beyond good fun. Bob Kennedy's Hickory Hill estate became headquarters of the cult because of the confining atmosphere of the White House.

Walt Rostow found himself striding over the dewy ten acres in Virginia as he talked about guerrilla warfare before breakfast. Max Taylor took to the new Hickory Hill tennis court.

Pierre Salinger was unceremoniously tossed in the Kennedy swimming pool as a fitting end to a huge lawn party. Teddy Kennedy dived in on his own accord, just out of sheer exuberance.

A journalist interviewing Bob Kennedy found himself striding up and down the side of the swimming pool shouting his questions as Bob swam. When one question offended Bob, he simply submerged, swam under water to the other side of the pool, crawled out and stalked off up the hill, leaving the perplexed newsman standing.

A Secret Service agent found himself singing nursery rhymes on board the Kennedy sailing sloop in Hyannis Port as it headed, brimming with children, for a picnic on the beach.

Don Wilson, the United States Information Agency's deputy director, met a Kennedy tennis challenge in his bare feet. Many a brave man plunged headlong into the rose bushes on the Hyannis Port lawn to catch a touch football pass. Guests of the Kennedys at Stowe, Vermont, could only win endorsement if they hurtled down near-vertical ski slopes. And those intimate friends who vacationed with Bob and Ethel found that 5 A.M. was a reasonable time at which to expect the first athletics—and there was no curfew.

The President did his back exercises, carefully prescribed by New York University's Dr. Hans Kraus, on the floor of his jet plane, in his bedroom and occasionally in the pocket-sized White

House gym. He frequently challenged his chubby Press Secretary to do pushups. He asked his entire staff at one point to lose five pounds each. After seeing some tough paratroopers at Fort Bragg, he prodded his own desk-bound military advisers into a fitness course.

White House staffers Ted Sorensen and Mike Feldman hurried downtown in the mornings for a tennis game before work. And Under Secretary of the Navy Paul Fay, a personal friend of the President's, became so fitness-conscious that, as he flew around the country for speaking engagements and inspection tours, he took to challenging the young gobs to pushup contests.

It was not only athletics that demanded such verve. Every activity was to be engaged at full throttle. When the word spread that John Kennedy read 1,200 words a minute and read everything in sight, White House staffers enrolled in speed reading courses, even set up a special class in the White House. Ian Fleming's mystery books were devoured, as were such other Kennedy favorites as *Melbourne* and vast quantities of history. One White House aide tried to assemble a shelf for all the books written by New Frontiersmen, no small task.

Loud and sloppy dress disappeared among and around the Kennedys. Pierre Salinger, after a struggle, gave up his California-type shirts with their pink, yellow, orange and green hues. Only in the most casual moments did he feel safe wearing them. On some occasions he was noted wearing a vest. The pendulum had swung.

The button-down shirt, which the President declared out of style, disappeared as well.

Naturalness became the rule. Bob and Ethel Kennedy came to Hyannis airport to pick up Central Intelligence Agency Director Allen Dulles and loaded him, to his delight, in a convertible full of children. When the stiff White House protocol made no sense, Kennedy simply ignored it. He lingered by the door at night to bid his party guests good night when the rule book said that he should have gone upstairs and let the guests find their own way out. He grabbed people and shoved them in the receiving lines when he thought they should be there, and rank and order meant nothing.

He could kid his famous guests, as he did the day he greeted India's Prime Minister Nehru in Newport. On the *Honey Fitz,* gliding by the great mansions of a past era, Kennedy casually waved to the huge homes and said, "I wanted you to see how the average American family lives."

Harry Truman and Bess were invited to stay overnight at the White House for the very simple reason that the Kennedys thought they might enjoy it. They did—immensely. Margaret and her husband came too.

The gaudy expense-account restaurants became less chic as the Kennedys established the smartness of dining at home. Night-clubbing was not on their agenda much, either. Nor was heavy drinking. The gentle sipping of a daiquiri or a bloody Mary was about as far as liquor went.

It was not what people were, it was what they could do. Under this rule a new official society was born. Those who had talent, not money alone, were asked to the White House. They included a vast spectrum, from workaday newsmen to titled foreigners.

By right of office the first couple can control official society. But sometimes in the past, as with Bess Truman and Mamie Eisenhower, they simply did not want to. As the luster of Jackie's entertaining became known, it became obvious that the Kennedys were now society.

The newspapers which arbitrate found little space for other events. A White House whing-ding swept all else off the pages. Caroline's birthday parties, Jackie's Virginia horseback riding, the President's cruises on the *Honey Fitz,* the first couple's house guests—these were the headline materials. The huge stiff embassy receptions, which had been forever and probably will continue forever, dwindled to mere paragraphs buried on the inside pages with the grocery ads.

The successful hostesses were those who got the President and his wife to their homes (such as Mrs. John Sherman Cooper, wife of the Republican senator from Kentucky) or, next in line, the Robert Kennedys (the Don Wilsons). Next important were the other members of the family, then came close friends, and then the frighteningly intelligent members of the New Frontier, such as Arthur Schlesinger, Jr., Walt Rostow and McGeorge Bundy.

Gone, or at least out of sight for the time being, were the mastodons who had ruled in previous eras simply by the heft of their bankbooks. Perle Mesta had taken flight after endorsing Nixon loudly and publicly, and she stayed in New York making plans to return to Washington after a decent interval. But when she finally did come back to the capital, she did not make the splash she had predicted. Something funny had happened to her on the way to the New Frontier.

Gwen Cafritz looked in every mail, but there was no invitation to any of the White House soirees. She threw her annual "Supreme Court" party in October and carelessly let it conflict with a White House affair. Not a single Supreme Court Justice showed up.

A gay party giver of lesser years, Scottie Lanahan, F. Scott Fitzgerald's daughter, also made the fatal miscalculation and gave a party on the same night the Kennedys were having one of their own intimate gatherings for the people they liked. Mrs. Lanahan got the third team, those not invited to the White House—hardly a smashing success.

Another of Mrs. Cafritz's affairs which managed to lure only a thin sprinkling of New Frontier talent was described by one of those who attended as "the most uninteresting collection of people that anybody could find anywhere."

The Kennedy group was described by one Washington society writer as "the richest, prettiest, most interesting" young people in the country. As a matter of fact, the praise was so lavish that it grew a little heavy.

Government was the code name. The Kennedys described what they were doing as the most interesting thing in the world. Public service was the challenge. Those who answered the call and did well got to know the Kennedys and whom the Kennedys liked were apt to be society.

Some of the rich young men around the nation heard the call. Paul (Red) Fay took a biting cut in salary when he left the family's lucrative construction firm in San Francisco and came back to be Under Secretary of the Navy at $20,000 per annum. So did Don Wilson when he gave up heading *Life* magazine's Washington bureau to work for the United States Information Agency.

There was another side to the picture, however. Kennedy's friend Bill Walton found that the demand and hence the price of his paintings went up as his association with the White House became known. Chuck Spaulding, who had joined with another young man to start an obscure investment office, suddenly became a noted New York investment banker in the newspaper columns. K. LeMoyne Billings, a New York advertising executive, found that his stature in trade rose in direct proportion to the degree he became known as a close friend of the President's. Correspondent Charles Bartlett found increased interest in his column "New Focus" when his old friend John Kennedy was elected and took office.

Money still helped around Washington, but it did not rule. An eager young couple with imagination and wit could lure the cream of the New Frontier into a tiny Georgetown garden for an evening of folk singing when the Cafritzes and the Mestas could not entice them to come out.

Almost forgotten in their mausoleums were the old, old Washington society. "We don't even cover those old ladies with canes anymore," acknowledged one society reporter.

Jackie's entertaining deserved its reputation, because she worked at it. Each affair was a new creation. She crawled on the floor among diagrams as she arranged the complex seating. She went over the menus minutely. She made sure to know what food each guest could and could not have.

There used to be an embarrassingly silent time at official functions as the guests were pushed into line to shake hands with the

President and his wife. Jackie added soothing music of the President's own red-coated Marine band to coax her guests through that half hour.

When Finland's President Urho Kaleva Kekkonen and his wife came to visit in October, they were ushered into the State Dining Room for lunch. It was decorated in blue and white flowers, the colors of the Finnish flag. The Marine band played Finlandia, and in the private quarters on a table Jackie had arranged the dolls which Mrs. Kekkonen had sent earlier as a present to Caroline. Aware from her study that Mrs. Kekkonen liked art and antiques, Jackie gave her a set of books on American art, antiques, homes and literature. And when the men went off to talk business, Jackie arranged for the Finnish lady to visit Mount Vernon and the National Gallery of Art.

In mid-November the Kennedys scored another first: Pablo Casals played in the East Room. The 84-year-old cellist had refused since his self-banishment from his native Spain in 1939 to play publicly in any country that recognized Franco. But as a special tribute to Kennedy, he had come back to the White House after fifty-seven years—the first time since he had played as a youth for Teddy Roosevelt.

American composers from across the land were invited to the white-tie affair. So were the leading patrons and critics of music. There were other noted guests, such as New York Mayor Robert Wagner and labor leader George Meany.

Casals was superb, and so were the praises that echoed for days. (Months later, still being complimented on the fact that her husband had done so much for music through the Casals performance, the story goes that Jackie kidded, "The only music he really appreciates is 'Hail to the Chief!' ")

Not only was this a new kind of society, it was a new tribute to culture.

The Kennedys both felt that American artists and performers should be honored by being invited to the White House, that American arts and skills should be displayed for the world to see in this manner. Culture was not only to be enjoyed in this country, but to be spread abroad as a peaceful tool in the cold war.

And then, of course, if John Kennedy was allowed to slip in a couple of reporters, some key congressmen, a labor bigwig or two, it did not really offend anyone and it certainly helped in the old grubby political war. . . .

Nuclear Testing and Disarmament

Radio and Television Address
to the American People

March 2, 1962

[Delivered from the President's Office
at 7 P.M.]

Good evening:

Seventeen years ago man unleashed the power of the atom. He thereby took into his mortal hands the power of self-extinction. Throughout the years that have followed, under three successive Presidents, the United States has sought to banish this weapon from the arsenals of individual nations. For of all the awesome responsibilities entrusted to this office, none is more somber to contemplate than the special statutory authority to employ nuclear arms in the defense of our people and freedom.

But until mankind has banished both war and its instruments of destruction, the United States must maintain an effective quantity and quality of nuclear weapons, so deployed and protected as to be capable of surviving any surprise attack and devastating the attacker. Only through such strength can we be certain of deterring a nuclear strike, or an overwhelming ground attack, upon our forces and our allies. Only through such strength can we in the free world—should that deterrent fail—face the tragedy of another war with any hope of survival. And that deterrent strength, if it is to be effective and credible when compared with that of any other nation, must embody the most modern, the most reliable and the most versatile nuclear weapons our research and development can produce.

The testing of new weapons and their effects is necessarily a part of that research and development process. Without tests—to experiment and verify—progress is limited. A nation which is refraining from tests obviously cannot match the gains of a nation conducting tests. And when all nuclear powers refrain from testing, the nuclear arms race is held in check.

That is why this nation has long urged an effective worldwide end to nuclear tests. And this is why in 1958 we voluntarily subscribed, as did the Soviet Union, to a nuclear test moratorium, during which neither side would conduct new nuclear tests, and both East and West would seek concrete plans for their control.

But on September first of last year, while the United States and the United Kingdom were negotiating in good faith in Geneva, the Soviet Union callously broke its moratorium with a two month series of tests of more than 40 nuclear weapons. Preparations for these tests had been secretly underway for many months. Accompanied by new threats and new tactics of terror, these tests—conducted mostly in the atmosphere—represented a major Soviet effort to put nuclear weapons back into the arms race.

Once it was apparent that new appeals and proposals were to no avail, I authorized on September fifth a resumption of U.S. nuclear tests underground, and I announced on November second—before the close of the Soviet series—that preparations were being ordered for a resumption of atmospheric tests, and that we would make whatever tests our security required in the light of Soviet gains.

This week, the National Security Council of the United States has completed its review of this subject. The scope of the Soviet tests has been carefully reviewed by the most competent scientists in the country. The scope and justification of proposed American tests have been carefully reviewed, determining which experiments can be safely deferred, which can be deleted, which can be combined or conducted underground, and which are essential to our military and scientific progress. Careful attention has been given to the limiting of radioactive fallout, and to the future course of arms control diplomacy, and to our obligations to other nations.

Every alternative was examined. Every avenue of obtaining Soviet agreement was explored. We were determined not to rush into imitating their tests. And we were equally determined to do only what our own security required us to do. Although the complex preparations have continued at full speed while these facts were being uncovered, no single decision of this Administration has been more thoroughly or more thoughtfully weighed.

Having carefully considered these findings—having received unanimous recommendations of the pertinent department and agency heads—and having observed the Soviet Union's refusal to accept any agreement which would inhibit its freedom to test extensively after preparing secretly—I have today authorized the Atomic Energy Commission and the Department of Defense to conduct a series of nuclear tests—beginning when our preparations are completed, in the latter part of April, and to be concluded as quickly as possible (within two or three months)—such series, involving only those tests which cannot be held underground, to take place in the atmosphere over the Pacific Ocean.

These tests are to be conducted under conditions which restrict the radioactive fallout to an absolute minimum, far less than the contamination created by last fall's Soviet series. . . .

Nevertheless, I find it deeply regrettable that any radioactive material must be added to the atmosphere—that even one individual's health may be risked in the foreseeable future. And however remote and infinitesimal those hazards may be, I still exceedingly regret the necessity of balancing these hazards against the hazards to hundreds of millions of lives which would be created by any relative decline in our nuclear strength.

In the absence of any major shift in Soviet policies, no American President—responsible for the freedom and the safety of so many people—could in good faith make any other decision. But because our nuclear posture affects the security of all Americans and all free men—because this issue has aroused such widespread concern—I want to share with you and all the world, to the fullest extent our security permits, all of the facts and the thoughts which have gone into this decision.

Many of these facts are hard to explain in simple terms—many are hard to face in a peaceful world—but these are facts which must be faced and must be understood.

II.

Had the Soviet tests of last fall merely reflected a new effort in intimidation and bluff, our security would not have been affected. But in fact they also reflected a highly sophisticated technology, the trial of novel designs and techniques, and some substantial gains in weaponry. Many of these tests were aimed at improving their defenses against missiles—others were proof tests, trying out existing weapons systems—but over one-half emphasized the development of new weapons, particularly those of greater explosive power. . . .

Last fall's tests, in and by themselves, did not give the Soviet Union superiority in nuclear power. They did, however, provide the Soviet laboratories with a mass of data and experience on which, over the next two or three years, they can base significant analyses, experiments, and extrapolations, preparing for the next test series which would confirm and advance their findings.

And I must report to you in all candor that further Soviet tests, in the absence of further Western progress, could well provide the Soviet Union with a nuclear attack and defense capability so powerful as to encourage aggressive designs. Were we to stand still while the Soviets surpassed us—or even appeared to surpass us—the Free

World's ability to deter, to survive and to respond to an all-out attack would be seriously weakened.

III.

The fact of the matter is that we cannot make similar strides without testing in the atmosphere as well as underground. For, in many areas of nuclear weapons research, we have reached the point where our progress is stifled without experiments in every environment. The information from our last series of atmospheric tests in 1958 has all been analyzed and re-analyzed. It cannot tell us more without new data. And it is in these very areas of research—missile penetration and missile defense—that further major Soviet tests, in the absence of further Western tests, might endanger our deterrent.

In addition to proof tests of existing systems, two different types of tests have therefore been decided upon. The *first* and most important are called "effects tests"—determining what effect an enemy nuclear explosion would have upon our ability to survive and respond. We are spending great sums of money on radar to alert our defenses and to develop possible anti-missile systems—on the communications which enable our command and control centers to direct a response—on hardening our missiles sites, shielding our missiles and warheads from defensive action, and providing them with electronic guidance systems to find their targets. But we cannot be certain how much of this preparation will turn out to be useless: blacked out, paralyzed or destroyed by the complex effects of a nuclear explosion. . . .

Secondly, we must test in the atmosphere to permit the development of those more advanced concepts and more effective, efficient weapons which, in the light of Soviet tests, are deemed essential to our security. Nuclear weapons technology is a constantly changing field. If our weapons are to be more secure, more flexible in their use and more selective in their impact—if we are to be alert to new breakthroughs, to experiment with new designs—if we are to maintain our scientific momentum and leadership—then our weapons

259

progress must not be limited to theory or to the confines of laboratories and caves. . . .

IV.

While we will be conducting far fewer tests than the Soviets, with far less fallout, there will still be those in other countries who will urge us to refrain from testing at all. Perhaps they forget that this country long refrained from testing, and sought to ban all tests, while the Soviets were secretly preparing new explosions. Perhaps they forget the Soviet threats of last autumn and their arbitrary rejection of all appeals and proposals, from both the United States and the United Nations. But those free peoples who value their freedom and their security, and look to our relative strength to shield them from danger—those who know of our good faith in seeking an end to testing and an end to the arms race—will, I am confident, want the United States to do whatever it must do to deter the threat of aggression.

If they felt we could be swayed by threats or intimidation—if they thought we could permit a repetition of last summer's deception —then surely they would lose faith in our will and our wisdom as well as our weaponry. I have no doubt that most of our friends around the world have shared my own hope that we would never find it necessary to test again—and my own belief that, in the long run, the only real security in this age of nuclear peril rests not in armament but in disarmament. But I am equally certain that they would insist on our testing once that is deemed necessary to protect free world security. They know we are not deciding to test for political or psychological reasons—and they also know that we cannot avoid such tests for political or psychological reasons.

V.

The leaders of the Soviet Union are also watching this decision. Should we fail to follow the dictates of our own security, they will chalk it up, not to goodwill, but to a failure of will—not to our confidence in Western superiority, but to our fear of world opinion, the very world opinion for which they showed such contempt. They could well be encouraged by such signs of weakness to seek another period of no testing without controls—another opportunity for stifling our progress while secretly preparing on the basis of last fall's experiments, for the new test series which might alter the balance of power. With such a one-sided advantage, why would they change their strategy, or refrain from testing, merely because we refrained? Why would they want to halt their drive to surpass us in nuclear technology? And why would they ever consider accepting a true test ban or mutual disarmament?

Our reasons for testing and our peaceful intentions are clear—so clear that even the Soviets could not objectively regard our resumption of tests, following their own resumption of tests, as provocative or preparatory for war. On the contrary, it is my hope that the prospects for peace may actually be strengthened by this decision —once the Soviet leaders realize that the West will no longer stand still, negotiating in good faith, while they reject inspection and are free to prepare for further tests. As new disarmament talks approach, the basic lesson for some three years and 353 negotiating sessions at Geneva is this—that the Soviets will not agree to an effective ban on nuclear tests as long as a new series of offers and prolonged negotiations, or a new uninspected moratorium, or a new agreement without controls, would enable them once again to prevent the West from testing while they prepare in secret.

But inasmuch as this choice is now no longer open to them, let us hope that they will take a different attitude on banning nuclear tests—that they will prefer to see the nuclear arms race checked instead of intensified, with all the dangers that that intensification brings: the spread of nuclear weapons to other nations; the constant increase in world tensions; the steady decrease in all prospects for disarmament; and, with it, a steady decrease in the security of us all.

VI.

If the Soviets would change their position, we will have an opportunity to learn it immediately. On the 14th of March, in Geneva,

Switzerland, a new 18-power conference on disarmament will begin. A statement of agreed principles has been worked out with the Soviets and endorsed by the U.N. In the long run, it is the constructive possibilities of this conference—and not the testing of new destructive weapons—on which rest the hopes of all mankind. However dim those hopes may sometimes seem, they can never be abandoned. And however far-off most steps toward disarmament appear, there are some that can be taken at once.

The United States will offer at the Geneva conference—not in the advance expectation they will be rejected, and not merely for purposes of propaganda—a series of concrete plans for a major "breakthrough to peace." We hope and believe that they will appeal to all nations opposed to war. . . .

In short, in the absence of a firm agreement that would halt nuclear tests by the latter part of April, we shall go ahead with our talks—striving for some new avenue of agreement—but we shall also go ahead with our tests. If, on the other hand, the Soviet Union should accept such a treaty in the opening months of the talks, that single step would be a monumental step toward peace. . . .

VII.

For our ultimate objective is not to test for the sake of testing. Our real objective is to make our own tests unnecessary, to prevent others from testing, to prevent the nuclear arms race from mushrooming out of control, to take the first steps toward general and complete disarmament. And that is why, in the last analysis, it is the leaders of the Soviet Union who must bear the heavy responsibility of choosing, in the weeks that lie ahead, whether we proceed with these steps—or proceed with new tests.

If they are convinced that their interests can no longer be served by the present course of events, then it is my fervent hope that they will agree to an effective treaty. But if they persist in rejecting all means of true inspection, then we shall be left with no choice but to keep our own defensive arsenal adequate for the security of all free men.

It is our hope and prayer that these grim, unwelcome tests will never have to be made—that these deadly weapons will never have to be fired—and that our preparations for war will bring about the preservation of peace. Our foremost aim is the control of force, not the pursuit of force, in a world made safe for mankind. But whatever the future brings, I am sworn to uphold and defend the freedom of the American people—and I intend to do whatever must be done to fulfill that solemn obligation.

Thank you—and good night.

On Returning from Europe

*Radio and Television Report
to the American People*

June 6, 1961

[Delivered from the President's Office
at 7 P.M.]

*In June, 1961, President Kennedy embarked upon a trip
to Europe. The focal point of the entire trip was his
confrontation with Russia's Premier Khrushchev at Vienna.
Many of the world's most delicate problems were on their
agenda for discussion, but Kennedy was not optimistic about
the chances of any significant breakthroughs in these areas.
But one of his main objectives was to gain a first-hand
understanding of his adversary, an undertaking which he deemed
indispensable in any appraisal of East-West conflicts. The
talks proved as fruitless—or more so—as Kennedy had
expected, but he did leave Vienna with a grasp of Khrushchev's
character that was later to stand him in good stead.*

Good evening, my fellow citizens:

I returned this morning from a weeklong trip to Europe and I want to report to you on that trip in full. It was in every sense an unforgettable experience. The people of Paris, of Vienna, of London, were generous in their greeting. They were heartwarming in their hospitality, and their graciousness to my wife is particularly appreciated.

We knew of course that the crowds and the shouts were meant in large measure for the country that we represented, which is regarded as the chief defender of freedom. Equally memorable was the pageantry of European history and their culture that is very much a part of any ceremonial reception, to lay a wreath at the Arc de Triomphe, to dine at Versailles, and Schönbrunn Palace, and with the Queen of England. These are the colorful memories that will remain with us for many years to come. Each of the three cities that we visited—Paris, Vienna, and London—have existed for many centuries, and each serves as a reminder that the Western civilization that we seek to preserve has flowered over many years, and has defended itself over many centuries. But this was not a ceremonial trip. Two aims of American foreign policy, above all others, were the reason for this trip: the unity of the free world, whose strength is the security of us all, and the eventual achievement of a lasting peace. My trip was devoted to the advancement of these two aims.

To strengthen the unity of the West, our journey opened in Paris and closed in London. My talks with General de Gaulle were profoundly encouraging to me. Certain differences in our attitudes on one or another problem became insignificant in view of our common commitment to defend freedom. Our alliance, I believe, became more secure; the friendship of our nation, I hope—with theirs—became firmer; and the relations between the two of us who bear responsibility became closer, and I hope were marked by confidence. I found General de Gaulle far more interested in our frankly stating our position, whether or not it was his own, than in appearing to agree with him when we do not. But he knows full well the true meaning of an alliance. He is after all the only major leader of World War II who still occupies a position of great responsibility. His life has been one of unusual dedication; he is a man of extraordinary personal character, symbolizing the new strength and the historic grandeur of France. Throughout our discussions he took the long view of France and the world at large. I found him a wise counselor for the future, and an informative guide to the history that he has helped to make. Thus we had a valuable meeting. . . .

General de Gaulle could not have been more cordial, and I could not have more confidence in any man. In addition to his individual strength of character, the French people as a whole showed vitality and energy which were both impressive and gratifying. Their recovery from the postwar period is dramatic; their productivity is increasing, and they are steadily building their stature in both Europe and Africa, and thus, I left Paris for Vienna with increased confidence in Western unity and strength.

The people of Vienna know what it is to live under occupation, and they know what it is to live in freedom. Their welcome to me as President of this country should be heartwarming to us all. I went to Vienna to meet the leader of the Soviet Union, Mr. Khrushchev. For two days we met in sober, intensive conversation, and I believe it is my obligation to the people, to the Congress, and to our allies to report on those conversations candidly and publicly.

Mr. Khrushchev and I had a very full and frank exchange of views on the major issues that now divide our two countries. I will tell you now that it was a very sober two days. There was no discourtesy, no loss of tempers, no threats or ultimatums by either side; no advantage or concession was either gained or given; no major decision was either planned or taken; no spectacular progress was either achieved or pretended.

This kind of informal exchange may not be as exciting as a full-fledged summit meeting with a fixed agenda and a large corps of advisers, where negotiations are attempted and new agreements sought, but this was not intended to be and was not such a meeting, nor did we plan any future summit meetings in Vienna.

But I found this meeting with Chairman Khrushchev, as somber as it was, to be immensely useful. I had read his speeches and of his policies. I had been advised on his views. I had been told by other leaders of the West, General de Gaulle, Chancellor Adenauer, Prime Minister Macmillan, what manner of man he was.

But I bear the responsibility of the President of the United States, and it is my duty to make decisions that no adviser and no ally can make for me. It is my obligation and responsibility to see that these decisions are as informed as possible, that they are based on as much direct, firsthand knowledge as possible.

I therefore thought it was of immense importance that I know Mr. Khrushchev, that I gain as much insight and understanding as I could on his present and future policies. At the same time, I wanted to make certain Mr. Khrushchev knew this country and its policies, that he understood our strength and our determination, and that he knew that we desired peace with all nations of every kind.

I wanted to present our views to him directly, precisely, realistically, and with an opportunity for discussion and clarification. This was done. No new aims were stated in private that have not been stated in public on either side. The gap between us was not, in such a short period, materially reduced, but at least the channels of communication were opened more fully, at least the chances of a dangerous misjudgment on either side should now be less, and at least the men on whose decisions the peace in part depends have agreed to remain in contact.

This is important, for neither of us tried to merely please the other, to agree merely to be agreeable, to say what the other wanted to hear. And just as our judicial system relies on witnesses appearing in court and on cross-examination, instead of hearsay testimony or affidavits on paper, so, too, was this direct give-and-take of immeasurable value in making clear and precise what we considered to be vital, for the facts of the matter are that the Soviets and ourselves give wholly different meanings to the same words—war, peace, democracy, and popular will.

We have wholly different views of right and wrong, of what is an internal affair and what is aggression, and, above all, we have wholly different concepts of where the world is and where it is going.

Only by such a discussion was it possible for me to be sure that Mr. Khrushchev knew how differently we view the present and the future. Our views contrasted sharply but at least we knew better at the end where we both stood. Neither of us was there to dictate a settlement or to convert the other to a cause or to concede our basic interests. Both of us were there, I think, because we realized that each nation has the power to inflict enormous damage upon the other, that such a war could and should be avoided if at all possible, since it would settle no dispute and prove no doctrine, and that care should thus be taken to prevent our conflicting interests from so directly confronting each other that war necessarily ensued. We believe in a system of national freedom and independence. He believes in an expanding and dynamic concept of world communism, and the question was whether these two systems can ever hope to live in peace without permitting any loss of security or any denial of the freedom of our friends. However difficult it may seem to answer this question in the affirmative as we approach so many harsh tests, I think we owe it to mankind to make every possible effort. That is why I considered the Vienna talks to be useful. The somber mood that they conveyed was not cause for elation or relaxation, nor was it cause for undue pessimism or fear. It simply demonstrated how much work we in the free world have to do and how long and hard a struggle must be our fate as Americans in this generation as the chief defenders of the cause of liberty. The one area which afforded some immediate prospect of accord was Laos. Both sides recognized the need to reduce the dangers in that situation. Both sides endorsed the concept of a neutral and independent Laos, much in the manner of Burma and Cambodia.

Of critical importance to the current conference on Laos in Geneva, both sides recognized the importance of an effective cease fire. It is urgent that this be translated into new attitudes at Geneva, enabling the International Control Commission to do its duty, to make certain that a cease-fire is enforced and maintained. I am hopeful that progress can be made on this matter in the coming days at Geneva, for that would greatly improve the international atmosphere.

No such hope emerged, however, with respect to the other deadlocked Geneva conference, seeking a treaty to ban nuclear tests. Mr. Khrushchev made it clear that there could not be a neutral administrator—in his opinion because no one was truly neutral; that a Soviet veto would have to apply to acts of enforcement; that inspection was only a subterfuge for espionage, in the absence of total disarmament; and that the present test ban negotiations appeared futile. In short, our hopes for an end to nuclear tests, for an end to the spread of nuclear weapons, and for some slowing down of the arms race have been struck a serious blow. Nevertheless, the stakes are too important for us to abandon the draft treaty we have offered at Geneva.

But our most somber talks were on the subject of Germany and Berlin. I made it clear to Mr. Khrushchev that the security of Western Europe and therefore our own security are deeply involved in our presence and our access rights to West Berlin, that those rights are based on law and not on sufferance, and that we are determined to maintain those rights at any risk, and thus meet our obligation to the people of West Berlin, and their right to choose their own future.

Mr. Khrushchev, in turn, presented his views in detail, and his presentation will be the subject of further communication. But we are not seeking to change the present situation. A binding German peace treaty is a matter for all who were at war with Germany, and we and our allies cannot abandon our obligations to the people of West Berlin.

Generally, Mr. Khrushchev did not talk in terms of war. He believes the world will move his way without resort to force. He spoke of his nation's achievements in space. He stressed his intention to outdo us in industrial production, to outtrade us, to prove to the world the superiority of his system over ours. Most of all, he predicted the triumph of communism in the new and less developed countries.

He was certain that the tide there was moving his way, that the revolution of rising peoples would eventually be a Communist revolution, and that the so-called wars of liberation, supported by the Kremlin, would replace the old methods of direct aggression and invasion.

In the 1940's and early fifties, the great danger was from Communist armies marching across free borders, which we saw in Korea. Our nuclear monopoly helped to prevent this in other areas. Now we face a new and different threat. We no longer have a nuclear monopoly. Their missiles, they believe, will hold off our missiles, and their troops can match our troops should we intervene in these so-called wars of liberation. Thus, the local conflict they support can turn in their favor through guerrillas or insurgents or subversion. A small group of disciplined Communists could exploit discontent and misery in a country where the average income may be $60 or $70 a year, and seize control, therefore, of an entire country without Communist troops ever crossing any international frontier. This is the Communist theory.

But I believe just as strongly that time will prove it wrong, that liberty and independence and self-determination—not communism —is the future of man, and that free men have the will and the resources to win the struggle for freedom. But it is clear that this struggle in this area of the new and poorer nations will be a continuing crisis of this decade.

Mr. Khrushchev made one point which I wish to pass on. He said there are many disorders throughout the world, and he should not be blamed for them all. He is quite right. It is easy to dismiss as Communist-inspired every anti-government or anti-American riot, every overthrow of a corrupt regime, or every mass protest against misery and despair. These are not all Communist inspired. The Communists move in to exploit them, to infiltrate their leadership, to ride their crest to victory. But the Communists did not create the conditions which caused them.

In short, the hopes for freedom in these areas which see so much poverty and illiteracy, so many children who are sick, so many children who die in the first year, so many families without homes, so many families without hope—the future for freedom in these areas rests with the local peoples and their government.

If they have the will to determine their own future, if their governments have the support of their own people, if their honest and progressive measures—helping their people—have inspired confidence and zeal, then no guerrilla or insurgent action can succeed. But where those conditions do not exist, a military guarantee against external attack from across a border offers little protection against internal decay.

Yet all this does not mean that our Nation and the West and the free world can only sit by. On the contrary, we have an historic opportunity to help these countries build their societies until they are so strong and broadly based that only an outside invasion would topple them, and that threat, we know, can be stopped.

We can train and equip their forces to resist Communist-supplied insurrections. We can help develop the industrial and agricultural base on which new living standards can be built. We can encourage better administration and better tax and land distribution and a better life for the people.

All this and more we can do because we have the talent and the resources to do it, if we will only use and share them. I know that there is a great deal of feeling in the United States that we have carried the burden of economic assistance long enough, but these countries that we are now supporting—stretching all the way along from the top of Europe through the Middle East, down through Saigon—are now subject to great efforts internally, in many of them, to seize control.

If we're not prepared to assist them in making a better life for their people, then I believe that the prospects for freedom in those areas are uncertain. We must, I believe, assist them if we are determined to meet with commitments of assistance our words against the Communist advance. The burden is heavy; we have carried it for many years. But I believe that this fight is not over. This battle goes on, and we have to play our part in it. And therefore I hope again that we will assist these people so that they can remain free.

It was fitting that Congress opened its hearings on the new foreign military and economic aid programs in Washington at the very time that Mr. Khrushchev's words in Vienna were demonstrating as nothing else could the need for that very program. It should be well run, effectively administered, but I believe we must do it, and I hope that you, the American people, will support it again, because I think it's vitally important to the security of these areas. There is no use talking against the Communist advance unless we're willing to meet our responsibilities, however burdensome they may be.

I do not justify this aid merely on the grounds of anti-Communism. It is a recognition of our opportunity and obligation to help these people be free, and we are not alone.

I found that the people of France, for example, were doing far more in Africa in the way of aiding independent nations than our own country was. But I know that foreign aid is a burden that is keenly felt and I can only say that we have no more crucial obligation now.

My stay in England was short but the visit gave me a chance to confer privately again with Prime Minister Macmillan, just as others of our party in Vienna were conferring yesterday with General de Gaulle and Chancellor Adenauer. We all agreed that there is work to be done in the West and from our conversations have come agreed steps to get on with that work. Our day in London, capped by a meeting with Queen Elizabeth and Prince Philip, was a strong reminder at the end of a long journey that the West remains united in its determination to hold to its standards.

May I conclude by saying simply that I am glad to be home. We have on this trip admired splendid places and seen stirring sights, but we are glad to be home. No demonstration of support abroad could mean so much as the support which you, the American people, have so generously given to our country. With that support

I am not fearful of the future. We must be patient. We must be determined. We must be courageous. We must accept both risks and burdens, but with the will and the work freedom will prevail.

Good night, and thank you very much.

from The Kennedy Wit

by Bill Adler

I do not think it entirely inappropriate to introduce myself to this audience. I am the man who accompanied Jacqueline Kennedy to Paris, and I have enjoyed it.

SHAPE Headquarters
Paris, France
June 2, 1961

I see nothing wrong with giving Robert some legal experience at Attorney General before he goes out to practice law.

Alfalfa Club
Washington, D.C.
January 21, 1961

from

With Kennedy

by Pierre Salinger

Chapter XIII

*The Kennedy-Khrushchev
Correspondence*

*John F. Kennedy and Pierre Salinger first became friends
through their association with the Senate Labor Relations
Committee, of which Kennedy was a member. He appointed
Salinger Press Secretary in 1959, and their personal friendship
grew along with their public duties. In* With Kennedy *Salinger
admittedly did not try to write a definitive history of the Kennedy
Administration, rather to offer a personal memoir of Kennedy
and his own personal association with him. Nevertheless,
Salinger's book did provide historians with some new data,
including that contained in the following chapter, the heretofore
unpublished "Kennedy-Khrushchev Correspondence."*

Friday, September 29, 1961, was a lazy fall day in Newport, Rhode Island. The President and his family were there for a brief vacation at the Narragansett Bay-front home of Mrs. Kennedy's mother and stepfather, Mr. and Mrs. Hugh D. Auchincloss.

I held a press briefing that morning at the Newport Naval Station. The big story of the day was Richard Nixon's decision to run for governor of California against incumbent Pat Brown—a miscalculation that was to wipe him out in 1964 as a presidential contender. The correspondents were looking for a White House angle.

"Does the President have any reaction to Mr. Nixon's announcement?"

"He does not," I replied.

"As a Californian, do you have a reaction?"

"No."

"Not even as a patriotic American?"

"No."

(The question was later put to the President directly at a press conference in Washington. What advice would he have given Nixon? "I would have been happy to tell him my opinion," JFK answered, "but he never asked me for it." Nixon, of course, wasn't a man to accept advice, much less solicit it. If he had, the President would have told him he was out of his mind. "He's only running to stay alive politically," he said to me after first learning of Nixon's decision. "He hasn't a chance of winning, but even if he did the risks are too great for the advantages he might win.")

After the briefing, I took off for an afternoon round of golf. When I got back to my quarters at the naval station, I had a call waiting from Georgi Bolshakov in New York City. He said it was urgent that he see me immediately and he was willing to charter a plane and fly up that evening.

I told him to hold off. I would call him back within an hour. We had twenty or thirty correspondents with us at Newport and I knew that a sudden appearance by the Russian editor might cause a minor sensation on a slow news day. I put in calls to the President and to Dean Rusk, who was conferring with Soviet Foreign Minister Andrei Gromyko on Laos and Berlin that afternoon in New York. Their best guess was that Bolshakov had a Soviet response to JFK's memorandum on the Laotian crisis that I had read to him and Kharlamov just four days earlier. But they agreed with me that he should not be seen in Newport. I got back to him in New York. He was most unhappy when I told him the earliest we could meet would be at three-thirty the following afternoon at the Carlyle Hotel in Manhattan.

"If you knew the importance of what I have," he said, "you wouldn't keep me waiting that long."

Bolshakov had a flair for the conspiratorial—and why not? Editing the magazine *USSR* and serving as an interpreter for visiting Russian officials were but two of his chores in Washington. He was also, according to the CIA, a top agent for the KGB, the Soviet international spy network.

I flew to New York the next day and met Secretary Rusk who was winding up his conference with Gromyko. We met at Rusk's suite at the Waldorf-Astoria. He was most eager to find out what Bolshakov had up his sleeve. If it was the Kremlin's answer to Laos, why all the mystery? Gromyko could have given that to him at their meeting that day. I left for the Carlyle after promising to call Rusk immediately after my session with the Russian spy. Bolshakov was at my door at exactly three-thirty. He had two newspapers under his arm. Hidden in the fold of one of them was a thick manila envelope. He took his time opening it.

"Here," he said. "You may read this. Then it is for the eyes of the President only."

It was a twenty-six page personal letter from Nikita S. Khrushchev to John F. Kennedy—the beginning of a secret correspondence that has no known parallel in the history of modern diplomacy. (The letters are now in the archives of the Kennedy Library. Their publication at a future time would depend on many factors—the state of U.S.-Soviet relations, possible injury to statesmen who may still be alive, and the risk that their publication might foreclose such personal and confidential exchanges between heads of state in the future.)

Khrushchev's first letter was a direct response on Laos but sections of it also dealt with the highly volatile situation in Berlin. Khrushchev was now ready to back off from the unconciliatory positions he had taken at Vienna. He saw no reason why negotiations in good faith could not produce settlements in both Southeast Asia and Germany. He was willing, if JFK was, to take another look at positions that had been frozen hard through fifteen years of cold war.

It was the most hopeful overture from Khrushchev since the release of the RB-47 pilots eight months earlier. I read the letter twice while Bolshakov sat smugly on the edge of the bed savoring my surprise. This first of many personal letters the Russian Premier was to write the American President was remarkable not only for its contents but for its candor. In contrast to the sterile gobbledegook that passes for high-level diplomatic correspondence, Khrushchev wrote with almost peasant simplicity and directness. He said, in effect, that you and I, Mr. President, are the leaders of two nations that are on a collision course. But because we are reasonable men, we agree that war between us is unthinkable. We have no choice but to put our heads together and find ways to live in peace.

Bolshakov had spent an entire night translating the letter from the Russian. But he also gave me the original in Russian to permit a comparison by our own translators. I was to deliver the letter to the President personally and to regard it as highly confidential. The only Russians in the United States who knew of it, Bolshakov said, were himself and Gromyko. Not even the Soviet ambassador to the United States, Mikhail Menshikov, had been told. The only Americans who knew were the President, the Secretary of State, and myself.

But Bolshakov had still another surprise for me. My recommendation to Mikhail Kharlamov that an important Soviet editor interview President Kennedy had been brought to the attention of

Premier Khrushchev. He was all for it. Either Aleksey Adzhubei or Pavel Sutukov of Pravda would fly over for that purpose within the next two months.

This was great news. But I told Bolshakov we would expect the interview to run in full in the Soviet Union, and after agreement on our part that the Russian translation was accurate. He saw no difficulties.

Two minutes after Bolshakov was out the door, I had the President on the line at Newport. "Get that letter over to Dean Rusk as quickly as possible," he said, "then bring it up here to me."

The Secretary of State was not at the Waldorf-Astoria but would be back at seven-thirty. I was waiting for him. He also read the letter twice but did not want to give JFK a snap reaction. It was agreed that he would take the letter to Washington that night and have a State Department messenger return it to me at seven-thirty the next morning at the Northeast Airlines terminal at La Guardia, where I would be waiting for a plane to Providence. I gave it to the President two hours later on his return to the Auchincloss' from church. Immediately after reading it, JFK spoke to Rusk in Washington. They agreed that I should contact Bolshakov and inform him that the President would respond promptly, probably within the week. This settled the fact that Bolshakov and I would again serve as couriers—a role we were to play many times in the future.

I held another press briefing at the naval station that afternoon. I didn't know the Secretary of State and I had been seen together in New York by a newspaperman and one of the first questions came as a surprise.

"Is there anything you can tell us about your meeting with Secretary Rusk yesterday?" I came up with the fastest "no" of my career, and they didn't press me.

On this autumn weekend, there came into being a system of personal and direct correspondence between the two heads of state that was to continue until the President's murder more than two years later. It was to prove most useful in preserving the peace. But it also forced upon JFK the most fateful decision of his life during the Cuban missile crisis a year later.

Khrushchev would always initiate the exchange of letters. If I was in Washington, I would have a call from Bolshakov, who would tell me simply that "there is a matter of urgency." We would agree on a rendezvous, either on a Washington street corner or in a bar. If I wasn't available, the Russian would contact the President's brother Bob, Ted Sorensen, or another White House staffer. When I was the courier and JFK's answer was ready, I would call Bolshakov and arrange to deliver it to him. He almost broke me up one night on a rainy street corner. After furtively slipping an envelope out of his pocket and into mine, he clapped a fraternal hand on my shoulder.

"Every man has his Russian," he said, "and I'm yours."

Early in November, Bolshakov told me Adzhubei had been chosen to interview the President, and he and I were to work out the arrangements. We quickly agreed on the date—November 25, and the place—Hyannis Port.

The chief editor of *Izvestia* arrived in Washington November 20 and I had a dinner party for him at my home. He brought gifts from his father-in-law—a Ukrainian blouse for my wife and a hamper of vodka and American brandy for me. With Adzhubei were Yuri Barsukov, an *Izvestia* correspondent in Washington, and the omnipresent Bolshakov. Among the American guests were John C. Guthrie, director of the Soviet desk at the State Department, and his wife.

After a round of toasts to Soviet-American friendship and to all heroes—living and dead—of both countries, we sat down to dinner. My wife had spent all afternoon preparing stroganoff, one of her specialties. But Adzhubei, still distrustful of the Salinger cuisine after my blood rare chicken on his last visit, said he wasn't hungry. I broke open a bottle of his father-in-law's brandy for him and he held forth conversationally while the rest of us ate.

Adzhubei was a unique Communist. His antagonism toward

the West was always tempered by a respect, which he never tried to conceal, for Western technology and culture. He bought his trim-fitting suits in London and was a fair authority on French wines and American motor cars.

"I'm a New Frontier Russian," he often told me, implying a contempt for the doctrinaire old guard in Russia that saw nothing redeeming in the non-Communist world.

Adzhubei was much taken with my son, Stephen, on his first visit to Falls Church—probably because of that impromptu violin recital on the Potomac—and we had pursued the idea of exchanging sons for a summer. Stephen would spend his vacation with the Adzhubeis in Moscow and his oldest, Nikita, would live with us in Virginia.

But nothing had come of our discussion. Adzhubei hadn't been able to sell it to his superiors and the FBI and Secret Service had told me the cost of maintaining a summer-long, twenty-four-hour-a-day vigil over Khrushchev's grandson would be staggering.

After his second or third brandy that evening, Adzhubei became more than a little critical of his father-in-law. He said Khrushchev had not given the Adzhubeis a wedding present or any other gift in all the fifteen years of their marriage.

"I went hunting with him once in the woods outside Moscow," Adzhubei said. "I had a severe pain on my right side but said nothing until it became unbearable. When it was apparent that I had acute appendicitis and would have to be rushed to a hospital, he said he hoped I would be all right. That was the only personal interest he has ever shown in me."

Adzhubei's general political theme that night was that the Soviet Union and the United States were the only important world powers and should resolve their differences without paying too much attention to their allies. Neither the French, the British, nor the West Germans were reliable friends, he continued, and we should not permit them to complicate our relations with the Kremlin. But he quickly dropped the subject when Guthrie asked him if the Soviets would be equally willing to discard allies that had been particularly troublesome to us—East Germany and China, for example.

There was a reference to the interest of the Kennedy family in the arts and Adzhubei cut in with the comment that America had no corner on culture. He spoke glowingly of Rachmaninoff, Chaliapin, and Tolstoi. When it was pointed out to him that all three were pre-revolutionary figures, he came back with Shostakovich—although admitting that he didn't care for his music personally.

We had a musicale of our own after dinner. Barsukov was an excellent pianist and accompanied Bolshakov, who sang magnificently. I performed a little Bach—but not without interruption.

My daughter Suzanne, then ten years old, had taken quite a liking to Adzhubei. Whenever he caught her peeking at him over the top of the piano or around a corner, he would leap from his chair and chase her wildly through the downstairs rooms. It was on that note of hilarity that we all said goodnight.

Adzhubei and I flew to Hyannis two days before the interview and took rooms at the Yachtsman Hotel. With us were Bolshakov, who would translate for Adzhubei; Alexander Akalovsky of the State Department, who would translate for the President; and Jack Romagna, the official White House stenotype reporter, who would prepare the English transcript. Akalovsky had been the translator of the Eisenhower-Khrushchev conversations at Camp David, the Nixon visit to the Soviet Union, and the Kennedy-Khrushchev "summit" at Vienna. He was our best.

Adzhubei and I were now agreed on all the ground rules. We would both have to approve the transcript and he was to run the interview in full—a promise he kept with one unimportant exception. I was disappointed when he told me the interview would appear only in the Moscow edition of *Izvestia,* but I was in no position to haggle.

I can best describe Adzhubei's mood as cocky. He was looking forward to the exchange with JFK and even offered to give me his questions in advance so the President would know what to expect. When I declined, he said he was even willing to ask questions I might suggest, to be certain JFK had an opportunity to develop particular points for the Russian audience. I declined that offer, too, and he shrugged, as if to say:

"Well, don't blame me if it doesn't go your way."

The night before the interview we had dinner together at the Captain's Table in Hyannis. I recall it only because of an incident involving Al Spivak, a White House correspondent for UPI. Spivak was sitting at a table across the dining room and came over to see me. He didn't catch my eye immediately, but Adzhubei was aware of his presence. Suddenly, he twisted around in his chair and shouted: "You agent!" This was Adzhubei's idea of a joke, but to this day, Spivak is known to some of his colleagues in the White House press corps as "The Agent."

The next morning the President and Mrs. Kennedy met us at the door of their home in Hyannis Port. She introduced Adzhubei and Bolshakov to Caroline and John, and then left us. The interview began at 10:20 A.M. in the sun-bright living room. The President sat in a rocking chair and the two Russians on a sofa facing him. Akalovsky and I sat to one side. There was a preliminary exchange of hopes that the interview would create a new atmosphere of understanding between their two countries. Then Adzhubei swung into his questions, which he had written on large white cards. He would ask them in Russian, wait for the translation, then steal a peek at the next question as the President spoke.

The next two hours were notable on many counts. First, the interview was totally unlike any that JFK had ever given to an American newsman. Adzhubei, a man of spectacular ego, would introduce almost every question with a propagandistic defense of the Soviet position before inviting JFK's view on the same issue. He would then comment rather incisively on the President's answer.

We knew this was likely to happen but were confident that the President would more than hold his own. Adzhubei was there not only as a reporter but as an important Communist official. That, and his relationship with Khrushchev, gave him little choice. He must try to come home with an interview in which the American President came off second best to the chief editor of *Izvestia*.

JFK, impatient with Adzhubei's propagandistic prelude to every question, accused him early in the interview of being both "a newspaperman and a politician." The editor was only briefly dismayed. "In our country every citizen is a politician, because we like our country very much. The young and the old like the socialist system of our country and we are ready to fight for it until its victorious end."

The President took the line that there would be much less to fight about if the Russians would demonstrate a sincere desire to negotiate a nuclear test ban and a realistic settlement of the Berlin question. Adzhubei said "coals from the last war" were still burning in "the heart of every Soviet citizen. . . . Thus, a solution of the question of a (German) peace treaty is the hope and tranquillity in the heart of every Soviet man. After all, we are still singing songs about those who did not come home from the war. I know that you participated in the war, that you are a hero of the war, and this is why I am talking to you in such lofty words."

JFK agreed that "the Soviet Union suffered more from World War II than any country . . . (but) I will say that the United States also suffered." In his own family, "my brother was killed in Europe —my sister's husband was killed in Europe. The point is that that war is over now. We want to prevent another war arising out of Germany. I think the important thing between the United States and the U.S.S.R. is not to create the kind of tension and pressure which, in the name of settling World War II, increases the chances of a conflict between the Soviet Union and its allies on one hand and the United States and its allies on the other."

Adzhubei could find no fault with that answer. "I will communicate your words to our readers with a feeling of satisfaction. We have always thought and still think of the Americans as realists." But we were not being realistic, he felt, in thinking that "the social changes which are happening in the world today are the result of actions in which Moscow has its hands."

The President was not at all certain that every country that had embraced Communism since World War II had done so voluntarily. "We have been under the impression that the Yalta Agreement and the Potsdam Agreement provided for a free choice for the peoples of Eastern Europe. They do not, in our opinion, have a free choice. You may argue that they may want to live under Communism, but if they do not they are not given the opportunity to change. We believe that if the Soviet Union . . . will permit the people of the world to live as they wish to live, relations between the Soviet Union and the United States will then be very satisfactory. . . ."

Late in the interview, Adzhubei foolishly set a trap for himself with one of his own questions. If the President were a Soviet Navy veteran of World War II, wouldn't he be gravely disturbed by the rearmament of West Germany?

JFK's answer was devastating. "If I were a Soviet veteran, I would see that West Germany now has only nine divisions, which is a fraction of the Soviet forces. Nine divisions. It has no nuclear weapons of its own. It has a very small Air Force—almost no Navy, I think perhaps two or three submarines. Its nine divisions are under the international control of NATO. . . . I don't believe West Germany is a military threat (to the Soviet Union). . . . Then I would look at the power of the United States and I would look at the power of the Soviet Union, and I would say that the important thing is for the Soviet Union and the United States not to get into a war which would destroy both of our systems."

The President added that "Chairman Khrushchev did not, nor did I, make the arrangements in 1945 in regard to Berlin," which he had described earlier as the issue most threatening to peace. "Our responsibility, given the situation, which is a difficult one, is to bring about peace, and I would believe it can be done. In short, if I were a Soviet naval officer, I would feel . . . that the important thing now is to reach an accord with the United States, our ally during that second war."

Adzhubei replied weakly that "you answered this question not as a veteran of the Soviet armed forces but as President of the United States, and that is quite natural."

On my own visit to the Soviet Union the next year, most of the comment on the interview centered on this one answer. It was the most hopeful statement yet from the new President that peace was possible and that he was willing to work for it. But, beyond that, the manner in which Adzhubei chose to preface his question gave tremendously more impact to the answer. The average Russian citizen knew that JFK was not only a Navy veteran but a hero of World War II, and his answer was that much more moving and convincing.

Although the interview was always cordial on the surface, it was apparent that the two principals did not hit it off personally. There was no warmth or humor at all—merely cold politeness. When it was over, the President was convinced he had done badly. He gestured for me to stay behind when Adzhubei said his perfunctory goodbyes and left with the translators for the hotel.

"That might have been a mistake," he said. "Your arrogant Russian friend got in as many shots as I did."

I suggested that he reserve judgment until he saw the transcript. When he did, he agreed with me that Adzhubei's clumsy polemics had made his own comments that much stronger.

I put Adzhubei, Bolshakov, and Akalovsky on an Air Force courier plane to New York with Romagna's transcript about five hours after the interview. There, Bolshakov translated the transcript into Russian and Akalovsky retranslated the Russian version into English to check its accuracy. The agreed translation was in Adzhubei's hands thirty-six hours later.

On November 28—three days after the interview—I got a two-word cable from Adzhubei:

INTERVJU OPUBLICKOVANO (INTERVIEW PUBLISHED).

It had been printed that day in the Moscow edition of *Izvestia*. I immediately released the transcript to AP, UPI, and all the foreign wire services and it ran the next day in every major country in the world. It was a sensation everywhere. Within hours, all copies of *Izvestia* were sold out in Moscow. Worn, much-read copies were still being passed hand-to-hand in Russia months later. The major point it had struck home to Soviet citizens was that John F. Kennedy was a reasonable and mature man. He had personal knowledge of the horrors of war. He was determined to avoid another. And he was certain it could be done. To the Russians, who had suffered the most casualty losses in World War II, this was the message, above all, they had been eager to hear from the young American leader.

The London *Daily Mail* called the interview "the most remarkable event of its kind for many years." A Norwegian paper described it as "sensational." The *Manchester Guardian* said it was "a remarkable attempt by the leaders of the western world to put the western case to the Soviet people." "The beginning of a new thaw in East-West relations," was the response of an editorialist in Sweden. In France it was hailed as a first step toward "an effective summit conference."

There was dissent, of course. The press in both East and West Germany found the interview lacking in concrete proposals. *Izvestia* itself did not comment but Tass, the Soviet news agency, also criticized the President for failing to suggest new alternatives in Berlin. It did praise, however, his "inclination toward serious talks." Red China damned it by ignoring it, a policy consistent with Peking's total opposition to the Khrushchev line. Radio Havana called JFK a hypocrite for picturing "war-mongering Yankees as little Angels." An important newspaper in India said that America's recognition of anti-Communist regimes, "however undemocratic," belied the President's commitment to self-determination in the interview.

But world reaction was at least 10 to 1 in favor. Here was a positive and hopeful indication that the world's two nuclear giants were now a little more willing to talk to each other.

JFK, as always, was a realist. "It was important for me to speak directly to the Russian people, if only to try to convince them that we're not all that bloodthirsty. But it was a propaganda stroke for Khrushchev, too. Just by letting the interview run, he took the steam out of the argument that the Kremlin is afraid to let the Russian people hear the truth.

"When you add it all up, maybe the biggest plus is that Khrushchev held still for it. Do you think he might be softening up a little?"

Adzhubei kept his promise to run the interview verbatim, with one exception that wasn't worth quibbling over. The English transcript quotes him as saying that Khrushchev's visit to America in 1959 was not "completely satisfactory." It came out in *Izvestia:* "The positive results of that trip were wrecked and brought to nothing by the well-known actions of the then American administration." His motive for changing it was obvious. His original statement left it in doubt whether Khrushchev or his host was responsible for the failure of his mission. I never chided Adzhubei for tampering with the transcript. I probably would have done the same if the quick-tempered Khrushchev had been my father-in-law.

Finally, there had been much low-level grumbling in the State Department that the interview should have been arranged through diplomatic channels, not by me. But a couple of days after the interview ran in *Izvestia,* I got a letter from Llewellyn E. Thompson, the United States ambassador to the U.S.S.R. I didn't know him at the time. But we became friends on my trip to the Soviet Union and even closer friends later around a series of poker tables.

His letter read: "Just a line to tell you how delighted I am with the President's interview with Adzhubei. I must confess I was very dubious about the exercise as I did not think they would publish such a forceful statement of our position, and anything less than that would have misled the Soviet people. While the interview has only been published in the Moscow *Izvestia,* this in itself covers a good many people. What particularly pleased me was the tone of the President's remarks, which has made a great impression on the Russians I know, while at the same time getting across our point of view on specific issues."

"Getting across our point of view"—that had been JFK's only purpose in granting the interview and he had succeeded. The next phase almost brought us to a television confrontation between President Kennedy and Premier Khrushchev.

from The Kennedy Wit

by Bill Adler

At a Democratic fund raising dinner in Miami honoring Senator George A. Smathers of Florida, President Kennedy made these remarks:

Senator Smathers has been one of my most valuable counselors at crucial moments. In 1952 when I was thinking of running for the United States Senate, I went to Senator Smathers and said, "George, what do you think?" He said, "Don't do it, can't win, bad year." [*That was the year Mr. Kennedy won his Senate seat.*]

In 1956, I didn't know whether I should run for vice president or not so I said, "George, what do you think?" And Senator Smathers replied, "It's your choice!" So I ran and lost.

In 1960 I was wondering whether I ought to run in the West

Virginia primary, but the Senator said, "Don't do it. That state you can't possibly carry."

And actually, the only time I really got nervous about the whole matter of Los Angeles was just before the balloting and George came up and said, "I think it looks pretty good for you."

The Nuclear
Test Ban Treaty

*Radio and Television Address
to the American People*

July 26, 1963

[Delivered from the President's office
at 7 P.M.]

Good evening, my fellow citizens:

I speak to you tonight in a spirit of hope. Eighteen years ago
the advent of nuclear weapons changed the course of the world as
well as the war. Since that time, all mankind has been struggling to
escape from the darkening prospect of mass destruction on earth.
In an age when both sides have come to possess enough nuclear
power to destroy the human race several times over, the world of
communism and the world of free choice have been caught up in a
vicious circle of conflicting ideology and interest. Each increase of
tension has produced an increase of arms; each increase of arms
has produced an increase of tension.

In these years, the United States and the Soviet Union have

frequently communicated suspicion and warnings to each other, but very rarely hope. Our representatives have met at the summit and at the brink; they have met in Washington and in Moscow; in Geneva and at the United Nations. But too often these meetings have produced only darkness, discord, or disillusion.

Yesterday a shaft of light cut into the darkness. Negotiations were concluded in Moscow on a treaty to ban all nuclear tests in the atmosphere, in outer space, and under water. For the first time, an agreement has been reached on bringing the forces of nuclear destruction under international control—a goal first sought in 1946 when Bernard Baruch presented a comprehensive control plan to the United Nations.

That plan, and many subsequent disarmament plans, large and small, have all been blocked by those opposed to international inspection. A ban on nuclear tests, however, requires on-the-spot inspection only for underground tests. This Nation now possesses a variety of techniques to detect the nuclear tests of other nations which are conducted in the air or under water, for such tests produce unmistakable signs which our modern instruments can pick up.

The treaty initialed yesterday, therefore, is a limited treaty which permits continued underground testing and prohibits only those tests that we ourselves can police. It requires no control posts, no onsite inspection, no international body.

We should also understand that it has other limits as well. Any nation which signs the treaty will have an opportunity to withdraw if it finds that extraordinary events related to the subject matter of the treaty have jeopardized its supreme interests; and no nation's right of self-defense will in any way be impaired. Nor does this treaty mean an end to the threat of nuclear war. It will not reduce nuclear stockpiles; it will not halt the production of nuclear weapons; it will not restrict their use in time of war.

Nevertheless, this limited treaty will radically reduce the nuclear testing which would otherwise be conducted on both sides; it will prohibit the United States, the United Kingdom, the Soviet Union, and all others who sign it, from engaging in the atmospheric tests which have so alarmed mankind; and it offers to all the world a welcome sign of hope.

For this is not a unilateral moratorium, but a specific and solemn legal obligation. While it will not prevent this Nation from testing underground, or from being ready to conduct atmospheric tests if the acts of others so require, it gives us a concrete opportunity to extend its coverage to other nations and later to other forms of nuclear tests.

This treaty is in part the product of Western patience and vigilance. We have made clear—most recently in Berlin and Cuba —our deep resolve to protect our security and our freedom against any form of aggression. We have also made clear our steadfast determination to limit the arms race. In three administrations, our soldiers and diplomats have worked together to this end, always supported by Great Britain. Prime Minister Macmillan joined with President Eisenhower in proposing a limited test ban in 1959, and again with me in 1961 and 1962.

But the achievement of this goal is not a victory for one side— it is a victory for mankind. It reflects no concessions either to or by the Soviet Union. It reflects simply our common recognition of the dangers in further testing.

This treaty is not the millennium. It will not resolve all conflicts, or cause the Communists to forego their ambitions, or eliminate the dangers of war. It will not reduce our need for arms or allies or programs of assistance to others. But it is an important first step—a step toward peace—a step toward reason—a step away from war.

Here is what this step can mean to you and to your children and your neighbors:

First, this treaty can be a step toward reduced world tension and broader areas of agreement. The Moscow talks have reached no agreement on any other subject, nor is this treaty conditioned on any other matter. Under Secretary Harriman made it clear that any non-aggression arrangements across the division in Europe would require full consultation with our allies and full attention to their interests. He also made clear our strong preference for a more comprehensive treaty banning all tests everywhere, and our ultimate hope for general and complete disarmament. The Soviet Government, however, is still unwilling to accept the inspection such goals require.

No one can predict with certainty, therefore, what further agreements, if any, can be built on the foundations of this one. They could include controls on preparations for surprise attack, or on numbers and type of armaments. There could be further limitations on the spread of nuclear weapons. The important point is that efforts to seek new agreements will go forward.

But the difficulty of predicting the next step is no reason to be reluctant about this step. Nuclear test ban negotiations have long been a symbol of East-West disagreement. If this treaty can also be a symbol—if it can symbolize the end of one era and the beginning of another—if both sides can by this treaty gain confidence and experience in peaceful collaboration—then this short and simple treaty may well become an historic mark in man's age-old pursuit of peace.

Western policies have long been designed to persuade the Soviet Union to renounce aggression, direct or indirect, so that their people and all people may live and let live in peace. The unlimited testing of new weapons of war cannot lead toward that end—but this treaty, if it can be followed by further progress, can clearly move in that direction.

I do not say that a world without aggression or threats of war would be an easy world. It will bring new problems, new challenges from the Communists, new dangers of relaxing our vigilance or of mistaking their intent.

But those dangers pale in comparison to those of the spiraling arms race and a collision course toward war. Since the beginning of history, war has been mankind's constant companion. It has been the rule, not the exception. Even a nation as young and as peace-loving as our own has fought through eight wars. And three times in the last two years and a half I have been required to report to you as President that this Nation and the Soviet Union stood on the verge of direct military confrontation—in Laos, in Berlin, and in Cuba.

A war today or tomorrow, if it led to nuclear war, would not be like any war in history. A full-scale nuclear exchange, lasting less than 60 minutes, with the weapons now in existence, could wipe out more than 300 million Americans, Europeans, and Russians, as well as untold numbers elsewhere. And the survivors, as Chairman Khrushchev warned the Communist Chinese, "the survivors would envy the dead." For they would inherit a world so devastated by explosions and poison and fire that today we cannot even conceive of its horrors. So let us try to turn the world away from war. Let us make the most of this opportunity, and every opportunity, to reduce tension, to slow down the perilous nuclear arms race, and to check the world's slide toward final annihilation.

Second, this treaty can be a step toward freeing the world from the fears and dangers of radioactive fallout. Our own atmospheric tests last year were conducted under conditions which restricted such fallout to an absolute minimum. But over the years the number and the yield of weapons tested have rapidly increased and so have the radioactive hazards from such testing. Continued unrestricted testing by the nuclear powers, joined in time by other nations which may be less adept in limiting pollution, will increasingly contaminate the air that all of us must breathe.

Even then, the number of children and grandchildren with cancer in their bones, with leukemia in their blood, or with poison in their lungs might seem statistically small to some, in comparison with natural health hazards. But this is not a natural health hazard —and it is not a statistical issue. The loss of even one human life, or the malformation of even one baby—who may be born long after we are gone—should be of concern to us all. Our children and grandchildren are not merely statistics toward which we can be indifferent.

Nor does this affect the nuclear powers alone. These tests befoul the air of all men and all nations, the committed and the uncommitted alike, without their knowledge and without their consent. That is why the continuation of atmospheric testing causes so many countries to regard all nuclear powers as equally evil; and we can hope that its prevention will enable those countries to see the world more clearly, while enabling all the world to breathe more easily.

Third, this treaty can be a step toward preventing the spread of nuclear weapons to nations not now possessing them. During the next several years, in addition to the four current nuclear powers, a small but significant number of nations will have the intellectual, physical, and financial resources to produce both nuclear weapons and the means of delivering them. In time, it is estimated many other nations will have either this capacity or other ways of obtaining nuclear warheads, even as missiles can be commercially purchased today.

I ask you to stop and think for a moment what it would mean to have nuclear weapons in so many hands of countries large and small, stable and unstable, responsible and irresponsible, scattered throughout the world. There would be no rest for anyone then, no stability, no real security, and no chance of effective disarmament. There would only be the increased necessity for the great powers to involve themselves in what otherwise would be local conflicts.

If only one thermonuclear bomb were to be dropped on any American, Russian, or any other city, whether it was launched by accident or design, by a madman or by an enemy, by a large nation or by a small, from any corner of the world, that one bomb could release more destructive power on the inhabitants of that one helpless city than all the bombs dropped in the Second World War.

Neither the United States nor the Soviet Union nor the United Kingdom nor France can look forward to that day with equanimity. We have a great obligation—all four nuclear powers have a great obligation—to use whatever time remains to prevent the spread of nuclear weapons, to persuade other countries not to test, transfer, acquire, possess, or produce such weapons.

This treaty can be the opening wedge in that campaign. It provides that none of the parties will assist other nations to test in the forbidden environments. It opens the door for further agreements on the control of nuclear weapons, and it is open for all nations, and already we have heard from a number of countries who wish to join with us promptly.

Fourth and finally, this treaty can limit the nuclear arms race in ways which, on balance, will strengthen our Nation's security far more than the continuation of unrestricted testing. For in today's world, a nation's security does not always increase as its arms increase, when its adversary is doing the same, and unlimited competition in the testing and development of new types of destructive nuclear weapons will not make the world safer for either side. Under this limited treaty, on the other hand, the testing of other nations could never be sufficient to offset the ability of our strategic forces to deter or survive a nuclear attack and to penetrate and destroy an aggressor's homeland.

We have, and under this treaty we will continue to have, the nuclear strength that we need. It is true that the Soviets have tested nuclear weapons of the yield higher than that which we thought to be necessary, but the hundred megaton bomb of which they spoke two years ago does not and will not change the balance of strategic power. The United States has chosen, deliberately, to concentrate on more mobile and more efficient weapons, with lower, but entirely sufficient yield, and our security is, therefore, not impaired by the treaty I am discussing.

It is also true, as Mr. Khrushchev would agree, that nations cannot afford in these matters to rely simply on the good faith of their adversaries. We have not, therefore, overlooked the risk of secret violations. . . .

Secret violations are possible and secret preparations for a sudden withdrawal are possible, and thus our own vigilance and strength must be maintained, as we remain ready to withdraw and to resume all forms of testing, if we must. But it would be a mistake to assume that this treaty will be quickly broken. The gains of illegal testing are obviously slight compared to their cost, and the hazard of discovery; and the nations which have initialed and will sign this treaty prefer it, in my judgment, to unrestricted testing as a matter of their own self-interests, for these nations, too, and all nations, have a stake in limiting the arms race, in holding the spread of nuclear weapons, and in breathing air that is not radioactive. While it may be theoretically possible to demonstrate the risks inherent in any treaty, and such risks in this treaty are small, the far greater risks to our security are the risks of unrestricted testing, the risk of a nuclear arms race, the risk of new nuclear powers, nuclear pollution, and nuclear war.

This limited test ban, in our most careful judgment, is safer by far for the United States than an unlimited nuclear arms race. For all these reasons, I am hopeful that this Nation will promptly approve the limited test ban treaty. There will, of course, be debate in the country and in the Senate. The Constitution wisely requires the advice and consent of the Senate to all treaties, and that consultation has already begun. All this is as it should be. A document which may mark an historic and constructive opportunity for the world deserves an historic and constructive debate.

It is my hope that all of you will take part in that debate, for this treaty is for all of us. It is particularly for our children and our grandchildren, and they have no lobby here in Washington. This debate will involve military, scientific, and political experts, but it must not be left to them alone. The right and the responsibility are yours.

If we are to open new doorways to peace, if we are to seize this rare opportunity for progress, if we are to be as bold and farsighted in our control of weapons as we have been in their invention, then let us now show all the world on this side of the wall and the other that a strong America also stands for peace. There is no cause for complacency.

We have learned in times past that the spirit of one moment or place can be gone in the next. We have been disappointed more than once, and we have no illusions now that there are shortcuts on the road to peace. At many points around the globe the Communists are continuing their efforts to exploit weakness and poverty. Their concentration of nuclear and conventional arms must still be deterred.

The familiar contest between choice and coercion, the familiar places of danger and conflict, are still there, in Cuba, in Southeast Asia, in Berlin, and all around the globe, still requiring all the strength and the vigilance that we can muster. Nothing could more greatly damage our cause than if we and our allies were to believe that peace has already been achieved, and that our strength and unity were no longer required.

But now, for the first time in many years, the path of peace may be open. No one can be certain what the future will bring. No one can say whether the time has come for an easing of the struggle. But history and our own conscience will judge us harsher if we do not now make every effort to test our hopes by action, and this is the place to begin. According to the ancient Chinese proverb, "A journey of a thousand miles must begin with a single step."

My fellow Americans, let us take that first step. Let us, if we can, step back from the shadows of war and seek out the way of peace. And if that journey is a thousand miles, or even more, let history record that we, in this land, at this time, took the first step.

Thank you and good night.

from

The Private Letters of
John F. Kennedy

by Robert G. Deindorfer

*Busy as he may be, the President likes to write personal notes to
ordinary people. Here are some of his warmest, wittiest letters.*

Many Americans look upon a personal letter signed by the President of the United States as one of life's most cherished prizes.

For a youngster (or sometimes even an oldster), a note signed by the President is like Christmas and the Fourth of July rolled into one. Yet the chance of a person's ever receiving a Presidential letter is exceedingly small, for Presidents have little time for such correspondence. However, John F. Kennedy, former newspaperman and Pulitzer Prize-winning author, has managed to step up the mail between 1600 Pennsylvania Avenue and the nation at large.

Today, and almost every day, out of the Presidential office flutters an exciting volume of 50 to 75 notes, thank-you's, signed photographs, a few letters written entirely by hand and others "warmed up" with hand-written postscripts.

Of the many "Sincerely, John F. Kennedy" letters that have been written since 1960, the following are among the friendliest, warmest and most gracious the President has composed.

Youth can be a bittersweet time. Sooner or later, for example, almost every red-blooded American boy will break a window, accidentally or otherwise. Jameson Forster, of Haverford, Pennsylvania, accidentally broke a window not long ago. In a refreshing letter to President Kennedy, Jameson described the calamity in some detail.

This is how the President responded:

Dear Jameson:

I was very glad to hear from you. So you broke a window trying to hit your brother with a shoe! I am one of a large family and I recall some of the small arguments I had with my brothers and sisters and the only way out of your situation is to tell your parents exactly what happened. Maybe you could offer to pay for a new windowpane by doing some extra chores your parents need to have done.

I like your suggestion that we give surplus food to countries where people are hungry. We have a program to do just that—it's called Food for Peace. But I am particularly glad that the idea occurred to you. If you and boys like you are thinking about people around the world who are hungry, then I think that we are likely to have a peaceful and plentiful world by the time you grow up.

Best of luck to you.

Some months ago Leonard Lyons, the syndicated newspaper columnist, happened to see a New York window display which featured signed photographs of several American Presidents, past and present. Lyons suspected that Kennedy might be wryly interested in the current evaluation of his own signature, along with the others. In a note to the White House he quoted the prices of the signed photos: George Washington—$175; Franklin D. Roosevelt—$75; U.S. Grant—$55; John F. Kennedy—$65.

Dear Leonard:

I appreciate your letter about the market on Kennedy signatures. It is hard to believe that the going price is so high now. In order not to depress the market any further, I will not sign this letter.

Every day, ten-year-old Steve Eicker used to take a seat right behind the man who drove the school bus in West Springfield, Massachusetts. Steve liked to watch him work the gearshift and spin the big steering wheel.

One morning the driver fell into the aisle with what turned out to be a fatal heart attack. At the time, the bus was moving along at about 20 miles an hour. Yet Steve hopped up into the driver's seat, took hold of the wheel and jammed his foot hard against the brake pedal. After he slowed the bus down he brought it safely to the curb without harm to the 45 young passengers.

Dear Steven:

You showed great courage and quickness of mind when you stopped the school bus. I know few people who could have acted so quickly and effectively.

You saved many of your schoolmates from harm. We are very proud of you, Steven. You show the qualities which will make you an outstanding citizen when you grow up. Good luck to you.

During a reception for visiting Brazilian students gathered in the White House garden last summer, the President invited his guests to ask any questions that came to mind. Before the session ended, slight, 20-year-old José Kehele said that aggressive American military goals reminded him of Hitler's Germany.

President Kennedy did not let the remark go unanswered. In blunt and emphatic tones he reminded the Brazilian that no rational man could possibly want war in an age of nuclear weapons—and also that America has constantly sought disarmament. The next day José Kehele received a personal letter from the President, written in longhand, on stationery headed "From the Desk of John F. Kennedy."

Dear José:

I want you to know that I was glad to have a chance to answer your question yesterday. We believe in free discussion of all these matters here.

Slowly, with wise and skillful hands, surgeons performed a delicate spinal fusion on Cheryl Gray last July. The operation wasn't much fun for the 14-year-old Maryland schoolgirl. As she lay in the hospital recuperating, word of her plight reached a man who's had some back problems himself.

Dear Cheryl:

I have just learned that you are in the hospital and I thought I would surprise you with this note.

Be brave and patient, Cheryl, and remember that even though the cast is most uncomfortable, it is helping you to grow into a strong and healthy young lady.

With my best good wishes.

In 1954 an Army court-martial convicted Lieutenant Michael Collins of burglary and assault—crimes he didn't commit—and sentenced him to ten years' imprisonment.

Over a long period Collins convinced others of his innocence—first the Secretary of the Army, who ordered all charges against him dismissed and his rights restored, and, recently, the United States Congress, which voted him $25,000 for the expense of winning vindication.

Dear Mr. Collins:

I know that no financial compensation can repay you for the twenty months of suffering following your improper conviction by court-martial; no correction of the military records can correct the injustice you sustained; and no re-offer of your reserve commission as a first lieutenant in the Army can remove the memory of when you were unfairly sentenced for a crime you did not commit.

But I'm happy to approve the bill passed by Congress, helping to restore you to your former rank and position and compensating you for the expenses incurred on your behalf.

Please accept my personal best wishes for a successful career in whatever you may decide to do.

It was bad enough that Russia conducted a series of nuclear tests late in 1961. Even worse, to eight-year-old Michelle Rochon, of Marine City, Michigan, was the fact that the tests were conducted close to the North Pole. In a letter to the President Michelle expressed a jittery concern over the test site. She received a reassuring answer:

Dear Michelle:

I was glad to get your letter about trying to stop the Russians from bombing the North Pole and risking the life of Santa Claus.

I share your concern about the atmospheric testing by the Soviet Union, not only for the North Pole, but for countries throughout the world.

However, you must not worry about Santa Claus. I talked with him yesterday and he is fine. He will be making his rounds this Christmas.

Young Wanda Bush lives in Montgomery, Alabama. She was in the hospital, and all too familiar with the agony of pain. Yet Wanda seldom lost her cheery good nature, not even when she was all by herself, and friends often marveled at her determination.

This spirit showed through every line of Wanda's touching letter to the President.

"Dear Mr. Kennedy," she wrote. "My name is Wanda Bush. I live at Montgomery, Alabama. The reason I'm writing you this letter is to let you know that my birthday is on May 29 too. I was fourteen.

"When I was four years old I had polio. I had to wear a brace on my right leg. When I was eleven years I had another attack of polio. This time I had to have an operation on my leg and foot. Now at the age of fourteen I am having to have another operation;

this time it's polio in my back. They operated three weeks ago. They thought I would never walk but I did. I'm doing fine now and the mane reason I'm doing so fine is because I found your birthday on mine. Tell your wife I said hello and I think she is the most beautiful woman in the world.

"Love you always, Wanda Bush."

It wasn't long before a clerk picked up Wanda's letter out of the volume of White House correspondence and sent it along to the President's attention.

> Dear Wanda:
>
> I noted from your kind letter that we share the same birth date and want to extend my greetings even though they are belated.
>
> It is good to know that you are doing so well following your operation. With courage like yours I am sure you will continue to improve very rapidly.
>
> Mrs. Kennedy joins me in sending warm best wishes.

In a hand-written postscript, the President added, "Best of good luck to you."

In the spring of 1962 a commercial airliner carrying seventeen passengers crashed in the rolling backland of Colombia. Among the victims were two young American Peace Corps volunteers, David Crozier, of West Plains, Missouri, and Larry Radley, of Chicago, who had been toiling on community development projects in Colombian villages.

As the first volunteers killed abroad, Crozier and Radley were the subject of glowing articles in the American and Latin-American press. The Peace Corps paused to honor its dead in an enduring fashion. The two field training centers in Puerto Rico officially became Camp Crozier and Camp Radley.

> Dear Mr. and Mrs. Crozier:
>
> There is no adequate comfort that a nation can offer the parents of a son who died serving in its cause.
>
> David gave willingly of himself not only to our country, but to

Colombia and to the town of Jardia, where his work has already become legendary.

As a Peace Corps volunteer, your son represented the finest traditions of this country. With his heart in his hands, he reached out to others to help, seeking no special privileges and no concessions. What God has given our land, he was willing to share with others.

I met David when he came to the White House on the eve of his Colombian service. He was one of the first volunteers I had met. I came away from those first meetings with the volunteers convinced that they had the ability to carry on the high hopes we had for the Peace Corps. Your son fulfilled these hopes. It is because of work like David's that the Peace Corps will be able to continue to serve in the cause of world peace and understanding.

His fellow Americans will remember David with great pride.

A postal clerk in the White House mail room was the first to notice the following letter. It was written by hand, in a clear but unmistakably juvenile script, on plain white, lined paper, addressed to the President.

"I know you are the busiest man in the United States, but I hoped that you could help my friend and classmate to get well faster. His name is Bruce Jenkins and he is twelve years old like I am and lives on a dairy farm like I do. Last Friday both of his legs were cut off when he was playing with his pet cow by the feed chopper. The doctors think he is getting better now but he can't play ball anymore so maybe you could write to him and encourage him to get well faster."

A number of aides and assistants routed Barbara Ann Bork's plea up through White House channels until, finally, it came to the attention of the President.

Dear Bruce:

Your very good friend, Barbara Ann Bork, has written to me of your unfortunate accident, and I wanted to send you a word of cheer and encouragement. Remember, Bruce, that each of us during our lives must fight battles we do not understand, but faith in God alone with patience and determination can always help us over some very rough places. Keep your spirits high, and know that you have my very best wishes.

Not long after the Inauguration, Edward Myers, of Maine's Saltwater Farms, sent the President a whimsical telegram:

MAY CRAIG SAYS THAT ED MUSKIE SAYS THAT YOU SAY WHITE HOUSE SUFFERING ACUTE SHORTAGE MAINE LOBSTERS. WE ARE OPPOSED TO DEPRESSED AREAS WHEREVER LOCATED. HAVE THEREFORE SHIPPED THIS MORNING RAILWAY EXPRESS SIXTEEN LIVE LOBSTERS IN BUSY EXECUTIVE SIZE SMALL ENOUGH TO EAT ONE-HANDED BIG ENOUGH TO SATISFY UNDERSTANDABLE CRAVING. ASK NOT WHAT YOU CAN DO FOR MAINE RATHER WHAT MAINE CAN DO FOR YOU.

Dear Mr. Myers:
Maine lobsters arrived in fine fettle. My sincere thanks for your prompt action to alleviate local distress. Having now consumed several, I am confident that an equitable solution could be found for any problems of surpluses ever faced by Saltwater Farms.

Late one afternoon last year, 13-year-old Emmett Bowers slowly wheeled his bicycle up a leafy street in Wilton, Iowa, delivering copies of the evening newspaper. It had been a long day, and he was anxious to get home. At a railway crossing, warning lights blinked red and the safety crossbar came banging down.

As Emmett waited at the crossing, he saw something he won't ever forget. Out on the railway tracks, not aware of a train approaching at 80 miles an hour, was a year-old baby who'd wandered away from a nearby home.

Emmett Bowers responded to the crisis with little or no concern for his own safety. He flung himself off his bike, sprinted directly in front of the train and pulled the infant off the tracks.

Dear Emmett:

I have just learned of the great courage you displayed in saving the life of young Larry Baker. I think all of us regard courage as perhaps the outstanding of human virtues and particularly, as in your case, when it requires immediate reaction—not a deliberate one. My heartiest congratulations to you.

When Professor John Kenneth Galbraith was named United States Ambassador to India, the celebrants didn't include Galbraith's son Peter. Like many another contented American schoolboy, Peter Galbraith had wistful reservations about sinking new roots far from the familiar scenes of his home.

Dear Peter:

I learn from your father that you are not very anxious to give up your school and friends for India. I think I know a little about how you feel. More than twenty years ago our family was similarly uprooted when we went to London, where my father was ambassador. My younger brothers and sisters were about your age. They had, like you, to exchange old friends for new ones.

But I think you will like your new friends and your new school in India. For anyone interested, as your father says you are, in animals, India must have the most fantastic possibilities. The range is from elephants to cobras, although I gather the cobras have to be handled professionally. Indians ride and play polo, so you will come back an experienced horseman.

But more important still, I think of the children of the people I am sending to other countries as my junior Peace Corps. You and your brothers will be helping out your parents to do a good job for our country, and you will be helping yourself by making many friends. I think perhaps this is what you will enjoy most of all.

My best wishes.

Among the millions of Americans impressed by President Kennedy's eloquent Inaugural Address was a teacher at the fashionable Dalton School in New York City, who told her students Kennedy's oratorical style was much like that of the great Roman orator, Cicero.

Eight girls volunteered to translate the address into Latin and although they didn't quite finish the translation before final examinations five months later, they did send the President a copy of what they had completed. With the help of a White House administrative assistant, the President replied in appropriate fashion—entirely in Latin, beginning, Johannes Filiugeraldi Kennediensis, Respublicae Praesidens, puellis Scholae Daltoni salutem plurimam dicit. (For those whose Latin—like ours—is rusty, here is the letter in translation.)

President John Fitzgerald Kennedy sends heartiest greetings to the girls of Dalton School.

Distinguished young ladies, I have received your letter, in which you mention the translation of my speech, and I have read over that translation. I am pleased and delighted with many features of it. I strongly admire your knowledge of the Latin language and your skillful eloquence in writing. The style of your translation seems to me to be praiseworthy and admirable; the fact is it has both richness and variety.

What is there which could be done by you which would not deserve approval? I thank you not only for your kindness but also because through your efforts you have made it possible for me to read my own speech speaking the Latin language.

Best wishes to you! From the city of Washington on the twenty-seventh of May in the year of Our Lord 1961.

from The Kennedy Wit

by Bill Adler

This state knows the issues of this campaign—Senior Citizens. Senator McNamara is chairman of the Senate Committee on Senior Citizens. I am vice chairman. We are both aging fast.

Warren, Michigan
October 26, 1960

The man in the audience said that I should tell Mr. Nixon that experience is what he will have left after this campaign is over. I don't know why we never think of these things.

First, let me say that you are my type of Democrat. My friends, Bob

Wagner, General Farley, Frank O'Connor, Pat Clancy—the Irish are very big out here. Jim Delaney—they really run a balanced ticket.

New York City
October 27, 1960

from

John F. Kennedy:
A Sense of Purpose

by Charles L. Markmann and
Mark Sherwin

Chapter 22

Reaching the People

*Charles Markmann and Mark Sherwin both have substantial
journalistic credentials, and have previously collaborated
on two books,* One Week in March *and* The Book
of Sports Cars. *In* John F. Kennedy: A Sense of
Purpose, *they try to answer the question of how well,
during the first year of his administration, Kennedy had
achieved or laid the groundwork for achieving the goals he had
set upon taking office. The following chapter is their analysis
of Kennedy's contribution to press relations and to the
entire field of public information.*

There was a time in this country when the President spoke publicly
only to the people and to the Congress, leaving the press to report,

interpret and comment without any manner of direct contact. There were only rare exceptions to this until Theodore Roosevelt lowered the barrier slightly by giving exclusive interviews to correspondents of favored newspapers. Subsequently editors became suspicious of his generosity because Roosevelt frequently used these "exclusives" as trial balloons, and when the public reaction proved unfavorable, he would deny that the interview had taken place and soundly denounce the correspondent, the editor and the newspaper. Wilson was the first to invite reporters to an official press conference in his office. On March 15, 1913, he faced 100 reporters (he had modestly expected only 25) and answered questions politely and cautiously. He did not permit discussion. He continued these sessions regularly, showing his annoyance with some persistent questioners and acting like a pedantic schoolmaster lecturing a group of inquisitive urchins. When World War I began, he stopped the press conferences altogether. Harding set up a system in which written questions were submitted in advance. He selected those he would answer, prohibited direct quotation, discarded all embarrassing questions and allowed no informal talk. Coolidge half-heartedly continued the sessions, which he, intentionally or naturally, made short, unproductive and dull. Hoover's press meetings were dry, unsatisfactory, and as the Depression became more acute, grew tense and bitter.

The pattern for the modern press conference was set by Franklin Roosevelt, who "enjoyed" the most hostile press any President ever had. He allowed, even encouraged, banter, chit-chat and a kind of informal intimacy the reporters had never experienced. He answered questions, advised, lectured, joked and informed, calling many correspondents by their first names, and was able without giving offense to parry inquiries that were awkward or to which he did not wish to reply directly. These "gab fests" became so legendary that on many occasions anti-Roosevelt publishers asked to be invited and came away completely charmed by the man, and, trying to justify their position, blamed all the New Deal excesses on "those brain trusters." Truman followed Roosevelt's program, but without his grace and agility, supplying instead peppery commentaries that could not be printed. Eisenhower, under the clever guidance of James Hagerty, broke precedent by allowing direct quotations but reserving the right to edit the transcript. Then, in 1955, Eisenhower opened the conference to photographers for the first time—television, newsreels and stills. It was a historic advance in pictorial journalism, but again the White House properly reserved the right to black out any exchange that could be misinterpreted. It is to the credit of Eisenhower and Hagerty that few scenes were edited despite the "fluffs" and ear-wrenching grammar.

Roosevelt discovered radio as an excellent way to bypass the press attacks on him, his Administration, his wife, his children and his dog. The "Fireside Chat" was his most effective weapon against the printed word. Kennedy, who enjoyed a better press than any of his Democratic predecessors, found the medium of television a powerful supplement in the task of rallying public opinion toward his long-range eight-year program. In this projection he was not unduly optimistic, considering a statement made by Nixon shortly after the end of the 100 days that "the odds favored President Kennedy's re-election in 1964 barring some major catastrophe."

During the campaign, Kennedy's forceful, energetic personality on television had won to his cause many doubters and reluctant voters. Therefore it was natural that his first television press conference should draw an enviably large audience. One week after he took office, Kennedy stood on the rostrum in the spacious auditorium of the new State Department Building facing 418 news men, a record attendance. He set the pattern by opening with a statement —the most startling ever made at a press conference. He announced: "Captains Freeman B. Olmstead and John R. McKone, members of the crew of the U.S.A.F. RB-47 aircraft who have been detained by Soviet authorities since July 1, 1960, have been released by the Soviet Government and are now en route to the United States." When the excitement had subsided, he continued with discussions of other plans, speaking quietly, incisively and clearly. Then he answered 31 questions in 38 minutes, impressing the reporters and the television audience with his knowledge of all matters that came up for discussion. He used his right arm in a waving motion as if to put a punctuation and emphasis to his replies. The news men were visibly impressed and the viewers at home were enthralled and enchanted with a President who seemed to know all the answers. And the intellectuals were delighted with a President who understood syntax and spoke in sentences.

As the news conferences on television continued, always beginning with announcements and statements from the President, the veteran reporters examined this new method and found several flaws. Aside from the fact that the conference lacked the give-and-take atmosphere of Roosevelt's and Truman's sessions, there was a growing resentment that the announcements shrank the time left for questions in the traditional 30 minutes. Since it was impolite to break into discussion while millions watched, reporters suffered the unhappy feeling that Kennedy was using the haphazard method of selecting his questioners to play favorites. The President was not at fault alone. Criticism was leveled at reporters who used the television scanners in the interest of publicizing themselves and asking trivial and unanswerable questions, for example: "Would you welcome a visit from Mr. Khrushchev in the next few weeks or months?" "Do you propose to spark from the White House the one-man movement started by a Republican relative of yours in Oklahoma to restore the sound dollar?" (The Republican was no relative.) "Have you determined whether any in the State Department helped to advance the Communist foothold in Cuba, and if so will you take steps to remove them from office?" The President managed to answer these and many other silly questions with poise and patience. And he impressed his listeners with his exact knowledge of a molasses shipment from Cuba and several other matters that appeared as if the questioner had specifically copied some obscure figures for the sake of demonstrating his erudition.

Nevertheless, the televised press conference served Kennedy well. Arthur Krock wrote in the *Times:*

In this revitalized atmosphere of government by a Chief Executive who has an intelligent and tireless interest in its over-all and detailed functioning, the White House news conferences themselves have become even more the instrument of the President. The questions grow fewer because Mr. Kennedy has employed them more as a platform to make important announcements of acts and policies. Through the projection of television, live or canned, this expansion of the President's role has well served the dual purpose of informing the United States and the world on the vital and timely matters and providing him with a better forum than has been built on that foundation before. And that is one of the most effective means of transmitting to the furthest reaches of the planet an impression of new vitality in Washington.

Kennedy's intense desire to arouse the people from their apathy of the "Easy Fifties" and to cast a brighter light in broad areas of ignorance showed some gratifying results. While the public opinion polls indicated his popularity was growing in a rather casual way, other statistics were even more heartening. The White House switchboard was 60 per cent busier than it was before Kennedy took office; mail arrived at the rate of 30,000 letters a week, and the same general attitude of awakening was reflected in the phone calls and mail received by Cabinet members. Yet there was the grave concern that the vibrant New Frontier might wear out its welcome with the easily distracted mass of television viewers who could retreat to their cowboy or gangster violence and just say: "Let Jack do it."

The President repeatedly told the people that the world looked to the United States for leadership despite Communist propaganda; that our leadership depended largely upon an informed electorate, and that no Administration could succeed if the country did not understand. He was openly disturbed by reports that only three in ten voters were aware of the major problems in foreign affairs and that two in ten could be considered reasonably well informed. In defense of this state of affairs it was noted that never before in the history of this nation had its foreign affairs been so perplexing, so varied and so complicated. The tones and shadings became increasingly confusing. The ordinary citizen could not understand why tiny Laos, so far away, was important. He had been conditioned by the films and television to understand the difference between the good guy and the bad guy. He felt secure in the single knowledge that Communism was the bad guy, Uncle Sam was the good guy. As for the rest, it was up to the man who was President.

In striving for the greater dissemination of information, Kennedy indicated that what we do not know is certain to hurt us. These words were to come back later in a different light when he addressed the American Newspaper Publishers' Association in New York. He began gently by asking the publishers to reconsider the meaning of freedom of the press. Then he outlined the "distinct" advantages that a closed totalitarian society held over an open society. "Its preparations," he said of the closed society, "are concealed, not published. Its mistakes are buried, not headlined. . . . No expenditure is questioned, no rumor is printed, no secret is revealed. It conducts the cold war, in short, with a wartime discipline no democracy could ever hope—or wish—to match."

The President went on to show that every democracy recognized the necessary restraints of national security—"and the question remains whether those restraints need to be more strictly observed if we are to oppose this kind of attack as well as outright invasion." He declared that this nation's foes had openly boasted of acquiring through American newspapers information they would otherwise hire agents to acquire through theft, bribery or espionage. "Details of this nation's covert preparations," he said, "to counter the enemy's covert operations have been available to every newspaper reader, friend and foe alike." He pointed out that the size, strength, the location and nature of our forces and weapons, and our plans and strategy for their use, had all been pinpointed in the press and other news media to a degree sufficient to satisfy any foreign power; and that, in at least one case, the publication of details concerning a secret mechanism by which satellites were followed required its alteration at the expense of considerable time and money.

"The newspapers which printed these stories," he said, "were loyal, patriotic, responsible and well-meaning. Had we been engaged in open warfare, they undoubtedly would not have published such items. But in the absence of open warfare, they recognized only the tests of journalism and not the tests of national security. And my question . . . is whether additional tests should now be adopted. That question is for you to answer.

"I have no intention of establishing a new Office of War Information to govern the flow of news. I am not suggesting any new forms of censorship or new types of security classifications. I have no easy answer to the dilemma I have posed, and I would not seek to impose it if I had one. But I am asking the members of the newspaper profession and the industry in this country to re-examine their own responsibilities—to consider the degree and the nature of the present danger—and to heed the duty of self restraint which that danger imposes upon us.

"Every newspaper now asks itself, with respect to every story: 'Is it news?' All I suggest is that it add the question: 'Is it in the interest of national security?' And I hope that every group in America—unions and business men and public officials at every level—will ask the same question of their endeavors, and subject their actions to this same exacting test.

"And should the press of America consider and recommend the voluntary assumption of specific new steps or machinery, I can assure you that we will cooperate wholeheartedly with those recommendations."

The President made clear to the publishers that he had no desire to stifle controversy or criticism, and that his Administration intended to be candid about its errors. He quoted an old adage that "an error does not become a mistake until you refuse to correct it." He quoted Solon, the Athenian law maker, who said that it was a crime for a citizen to shrink from controversy. The publishers listened politely and even laughed when he said he had not come to "deliver the usual assault on the so-called one-party press. On the contrary, in recent months I have rarely heard any complaints about political bias except from a few Republicans."

The reaction was as expected from a press traditionally suspicious of any move to control it—even benevolently.

"There is no need for further restrictive machinery," said the

New York *Herald Tribune*. "In days of peril especially, the country needs more facts, not fewer. In the long run, competent, thorough and aggressive news reporting is the uncompromising servant of the national interest—even though it may be momentarily embarrassing to the Government."

The Portland *Oregonian* made the point that what is needed "far more is discipline among government officials, both civilian and military; first, to keep the people properly informed; second, to guard legitimate secrets from leaks, lies, misinterpretation and inter-agency sabotage."

The Newark *Evening News* asked who was to define the national interest. "The Press believes the public's right to know is a fundamental of democratic government. But where does this right collide with national security? If Mr. Kennedy . . . can tell us, he will not find the press uncooperative."

The Louisville *Courier-Journal* said the President "did not and probably could not spell out what he meant . . . for self-restraint, like virtue, is a matter that lends itself to individual interpretation."

The Nashville *Tennesseean* said: "There is not an ethical newspaper publisher or editor . . . who is not ready to recognize that any war, cold or hot, presents new problems and responsibilities. . . . Rights of the free press are not going to be tampered with, but patriotic cooperation . . . can be taken for granted."

If Kennedy intended to enter into debate with the editorial writers, he did not get the immediate opportunity because at this time the Cuban adventure exploded all over the front pages, keeping him and his press secretary fully occupied. Salinger himself was nursing wounds suffered at a panel session of the American Society of Newspaper Editors where Peter Lisagor, Washington bureau chief of the Chicago *Daily News,* had finally openly voiced the complaint that reporters were "little more than props for the TV press conference." Lisagor and others said it would "be nice to know when the Irish temper behind the Harvard facade had been excited. This could be accomplished by sitting a little closer to the President." The normally good-humored Salinger replied rather testily that "people who long for the good old days of F.D.R. are unrealistic. Television is here to stay." It was only natural that Salinger should be subject to comparison with his predecessor. White House correspondents felt that Salinger had not yet achieved "the polish and sure-footedness of Hagerty"; that he properly spoke less for Kennedy than Hagerty did for Eisenhower; that he often ignored telephone calls; that he was frequently late in holding his twice-a-day press briefings and that he was often not certain of his information. But all agreed that "Plucky Pierre," as he was sometimes called behind his ample back, did a prodigious amount of work, was willing to admit errors and definitely made no attempt to create a wall around the President. Salinger's own appraisal of his work so far was: "I think the people are getting a closer view of the President than they've ever had—and that's just what we want."

The closer view evidently favored Kennedy, as private and public polls showed an ever-increasing popularity and, what was even more encouraging, a genuine sympathy for his burdens of office. He made it a practice on some quiet weekend afternoons, rare though they were, to walk into the press room, which is really a large anteroom to the executive offices, and have a casual chat with reporters. Such visits were generally not mentioned and definitely were not to be construed as any form of press conference, briefing or background session. Shortly after the Cuban mishap, someone remarked that the Gallup Poll indicated that his popularity had reached a new peak. "My God," he exclaimed, "it's as bad as Eisenhower. The worse I do, the more popular I get."

The President
and the Press

Address Before the American
Newspaper Publishers Association,
New York City

April 27, 1961

Mr. Chairman [Palmer Hoyt, Denver *Post*], *ladies and gentlemen:*

I appreciate very much your generous invitation to be here tonight.

You bear heavy responsibilities these days and an article I read some time ago reminded me of how particularly heavily the burdens of present-day events bear upon your profession.

You may remember that in 1851, the New York *Herald Tribune*, under the sponsorship and publishing of Horace Greeley, employed as its London correspondent an obscure journalist by the name of Karl Marx.

We are told that foreign correspondent Marx, stone broke, and with a family ill and undernourished, constantly appealed to Greeley and Managing Editor Charles Dana for an increase in his munificent salary of $5 per installment, a salary which he and Engels ungratefully labeled as the "lousiest petty bourgeois cheating."

But when all his financial appeals were refused, Marx looked around for other means of livelihood and fame, eventually terminating his relationship with the *Tribune* and devoting his talents full time to the cause that would bequeath to the world the seeds of Leninism, Stalinism, revolution and the cold war.

If only this capitalistic New York newspaper had treated him more kindly; if only Marx had remained a foreign correspondent, history might have been different. And I hope all publishers will bear this lesson in mind the next time they receive a poverty-stricken appeal for a small increase in the expense account from an obscure newspaper man.

I have selected as the title of my remarks tonight "The President and the Press." Some may suggest that this would be more naturally worded "The President Versus the Press." But those are not my sentiments tonight.

It is true, however, that when a well-known diplomat from another country demanded recently that our State Department repudiate certain newspaper attacks on his colleague it was unnecessary for us to reply that this Administration was not responsible for the press, for the press had already made it clear that it was not responsible for this Administration.

Nevertheless, my purpose here tonight is not to deliver the usual assault on the so-called one-party press. On the contrary, in recent months I have rarely heard any complaints about political bias in the press except from a few Republicans. Nor is it my purpose here tonight to discuss or defend the televising of Presidential press conferences. I think it is highly beneficial to have some 20,000,000 Americans regularly sit in on these conferences to observe, if I may say so, the incisive, the intelligent and the courteous qualities displayed by your Washington correspondents.

Nor, finally, are these remarks intended to examine the proper degree of privacy which the press should allow to any President and his family.

If in the last few months your White House reporters and photographers have been attending church services with regularity, that has surely done them no harm.

On the other hand, I realize that your staff and wire service photographers may be complaining that they do not enjoy the same privileges at the local golf courses which they once did.

It is true that my predecessor did not object as I do to pictures of one's golfing skill in action. But neither on the other hand did he ever bean a Secret Service man.

My topic tonight is a more sober one of concern to publishers as well as editors.

I want to talk about our common responsibilities in the face of a common danger. The events of recent weeks may have helped to illuminate that challenge for some; but the dimensions of its threat have loomed large on the horizon for many years. Whatever our hopes may be for the future—for reducing this threat or living with it—there is no escaping either the gravity or the totality of its challenge to our survival and to our security—a challenge that confronts us in unaccustomed ways in every sphere of human activity.

This deadly challenge imposes upon our society two requirements of direct concern both to the press and to the President—two requirements that may seem almost contradictory in tone, but which must be reconciled and fulfilled if we are to meet this national peril. I refer, *first*, to the need for far greater public information; and, *second*, to the need for far greater official secrecy.

I.

The very word "secrecy" is repugnant in a free and open society; and we are as a people inherently and historically opposed to secret societies, to secret oaths and to secret proceedings. We decided long ago that the dangers of excessive and unwarranted concealment of pertinent facts far outweighed the dangers which are cited to justify it. Even today, there is little value in opposing the threat of a closed society by imitating its arbitrary restrictions. Even today, there is little value in insuring the survival of our nation if our traditions do not survive with it. And there is very grave danger that an announced need for increased security will be seized upon by those anxious to expand its meaning to the very limits of official censorship and concealment. That I do not intend to permit to the extent that it is in my control. And no official of my Administration, whether his rank is high or low, civilian or military, should interpret my words here tonight as an excuse to censor the news, to stifle dissent, or to cover up our mistakes or to withhold from the press and the public the facts they deserve to know.

But I do ask every publisher, every editor, and every newsman in the nation to reexamine his own standards, and to recognize the nature of our country's peril. In time of war, the government and the press have customarily joined in an effort, based largely on self-discipline, to prevent unauthorized disclosures to the enemy. In time of "clear and present danger," the courts have held that even the privileged rights of the First Amendment must yield to the public's need for national security.

Today no war has been declared—and however fierce the struggle may be, it may never be declared in the traditional fashion. Our way of life is under attack. Those who make themselves our enemy are advancing around the globe. The survival of our friends is in danger. And yet no war has been declared, no borders have been crossed by marching troops, no missiles have been fired.

If the press is awaiting a declaration of war before it imposes the self-discipline of combat conditions, then I can only say that no war ever posed a greater threat to our security. If you are awaiting a finding of "clear and present danger," then I can only say that the danger has never been more clear and its presence has never been more imminent.

It requires a change in outlook, a change in tactics, a change in missions—by the government, by the people, by every businessman or labor leader, and by every newspaper. For we are opposed around the world by a monolithic and ruthless conspiracy that relies primarily on covert means for expanding its sphere of influence—on infiltration instead of invasion, on subversion instead of elections, on intimidation instead of free choice, on guerrillas by night instead of armies by day. It is a system which has conscripted vast human and material resources into the building of a tightly knit, highly efficient machine that combines military, diplomatic, intelligence, economic, scientific and political operations.

Its preparations are concealed, not published. Its mistakes are buried, not headlined. Its dissenters are silenced, not praised. No expenditure is questioned, no rumor is printed, no secret is revealed. It conducts the Cold War, in short, with a war-time discipline no democracy would ever hope or wish to match.

Nevertheless, every democracy recognizes the necessary restraints of national security—and the question remains whether those restraints need to be more strictly observed if we are to oppose this kind of attack as well as outright invasion.

For the facts of the matter are that this Nation's foes have openly boasted of acquiring through our newspapers information they would otherwise hire agents to acquire through theft, bribery and espionage; that details of this Nation's covert preparations to counter the enemy's covert operations have been available to every newspaper reader, friend and foe alike; that the size, the strength, the location and the nature of our forces and weapons, and our plans and strategy for their use, have all been pinpointed in the press and other news media to a degree sufficient to satisfy any foreign power; and that, in at least one case, the publication of details concerning a secret mechanism whereby satellites were followed required its alteration at the expense of considerable time and money.

The newspapers which printed these stories were loyal, patriotic, responsible and well-meaning. Had we been engaged in open warfare, they undoubtedly would not have published such items. But in the absence of open warfare, they recognized only the tests of journalism and not the tests of national security. And my question tonight is whether additional tests should not now be adopted.

That question is for you alone to answer. No public official should answer it for you. No governmental plan should impose its restraints against your will. But I would be failing in my duty to the Nation, in considering all of the responsibilities that we now bear and all of the means at hand to meet those responsibilities, if I did not commend this problem to your attention, and urge its thoughtful consideration.

On many earlier occasions, I have said—and your newspapers have constantly said—that these are times that appeal to every citizen's sense of sacrifice and self-discipline. They call out to every citizen to weigh his rights and comforts against his obligations to the common good. I cannot now believe that those citizens who serve in the newspaper business consider themselves exempt from that appeal.

I have no intention of establishing a new Office of War Information to govern the flow of news. I am not suggesting any new forms of censorship or new types of security classifications. I have no easy answer to the dilemma that I have posed, and would not seek to impose if it I had one. But I am asking the members of the newspaper profession and the industry in this country to reexamine their own responsibilities, to consider the degree and the nature of the present danger, and to heed the duty of self-restraint which that danger imposes upon us all.

Every newspaper now asks itself, with respect to every story: "Is it news?" All I suggest is that you add the question: "Is it in the interest of the national security?" And I hope that every group in America—unions and businessmen and public officials at every level—will ask the same question of their endeavors, and subject their actions to this same exacting test.

And should the press of America consider and recommend the voluntary assumption of specific new steps or machinery, I can assure you that we will cooperate whole-heartedly with those recommendations.

Perhaps there will be no recommendations. Perhaps there is no answer to the dilemma faced by a free and open society in a cold and secret war. In times of peace, any discussion of this subject, and any action that results, are both painful and without precedent. But this is a time of peace and peril which knows no precedent in history.

II.

It is the unprecedented nature of this challenge that also gives rise to your second obligation—an obligation which I share. And that is our obligation to inform and alert the American people— to make certain that they possess all the facts that they need, and understand them as well—the perils, the prospects, the purposes of our program and the choices that we face.

No President should fear public scrutiny of his program. For from that scrutiny comes understanding; and from that understanding comes support or opposition. And both are necessary. I am not asking your newspapers to support the Administration, but I am asking your help in the tremendous task of informing and alerting the American people. For I have complete confidence in the response and dedication of our citizens whenever they are fully informed.

I not only could not stifle controversy among your readers—I welcome it. This Administration intends to be candid about its errors; for as a wise man once said: "An error doesn't become a mistake until you refuse to correct it." We intend to accept full responsibility for our errors; and we expect you to point them out when we miss them.

Without debate, without criticism, no Administration and no country can succeed—and no republic can survive. That is why the Athenian law-maker Solon decreed it a crime for any citizen to shrink from controversy, and that is why our press was protected by the First Amendment—the only business in America specifically protected by the Constitution—not primarily to amuse and entertain, not to emphasize the trivial and the sentimental, not to simply "give the public what it wants"—but to inform, to arouse, to reflect, to state our dangers and our opportunities, to indicate our crises and our choices, to lead, mold, educate, and sometimes even anger public opinion.

This means greater coverage and analysis of international news —for it is no longer far away and foreign but close at hand and local. It means greater attention to improved understanding of the news as well as improved transmission. And it means, finally, that government at all levels must meet its obligation to provide you with the fullest possible information outside the narrowest limits of national security—and we intend to do it.

III.

It was early in the Seventeenth Century that Francis Bacon remarked on three recent inventions already transforming the world: the compass, gunpowder and the printing press. Now the links between the nations first forged by the compass have made us all citizens of the world, the hopes and threats of one becoming the hopes and threats of us all. In that one world's efforts to live together, the evolution of gunpowder to its ultimate limit has warned mankind of the terrible consequences of failure.

And so it is to the printing press—to the recorder of man's deeds, the keeper of his conscience, the courier of his news—that we look for strength and assistance, confident that with your help man will be what he was born to be: free and independent.

from

White House Nannie

by Maud Shaw

Chapter VII

Maud Shaw, an English "nannie" from Kent, became the Kennedys'
governess shortly before the birth of the then-Senator Kennedy's
daughter, Caroline. She stayed with the family for seven years,
being with them in the White House and traveling with them to
vacation spots like Hyannis Port. She became a part of the family's
intimate home life, and her book reveals part of the private
character of John Kennedy, father of two delightfully lovable
children.

Little Caroline was the first person to confirm to Senator Kennedy
that he was, in fact, President Kennedy, and I think I shall always

remember with pride how it came about—and his quiet, simple reaction to the news that realized his greatest hope.

It happened the morning after America had gone to the polls to choose between John F. Kennedy and Richard Nixon for the Presidency. At about seven-fifteen that morning, Caroline woke me in my room in the Kennedy home in Hyannis Port, and, after I had given her a quick breakfast, she asked to go and see her Daddy in his room.

It was a sunny morning. The November day was bright and warm, and I awoke with a feeling of intense excitement. I had gone to bed shortly before one in the morning after listening to the election results coming in on television. The voting was so close that no one expected a final result before breakfasttime, and while I prepared Caroline's cornflakes and eggs, I was wondering what the outcome would be.

Caroline and I had breakfast together in her room. She was quite happy and cheerful as ever, not quite realizing how important this day was to her father, of course. I got up from the table, waiting for Caroline to finish her meal, and walked across to the window.

And then, on the lawn outside the front of the house, I noticed a man in a dark suit, just standing there. He wasn't going anywhere; he just kept looking around rather carefully, taking an occasional glance toward the house. Who could it possibly be standing out on the lawn? He certainly was not one of Mr. Kennedy's aides who had been with him through the election campaign. And then I realized. He was a Secret Service man! The President's bodyguard.

I realized then that Senator Kennedy must have won.

Caroline came over to the window then and asked who the man was.

"He's a friend of your Daddy's," I told her.

She nodded, unconcerned. "May I go and see Daddy now?"

"Yes, right away," I said. "But when you go and wake him up, I want you to give him a nice surprise. Will you go in and say 'Good morning, Mr. President' this time?"

Caroline nodded eagerly. It seemed a good time to her.

"Will he like that?" she asked.

"Yes, I think he'll be very pleased," I said. I took her hand and led her along the corridor to Senator Kennedy's room, knocked gently on the door, opened it and let Caroline in.

The new President was just a hump in the bedclothes, but Caroline shot across the room, jumped on the bed and pulled the blankets from her father's tousled head. He grunted, opened his eyes and smiled at his daughter.

Caroline played her part perfectly and with good timing.

She said nothing until he had given her a hug and a kiss.

"Good morning, Mr. President," she said, her eyes shining with delight.

"Well now, is that right?" Caroline looked over to where I stood in the doorway, and her father's glance followed hers.

"Am I in, Miss Shaw?" he asked.

"Of course you are, Mr. President," I said.

He looked at his watch a bit doubtfully. "Well, I wasn't in the White House for sure at four-thirty this morning."

"Oh, I'm sure you've been elected, sir," I said.

He sat up in bed then and looked almost sternly at me. "Now you just go back to the television set," he said, "and wait there until the result is confirmed, and then come back and tell me the final figures."

"Yes, sir," I said.

I hurried back to the nursery and switched on the big TV set. I switched from channel to channel, where all the newscasters were giving the latest results. According to their figures it was neck and neck, and the whole election would be decided on the result from California, Nixon's home state.

Within five minutes the result was through, and the election of the President could be definitely confirmed. I jotted down the figures and fairly skipped back to Mr. Kennedy's room. When I burst in he was playing and talking to Caroline, apparently quite calm and unconcerned.

I felt tears of happiness pricking my eyes as I stopped a few paces inside the room.

"Mr. President," I said, "you have been elected."

I read out the figures, showing that he had won. You could see the deep pleasure in his face, puffish around the eyes but still boyish and worry-free, despite the enormous burden of the campaign and the fact that he had had only four hours' sleep.

He just nodded slowly and said quietly: "Well, there we are then."

This was very typical of the man. Even though this was the summit of his ambitions, he took it all calmly. No doubt his serene reaction to being finally elected was partly due to the sheer exhaustion of the Presidential campaign, for he never seemed to be at home during all those hectic weeks, and when I did see him during that time his face looked pale with fatigue.

I don't think I ever saw him lose his temper throughout the five years I knew him. Even when something made him angry, he would listen quietly to an explanation and, if it was reasonable, would accept it and drop the subject. I remember this happening one time when we had moved into the White House and he complained to me about the children making too much noise and upsetting some important State visitors. What had happened was that during the visit of Ben Bella, the then-President of Algeria, to the White House, Caroline's school had been let out to play on the White House roof during recess. I don't know quite how this was allowed, but anyway the children made quite a noise, it seems, while Ben Bella was making a speech on the lawns down below.

It all caused a bit of a stir in the White House, and although, naturally, the President did not tell me about it, he did ask me that evening to keep the children out of the way the next day, when Marshal Tito of Yugoslavia was due to make a speech on the White House lawn.

That morning Caroline went off to school, and I gathered that the teachers had been told not to let the children out during recess. So I had only little John to worry about. Of course, while all the preparations were going on down on the lawn, he wanted to go out on the Truman Balcony and have a look. I didn't think there was any harm in it, so I let him out. He loved that, staring at the men putting the platforms and microphones in place and watching the television and film cameras being lined up.

He was dressed up with a couple of six-shooters in his belt and was having a fine old time. Then one of his toy guns fell off his belt, clattered onto the balcony and dropped through the railings down among the technicians below. I did not think any more about it, and about a quarter of an hour before the ceremony was due to start, I thought my best plan was to take John away from the White House. So I called up the Secret Service detail and asked them to fetch a car around for us. Ten minutes later we were on our way to Dumbarton Oaks for a walk in the gardens there.

But that evening I was horrified to learn that the little incident of John dropping his gun had been caught by one of the film cameras down below and inserted into a newsreel of the Tito speech, making it appear that John had been up on the balcony playing about throughout the ceremony. All the newspapers made a big thing of it, saying John had dropped his gun on Tito's head. The following morning, the President called me into his office after Caroline had gone up to school.

"Miss Shaw," he began, "I thought I asked you to keep John-John out of sight yesterday."

"Yes, you did, Mr. President," I said. "And I did take him away from the White House during the ceremony. I assure you we were at Dumbarton Oaks when he was supposed to be dropping his gun on President Tito's head."

"Is that right?" he said in surprise.

"Yes, Mr. President. You can check with the Secret Service detail."

He nodded. Then smiled. "All right, then. Thank you."

And that was the end of the affair. He retained this charm and coolness in spite of everything, even when, as Senator Kennedy, he was fighting bitterly to become President of the United States, and was forever traveling, talking, speechmaking, and handshaking.

There was always pressure on him, and he could not escape it when he had become President-elect and had gone away on his own for a rest at his father's home in Palm Beach.

Mrs. Kennedy had stayed behind with Caroline and myself at 3307 N Street, and the President-elect was scarcely gone for an hour or so when the strain of the campaign started to have its effect on his wife. For it was then that she called up to me from her bedroom on the second floor.

"Can you come quickly, Miss Shaw?"

I knew it had started, that it was time for a trip to the hospital to have the baby.

Why England Slept

by JOHN F. KENNEDY

A book review from The New York Times,
August 3, 1940

by Thomas C. Linn

A study of the reasons for Britain's lack of preparedness against German military might ought to interest many people in the United States, especially in Washington, D.C. For as John F. Kennedy points out in his book *Why England Slept,* that country has been the "testing ground" of democratic efforts to cope with totalitarian force. It is from Britain's experience that the United States must profit if democracy is to be maintained here against totalitarian threats. . . .

Since John F. Kennedy is a son of Ambassador Joseph P. Kennedy, this book originated under fortunate auspices. For of all the Americans who have had advantageous positions for studying European affairs in the last few years, those in the American Embassy in London have been among the most favored. Not all young men enjoying such advantages, however, would have shown the will or ability to turn them to such useful literary ends. Young Mr. Kennedy also spent some time in the American Embassy in Paris, studied at the University of London, and is a cum laude graduate in international relations at Harvard University.

This is no time for anyone to find fault with individual British statesmen for what they may have contributed to Britain's present plight. Mr. Kennedy is not interested in finding scapegoats but in pointing out for the education of his fellow-countrymen the reasons for Britain's tardy rearmament so that similar mistakes may be avoided here. . . .

The basic reason for Britain's delayed rearmament, according to Mr. Kennedy, is inherent in the democratic form of government. Contrasting the weakness of democracy in competing with the totalitarian system, he writes, "Democracy is the superior form of government, because it is based on respect for man as a reasonable being. For the long run, then, democracy is superior.

"But for the short run, democracy has great weaknesses. When it competes with a system of government which cares nothing for permanency, a system built primarily for war, democracy, which is built primarily for peace, is at a disadvantage. And democracy must recognize its weaknesses; it must learn to safeguard its institutions if it hopes to survive." . . .

Armament was retarded by various factors which were peculiar to England. Mr. Kennedy thinks that the country was unfortunate in its choice of men to head the government during this critical period, that there was a lack of progressive younger leadership caused by the loss of a generation in the World War, that the English parliamentary system increased the difficulty of rearmament, as did the strong public sentiment in favor of the League of Nations, and as did also "the closeness to the government of the English aristocracy, which was opposed strongly to war."

It is, of course, too early for any final appraisal of the men and the circumstances that shaped England's policy during the last decade. The information is by no means obtainable yet for such an undertaking. Mr. Kennedy has made a careful analysis from the records that are available. His factual and unemotional approach to the problem is praiseworthy, and his conclusions ought to be weighed carefully in this country. . . .

Why Britain Slept While Hitler Prepared for War

JOHN F. KENNEDY, A SON OF OUR
AMBASSADOR, OFFERS A CLEAR-HEADED
AND REALISTIC EXPLANATION

A book review from The New York Times
August 11, 1940

by S. T. Williamson

In a foreword to this excellent examination of how Britain arrived at her present fix, Henry R. Luce, *Life-Time-Fortune* editor, who is no mean appraiser of young genius, writes: "In recent months there has been a certain amount of alarm concerning the 'attitude' of the younger generation. If John Kennedy is characteristic of the younger generation—and I believe he is—many of us would be happy to have the destinies of this Republic handed over to his generation at once."

John F. Kennedy is a son of the American Ambassador to the Court of St. James. He spent some time in our London and Paris Embassies and studied for a short while at the University of London. He's a little over a year out of Harvard and hasn't yet reached his middle twenties: yet he has written a book of such painstaking scholarship, such mature understanding and fair-mindedness and of such penetrating and timely conclusions, that it is a notable textbook for our times. This reviewer has seen no other discussion of pre-war Britain which sheds more light and generates less heated partisanship than Mr. Kennedy's book. This young man from Boston has a clear-headed, realistic, unhysterical message for his countrymen —and for his elders.

He has taken the hard way and the thorough way to show how and why Britain slept while Germany whetted her sword. He might have heaped a thesaurus-load of adjectives of contempt and ridicule upon Stanley Baldwin and Neville Chamberlain. . . .

"I believe that it is one of democracy's failings that it seeks to make scapegoats for its own weaknesses," Mr. Kennedy writes. "It frequently forgets the reasons for its previous point of view; it cannot understand how it could have believed as it formerly did. Seeking to explain this, it places the blame upon the men who were then in office." . . .

He draws these lessons for the United States from Britain's costly slumber: "Democracy must recognize its weaknesses: it must learn to safeguard its institutions if it hopes to survive. . . . We must keep our armaments equal to our commitments. Munich should teach us that; we must realize that any bluff will be called. We cannot tell anyone to keep out of our hemisphere unless our armaments *and the people behind those armaments* [these are Kennedy italics] are prepared to back up the command even to the ultimate point of war. There must be no doubt in anyone's mind, the decision must be automatic; if we debate, if we hesitate, if we question, it will be too late."

It may be recalled that after the Germans invaded Poland they made a big fuss over some "documents" they said they had discovered in Polish archives. One Polish diplomat was quoted as warning his home office that Ambassador Joe Kennedy's son John had great influence with the President, that Mr. Roosevelt listened to his views with respect. Let us hope that at least this document is genuine; and that a few million others listen, too.

from

The Founding Father

by Richard J. Whalen

Chapter 23
Tea Parties and Old Scores

Richard Whalen is a former associate editor of Fortune
magazine and has contributed frequently to Time *magazine and
the* Wall Street Journal. The Founding Father *is his first book,
a fascinating biography of Joseph P. Kennedy, multi-millionaire
businessman, politician, and paterfamilias. The chapter reproduced
here deals with the early political career of his son, a relative
newcomer to Massachusetts politics, John F. Kennedy.*

As early as 1949, Jack Kennedy, though scarcely more than a freshman congressman, began running hard for higher office. It had
taken only one term in the House for him to become bored with
the tortoiselike pace of the seniority system. Restless and impatient,

he found the satisfactions of the settled legislative life distinctly inferior to the excitement of capturing higher rank. What office he wanted, when he would seek it, and who his opponent would be— these questions were left to be decided by future opportunity.

Each Thursday evening, he flew from Washington to Boston, was met at the airport by his office manager, Frank Morrissey, and set off in a chauffeur-driven car for a long weekend of speech-making across the state. On the following Monday evening, the undeclared candidate caught a plane back to the capital and resumed his congressional duties for another three days. As a leading member of the "Tuesday-to-Thursday Club" of Eastern congressmen and a notable absentee, Jack found little time to distinguish himself in the House. But by early 1952, he had crisscrossed Massachusetts dozens of times, introducing the name of Kennedy to voters in almost all of the state's three hundred and fifty-one cities and towns.

When he embarked on this long preliminary campaign, he considered trying for the governorship in 1950, when the Democratic incumbent, Paul Dever, came up for reelection. State issues and politics were uninviting, but the executive position would make an excellent springboard to national office. Gradually, however, Jack changed his mind and moved toward a direct leap to the Senate in 1952. The way was cleared when Governor Dever, the logical challenger to Republican Senator Henry Cabot Lodge, fearful of the latter's popularity, chose to stay in the governor's mansion. Thirty-four-year-old Congressman Kennedy promptly announced his candidacy.

Most of the Bay State's professional politicians regarded it as a foolhardy move, likely to end in humiliating defeat. Lodge himself was supremely confident, and passed a message to Joe Kennedy through a mutual friend. "Lodge was considered unbeatable," Kennedy later remembered. "Do you know what Lodge said? He told Arthur Krock to 'tell Joe not to waste his money on Jack because he can't win. I'm going to win by three hundred thousand votes.' "

On the strength of Lodge's past performance, his boast was not extravagant. Since his first Senate victory in 1936, he had soundly beaten three popular Irish politicians—Jim Curley, Joseph Casey, and David I. Walsh. To achieve such triumphs in heavily Irish Massachusetts, it was necessary for him to attract the votes of loyal Democrats. Their defection reflected the changing Irish attitude toward the once-hated Brahmins. The envy and enmity of the nineteenth century steadily had given way to sentimental admiration and emulation. The descendants of Irish servants consciously aped the manners and outlook of the old ruling class, which kept its place on top even after its power waned. With the political emergence of late-arriving ethnic groups, such as the Italians, the Irish identified themselves with the Yankee remnant and made common cause against the newcomers. The deep-seated Irish awe of the great Yankee families both annoyed and impressed Joe Kennedy. "All I ever heard when I was growing up in Boston," he recalled, "was how Lodge's grandfather had helped to put the stained glass windows into the Gate of Heaven Church in South Boston and they were still talking about those same stained glass windows in 1952."

To such would-be challengers as Governor Dever, the chief discouragement was the aura of aristocracy surrounding Lodge. His grandfather, the first Senator Henry Cabot Lodge, had held sway in Massachusetts for two decades. He had demonstrated his mastery in the Senate by leading the fight against Wilson's dream of bringing America into the League of Nations. Farther back in imposing array were the earlier founders and shapers of the Lodge family, the men who had amassed the wealth and garnered the fame on which their descendant, the present Senator Lodge, stood so securely. His high office seemed part of an established station in life which humbly born, self-made Irishmen, be they as clever as Curley or as forceful as Walsh, seemed powerless to overthrow.

In contrast, Jack Kennedy met Lodge as a self-confident equal. It was true that his grandfather, "Honey Fitz," had been defeated by Lodge's grandfather in the hard-fought 1916 election. But the following generations had seen a spectacular advance in the standing of the challenger's family, until the new riches of the Kennedys far overshadowed the ancient wealth of the Lodges. And the patina-encrusted prestige of the old Yankee family seemed dull by contrast with the glitter of the celebrated Kennedys. Moreover, the famous men from whom Lodge was descended were only austere figures in fading portraits, while Jack Kennedy's father was robustly alive, a fiercely ambitious family founder of the type not seen in Boston since the days of Lodge's great-grandfather. Those who regarded Lodge as the clear favorite failed to grasp the true nature of the Kennedy-Lodge encounter.

Sociology, not politics, would explain the campaign. The opponents might have come from the same mold, so striking were the similarities between them. Both were youthful, Harvard-bred millionaires who had dabbled in journalism early in their careers. Both had been decorated for bravery in World War II. Both were moderately liberal in their political views. As the gentlemanly campaign would reveal, there were few meaningful issues on which they differed. ("Honey Fitz," in the 1916 campaign, had made a frank appeal to class antagonism, saying of Lodge: "The robber baron is still his highest ideal and his dearest friend.")

By the ordinary criteria of politics, the voters in 1952 had reason to favor the able, experienced incumbent. Paradoxically, it was the very lack of outward differences between the two men that made Jack Kennedy an attractive candidate. He was, in Governor Dever's phrase, "the first Irish Brahmin." The Irish of Massachusetts, long a psychologically downtrodden majority, at last could purge themselves of lingering feelings of inferiority by voting for a candidate who, save for his Irish ancestry, was indistinguishable from his aristocratic Yankee opponent.

In family councils, Joe Kennedy advised his son to take on Lodge, saying, "When you've beaten him, you've beaten the best. Why try for something less?" That confident remark would be widely quoted as typical of the Kennedy fighting spirit, but it disclosed only part of the truth about how Kennedy fought. He never committed himself and his resources to a quixotic battle. He fought to win, but only after being convinced there was a chance of winning. For a year and a half before the 1952 campaign, a pair of paid, fulltime Kennedy advance men toured the state, sounding out opinions, wooing local politicians, lining up likely volunteer workers. In addition to their detailed reports, Kennedy carefully weighed the findings of private polls. "You wonder why we're taking on Lodge," he confided to a friend. "We've taken polls. He'll be easier to beat than Leverett Saltonstall." Only after his cool head had confirmed his heart's desire did Kennedy encourage his son to go ahead.

In their recollections of 1952, father and son differed on the role the elder Kennedy played in the campaign. As Jack remembered that summer and fall, his father had stayed on the sidelines at Hyannis Port. However, Joe Kennedy recalled that he had been in Boston—and so he had. Jack's attempt to minimize his father's contribution was part of his general defensiveness about how he had won, and why. As he said several years afterward, "People say, 'Kennedy bought the election. Kennedy could never have been elected if his father hadn't been a millionaire.' Well, it wasn't the Kennedy name and the Kennedy money that won that election. I beat Lodge because I hustled for three years. I worked for what I got."

Work he did. But whether or not he acknowledged it, the name and wealth bestowed on him by his father made victory possible. At the time, Joe Kennedy acted as though he was fully aware of this fact. "The father was the distinct boss in every way," said one who attended pre-campaign strategy meetings at the Kennedy home on Cape Cod in the spring of 1952. "He dominated everything, even told everyone where to sit. They (were) just children in that house."

It was evident to outsiders that Jack, in his father's presence, felt the need gently to assert his authority. Running down a list of assignments at an early planning session, the candidate facetiously delegated to his father the task of making all the money. "We concede you that role," he said.

As in 1946, Joe Kennedy went ahead in his usual fashion, asking no one's permission and sometimes acting without his son's knowledge. "The father was a tremendous factor in the campaign," said a Boston lawyer and campaign worker. "He remained out of public view. He didn't run things, but they happened according to his plans. He cast the die."

Once again, Kennedy recruited campaign personnel. The new battle demanded the mobilization of specialized skills. The first adviser hired was Ralph Coglan, a former St. Louis newspaperman who, while sharing Louis Lyons' sensational 1940 interview, treated it as "off-the-record" and thereby won the Ambassador's gratitude. Kennedy thought the 1952 Democratic National Convention offered an opportunity for his son to gain attention, and he assigned Coglan to devise ways of putting the spotlight on Jack, in spite of the fact that he was a very minor party figure and not even a member of the Massachusetts delegation. With remarkable frequency, the television cameras at the Chicago convention caught the young Congressman for seemingly impromptu interviews, which duly impressed the viewers—and voters—back in the Bay State.

Quiet, mild-mannered Mark Dalton, who had managed Jack's previous campaigns for the House, loyally returned to his post. By 1952, Dalton's law practice had grown to the point where he no longer could afford the sacrifice of working as an unpaid volunteer, and so he agreed to take a salary. This new arrangement lasted just two weeks. "Dalton was at his desk, smoking a pipe, when Joe Kennedy breezed in," said one who witnessed the scene. "The old man spread all the books on the desk in front of him, studied them for about five minutes without saying a word, then he shoved his finger in Dalton's face and yelled: 'Dalton, you've spent ten thousand dollars of my money and you haven't accomplished a damn thing.' The next day Dalton was gone."

Money, as such, had nothing to do with Dalton's abrupt departure. Once again, Kennedy's retainer, John Ford, was serving as overseer of campaign finances, so Kennedy knew very well whom to blame if funds were misspent. His outburst may have been intended as a reminder to the hard-working Dalton that, having accepted a salary, he now became just another of Kennedy's employees.

Twenty-six-year-old Bobby Kennedy, fresh from the University of Virginia Law School, became campaign manager. "When Bobby came in," an insider said later, "we knew it was the old man taking over. What had Bobby done up to that time politically? Nothing. Not a damn thing and all of a sudden he was there as campaign manager, waving the banners." At the very least, the choice provided further proof, if any was needed, that Kennedys preferred to deal with Kennedys.

The inexperienced Bobby showed little deference toward older politicians. As much a stranger in Boston as his older brother had been, he knew almost none of the local powers. One very prominent Boston political figure paid a visit to the newly opened Kennedy headquarters and was astounded to discover that no one, not even the candidate's manager, recognized him. "You're asking me who I am?" he shouted. "You mean to say nobody here knows me? And you call this a political headquarters?" Annoyed, Bobby threw the caller out.

Some professionals found the young amateur insufferable. Governor Dever was running for reelection and his campaign was linked with Jack Kennedy's. One day, Bobby stormed into Dever's office and began to berate him for what he considered a mistake in strategy. Dever angrily cut him short and showed him the door. Then he telephoned the Ambassador: "I know you're an important man around here and all that, but I'm telling you this and I mean it. Keep that fresh kid of yours out of my sight from here on in."

Early in the campaign, the elder Kennedy visited Jim Curley and asked him to make a radio speech in support of his son. On hearing this request, Curley must have looked at his caller in amazement. In 1947, Mayor Curley had been convicted of using the mails to defraud in war contracts and had been sentenced to jail despite his plea to the judge that he was suffering from nine separate ailments, including an impending cerebral hemorrhage. Still serving as Mayor of Boston from behind the bars of the Danbury penitentiary, he sent out an S.O.S. to the state's sympathetic political chieftains. House Speaker John McCormack drew up a petition to President Truman asking Curley's pardon, and promptly got the signatures of Massachusetts representatives, Republicans and Democrats alike. All of them except freshman Jack Kennedy, who regarded Curley's illness as implausible and refused to sign. Freed when Truman commuted his sentence, Curley thereafter felt he owed the Kennedys less than nothing. But Joe Kennedy was persistent. "When I refused (to speak for his son) on the grounds that were I to do so I would have to do likewise for other candidates," Curley wrote in his autobiography, *I'd Do It Again*, "he (Kennedy) asked if I would agree not to speak against him. I assented. . . ." Kennedy was never one to go away empty handed.

Jack Kennedy's 1952 campaign, wrote Ralph G. Martin and Ed Plaut in their book, *Front Runner, Dark Horse*, "was the most methodical, the most scientific, the most thoroughly detailed, the most intricate, the most disciplined and smoothly working statewide campaign in Massachusetts history—and possibly anywhere else." Busy behind the scenes at the center of his enterprise, incessantly demanding perfection, was Joe Kennedy. "The Ambassador worked around the clock," said one of the speech-writers he brought to Boston. "He was always consulting people, getting reports, looking into problems. Should Jack go on TV with this issue? What kind of an ad should he run on something else? He'd call in experts, get opinions, have ideas worked up."

It was understood by all concerned that the candidate would make the final decisions, but the alternatives set before him usually were framed by his father's hand-picked "brain-trust." When unmade decisions piled up, as often happened in those hectic days, there was no question about where to turn. "Sometimes you couldn't get anybody to make a decision," a worker recalled. "You'd have to call the old man. Then you'd get a decision."

The 1952 campaign, though broader and more complex, divided into essentially the same two sides as the race for the House six years earlier. The candidate, under the nominal managership of his brother and surrounded by a phalanx of energetic young men, carried the battle to the far corners of the state. Back in Boston, unseen but hard at work, were the specialists and professionals on the elder Kennedy's payroll. Those who slipped in and out of his suite at the Ritz-Carlton included Jim Landis; Lynn Johnson, a lawyer from the Kennedy headquarters in Manhattan; John Harriman, on leave from his job as a financial writer on the *Boston Globe,* and Sargent Shriver, formerly on the staff of *Newsweek* and more recently a dollar-a-year man at the Department of Justice, where he had assisted Eunice Kennedy in a study of juvenile delinquency. Many others also were active, coming forward as their talents were needed.

At work throughout Massachusetts were two hundred and eighty-six "secretaries," backed by an army of more than twenty thousand volunteers. Jack Kennedy had had no opposition in the Democratic primary, thus losing an opportunity to test-run his newly built machine, but he did require twenty-five hundred signatures on his nomination papers. Someone suggested the workers should be encouraged to get as many signatures as possible. They collected more than a hundred times the number required—a record 262,324. A measure of the money spent on the campaign was the fact that each person who signed received a thank-you letter.

The magnitude of the Kennedy publicity effort was staggering. Distributed across the state were nine hundred thousand copies of an eight-page tabloid featuring drawings of Lieutenant Kennedy rescuing his shipmates in the Pacific. On the facing page was a photograph of young Joe Kennedy, whose fatal war mission was described under this headline: "John Fulfills Dream of Brother Joe Who Met Death in the Sky Over the English Channel." Inserted in each paper was a *Reader's Digest* reprint of John Hersey's article on the saga of *PT-109,* which originally had appeared in *The New Yorker.*

Still, the most impressive feature in this vast campaign—indeed, the Kennedy hallmark—was painstaking attention to small detail. In June, Boston's Mayor John B. Hynes appeared at a rally at the Copley-Plaza launching Jack Kennedy's campaign. "The speeches were televised," Hynes later recalled, "and for the first time I saw a Teleprompter. In fact, there were *two* of them, and I wondered why." When one broke down and the other kept the show running smoothly, Hynes realized he was in the company of perfectionists. . . .

Through the campaign, those around Jack often doubted his ability to bear up physically. His spinal operation had failed to heal properly, and he was in almost constant pain. On his trip with Bobby and Pat in 1951, he had become seriously ill, and was flown to a military hospital on Okinawa with a temperature above 106 degrees. ("They didn't think he would live," Bobby later recalled.) Midway through the campaign, Jack was unable to move without crutches, but he refused to admit his body's weakness. "He hated to appear in public on his crutches," said a friend who traveled with him. "When we came to the door of a hall where he was to make a speech, he'd hand the crutches to one of us and throw his shoulders back and march down the aisle as straight as a West Point cadet. How he did it, I'll never know."

An unfailing source of strength was the support he received from his family. "Each Kennedy," a reporter once observed, "takes pride in the achievements of the others. Each, instinctively, had rather win the approval of the family than of outsiders. And when an outsider threatens to thwart the ambitions of any of them, the whole family forms a close-packed ring, horns lowered, like a herd of bison beset by wolves." Accused of being self-centered, the Kennedys also were respected for their remarkable solidarity. "I don't worry about Jack Kennedy. I don't worry about Kennedy's money," moaned a Lodge supporter. "It's that family of his . . . they're all over the state."

Lodge, who had been busy working for Eisenhower, belatedly recognized his peril and came hurrying back to Massachusetts two months before the election. By that time, members of the Kennedy family had shaken the hands of some two million voters. During the campaign, no fewer than thirty-three formal receptions were given, attended by an estimated seventy-five thousand persons, almost all of them women. Rose Kennedy came directly from Paris for the first reception, arriving from New York's Idlewild Airport in a chauffeured limousine. Jack's standard appeal was brief and boyish. "In the first place," he told the ladies, "for some strange reason, there are more women than men in Massachusetts, and they live longer. Secondly, my grandfather, the late John F. Fitzgerald, ran for the United States Senate thirty-six years ago against my opponent's grandfather, Henry Cabot Lodge, and he lost by only thirty thousand votes in an election where women were not allowed to vote. I hope that by impressing the female electorate I can more than take up the slack."

The handsome young congressman made a dazzling impression: an estimated 80 percent of his volunteer workers were signed up at the receptions. "What is there about Jack Kennedy," a Republican visitor was heard to ask, "that makes every Catholic girl in Boston between eighteen and twenty-eight think it's a holy crusade to get him elected?" Women of all ages were awed by the family's trappings of wealth and power. A veteran newspaperman cynically remarked that "it was all they could do to keep those old gals who came to the affairs from curtsying. They had every tendency to drop to one knee."

The candidate's brothers and sisters rang doorbells, made speeches, attended house parties, and twice appeared on a family television program, "Coffee with the Kennedys." But the star of the family campaign troupe turned out to be Rose. Jack's organization was weakest in Boston, and his father summoned a seasoned professional, State Senator John Powers, to take the situation in hand.

"I told him," said Powers, "that he was right about Boston. I said to him, 'Joe, the fight's falling off and it needs something to pick it up.' I asked him for permission to use Mrs. Kennedy. He answered, 'But Johnny, she's a grandmother!' "

" 'That's all right,' I told him, 'she's a Gold Star mother, the mother of a war hero and a congressman, the wife of an Ambassador, the daughter of a mayor and a congressman, the daughter-in-law of a state senator and representative and she's beautiful and she's a Kennedy. Let me have her.' And he thought it over and finally said, 'Well, take it slow with her.' "

Joe's concern was misplaced. The daughter of "Honey Fitz" knew exactly what to say and do, no matter what the audience. Before a group of Italian women in Boston's North End, she appeared as a girl who had grown up in the neighborhood, the mother of nine children. She greeted her audience with a few words of Italian, and then showed the card index file she had used to keep track of her children's illnesses, vaccinations, and dental work. She might wear a simple black dress and a single strand of pearls. In her limousine en route to a gathering of Chestnut Hill matrons, she would don jewelry and a mink stole, as befit the Ambassador's lady. After speaking for a few minutes about her son, Rose would say, "Now, let me tell you about the new dresses I saw in Paris last month."

On election night, the workers at Kennedy headquarters watched tensely as a year and a half of planning, and more than six months of unremitting effort, were put to the test. Hour by hour, the returns swayed back and forth. By early morning, it was clear that Eisenhower would sweep the state. Lodge might ride Ike's landslide to victory. But Jack Kennedy remained serene, never doubting that he would win. At six o'clock in the morning, Lodge conceded. The final returns showed that while Eisenhower was swamping Stevenson, and Dever was being narrowly defeated by Christian Herter for the governorship, Kennedy had pulled a stunning upset, defeating Lodge by more than seventy thousand votes.

Had Joe Kennedy bought his son's election? Many would argue that he had. Estimates of the Kennedy spending ran up to a wildly improbable several million dollars. It was true that Kennedy had outspent Lodge by a substantial margin. The various Kennedy committees, operating independently of the Democratic party fund-raising groups, officially reported expenses of just under $350,000. The whole cost of the Kennedy campaign was probably well above half a million dollars—how much above, no one would ever know. Officially, Lodge reported expenses of only $59,000. In addition, he benefited heavily from the Republican party's record million-dollar spending for the state ticket.

"It was those damned tea parties," Lodge said afterward. In a sense, he was right. He had been defeated by a young patrician whose rise was shared vicariously by thousands of Irish-Americans. Where their grandfathers had dreamed of awakening as Yankee overlords, now they might dream of becoming Kennedys. Into the family's victory went money, hard work, and a long, unforgiving memory. Said Rose Fitzgerald Kennedy following the election: "At last, the Fitzgeralds have evened the score with the Lodges!"

After his nomination as Democratic candidate for President in 1956, Adlai Stevenson broke precedent by declining to announce a preference for a running-mate. There ensued a tense and hard-fought battle for the post between Senators John F. Kennedy and Estes Kefauver. The outcome was still up in the air in the second ballot, when Tennessee suddenly switched its votes to Kefauver, thereby starting a movement whose momentum carried Kefauver to a majority and victory. Kennedy accepted his defeat gracefully, philosophically, and with the comforting knowledge that he had made a lasting impression on the nation's millions of television viewers. Historians agree in retrospect that, politically speaking, events turned out for the best for Kennedy, as the Democrats were decisively beaten at the polls that year. The following editorial discusses one very important aspect of John Kennedy's performance at the Chicago convention.

Senator Kennedy
and the Convention

from an editorial in AMERICA,
September 4, 1956

Those slack summer TV programs got some brisk competition in mid-August when the cameras turned to the spontaneous doings at Chicago. We shall soon forget the brass bands, the parades and the inflated periods of the keynote address. But it is not likely that TV viewers will forget those tense moments on August 16 when Senators John F. Kennedy and Estes Kefauver ran their breath-taking race for the Vice-Presidential nomination. This was the best of all the unrehearsed drama at Chicago.

Still young at 39, Senator Kennedy lost the race in a photo finish. He lost graciously, calmly and with dignity. He will un-doubtedly be heard from again, at or before the next national con-vention of the Democratic party.

Of recent weeks Mr. Kennedy's Catholic faith has been the starting point for discreet but prolonged speculation by politicians, newspapers and the general public. As votes piled up for the young Senator at the convention, few needed to be reminded that he is a Catholic. The entire country realized that his victory would have placed him—in these days of the heightened importance of the Vice Presidency—in much the same spot where the late Alfred E. Smith stood in 1928.

In a quick shift of votes at the height of this contest, Mr. Kennedy lost. But one thing seems sure. His religion was not a bar to his nomination. Nor, had he been nominated, would it have hindered his election. With states like Georgia and Texas pledging him their votes, it should have been clear to everyone that the rancors of the 1928 campaign are finally laid to rest. Now, of course, one can only guess at the added strength Mr. Kennedy's name and religious affiliation would or would not have given the Democrats next November, had he won out over the Senator from Tennessee. But there is no question that the choice was based on politics, not religion.

Perhaps religious sociologists will someday unravel the skeins of fears, misconceptions and prejudices which until now have made it so unlikely that a Catholic candidate should seriously aspire to the highest reaches of public office in the United States. The Ottawa *Journal*, a secular daily, remarked on this strange U.S. phenomenon a month before the convention, noting how odd it was that Mr. Kennedy's religion was making so many headlines on this side of the border. The *Journal* found Canada's record "strikingly in contrast," listed Canada's three Catholic Prime Ministers and five Catholic Chief Justices and pointed out that British Columbia and Nova Scotia, two of Canada's most Protestant and Anglo-Saxon provinces, have had Catholic premiers.

REMNANTS OF PREJUDICE

Oddly enough, though so few U.S. Catholics have in the past been even considered for the highest post in our Government, no one ever questions the fact that the political counsel and vote-getting ability of Catholics like James A. Farley, Carmine G. De Sapio, Paul M. Butler and James A. Finnigan are commodities to be called on every election year. What has perpetuated the unwritten law that an American Catholic can be a king-maker but never a king? The sociologists will have to puzzle that one out.

Now, however, the day of dreary discrimination is over. At times, of course, someone will turn out—as did the *Christian Century* on August 15—a musty pocket filled with old soiled prejudice and forgotten hatreds. But today that sort of thing is dated and indecent. The Chicago convention made this luminously clear.

The issue of John Kennedy's Catholicism was—regardless of justification—a major issue in the Presidential campaign of 1960. It had long since been brought largely into the open, but still remained unclarified, as vague rumors of a Washington subservient to the will of Rome began to gain the public ear toward the waning months of summer. This speech, delivered to the Greater Houston (Texas) Ministerial Association on September 12, 1960, put the issue in its proper perspective, and removed all doubts concerning Kennedy's religion and its bearing on the Presidency. It was a firm, honest, eloquent, and probably decisive address.

On Church and State

Remarks of Senator John F. Kennedy
Addressed to Greater Houston
Ministerial Association

Houston, Texas,
September 12, 1960

I am grateful for your generous invitation to state my views.

While the so-called religious issue is necessarily and properly the chief topic here tonight, I want to emphasize from the outset that I believe that we have far more critical issues in the 1960 election: the spread of Communist influence, until it now festers only ninety miles off the coast of Florida—the humiliating treatment of our President and Vice-President by those who no longer respect our power—the hungry children I saw in West Virginia, the old people who cannot pay their doctor's bills, the families forced to give up their farms—an America with too many slums, with too few schools, and too late to the moon and outer space.

These are the real issues which should decide this campaign.

And they are not religious issues—for war and hunger and ignorance and despair know no religious barrier.

But because I am a Catholic, and no Catholic has ever been elected President, the real issues in this campaign have been obscured—perhaps deliberately in some quarters less responsible than this. So it is apparently necessary for me to state once again—not what kind of church I believe in, for that should be important only to me, but what kind of America I believe in.

I believe in an America where the separation of church and state is absolute—where no Catholic prelate would tell the President (should he be a Catholic) how to act and no Protestant minister would tell his parishioners for whom to vote—where no church or church school is granted any public funds or political preference —and where no man is denied public office merely because his religion differs from the President who might appoint him or the people who might elect him.

I believe in an America that is officially neither Catholic, Protestant, nor Jewish—where no public official either requests or accepts instructions on public policy from the Pope, the National Council of Churches or any other ecclesiastical source—where no religious body seeks to impose its will directly or indirectly upon the general populace or the public acts of its officials—and where religious liberty is so indivisible that an act against one church is treated as an act against all.

For while this year it may be a Catholic against whom the finger of suspicion is pointed, in other years it has been, and may someday be again, a Jew—or a Quaker—or a Unitarian—or a Baptist. It was Virginia's harassment of Baptist preachers, for example, that led to Jefferson's statute of religious freedom. Today, I may be the victim—but tomorrow it may be you—until the whole fabric of our harmonious society is ripped apart at a time of great national peril.

Finally, I believe in an America where religious intolerance will someday end—where all men and all churches are treated as equal —where every man has the right to attend or not attend the church of his choice—where there is no Catholic vote, no bloc voting of any kind—and where Catholics, Protestants and Jews, at both the lay and the pastoral level, will refrain from those attitudes of disdain and division which have so often marred their works in the past, and promote instead the American ideal of brotherhood.

That is the kind of America in which I believe. And it represents the kind of Presidency in which I believe—a great office that must be neither humbled by making it the instrument of any religious group, nor tarnished by arbitrarily withholding it, its occupancy, from the members of any religious group. I believe in a President whose views on religion are his own private affair, neither imposed upon him by the nation nor imposed by the nation upon him as a condition to holding that office.

I would not look with favor upon a President working to subvert the First Amendment's guarantees of religious liberty (nor would our system of checks and balances permit him to do so). And neither do I look with favor upon those who would work to subvert Article VI of the Constitution by requiring a religious test—even by indirection—for if they disagree with that safeguard, they should be openly working to repeal it.

I want a chief executive whose public acts are responsible to all and obligated to none—who can attend any ceremony, service, or dinner his office may appropriately require him to fulfill—and whose fulfillment of his Presidential office is not limited or conditioned by any religious oath, ritual or obligation.

This is the kind of America I believe in—and this is the kind of America I fought for in the South Pacific and the kind my brother died for in Europe. No one suggested then that we might have a "divided loyalty," that we did "not believe in liberty" or that we belonged to a disloyal group that threatened "the freedoms for which our forefathers died."

And in fact this is the kind of America for which our forefathers did die when they fled here to escape religious test oaths that denied office to members of less favored churches, when they fought for the Constitution, the Bill of Rights, the Virginia Statute of Religious Freedom—and when they fought at the shrine I visited today—the Alamo. For side by side with Bowie and Crockett died Fuentes and McCafferty and Bailey and Bedillio and Carey— but no one knows whether they were Catholics or not. For there was no religious test there.

I ask you tonight to follow in that tradition, to judge me on the basis of fourteen years in the Congress—on my declared stands against an ambassador to the Vatican, against unconstitutional aid to parochial schools, and against any boycott of the public schools (which I attended myself)—instead of judging me on the basis of these pamphlets and publications we have all seen that carefully select quotations out of context from the statements of Catholic Church leaders, usually in other countries, frequently in other centuries, and rarely relevant to any situation here—and always omitting, of course, that statement of the American bishops in 1948 which strongly endorsed church-state separation.

I do not consider these other quotations binding upon my public acts—why should you? But let me say, with respect to other countries, that I am wholly opposed to the state being used by any religious group, Catholic or Protestant, to compel, prohibit or persecute the free exercise of any other religion. And that goes for any persecution at any time, by anyone, in any country.

And I hope that you and I condemn with equal fervor those nations which deny their Presidency to Protestants and those which deny it to Catholics. And rather than cite the misdeed of those who differ, I would also cite the record of the Catholic Church in such nations as France and Ireland—and the independence of such statesmen as De Gaulle and Adenauer.

But let me stress again that these are my views—for, contrary to common newspaper usage, I am not the Catholic candidate for President. I am the Democratic Party's candidate for President, who happens also to be a Catholic.

I do not speak for my church on public matters—and the church does not speak for me.

Whatever issue may come before me as President, if I should

be elected—on birth control, divorce, censorship, gambling, or any other subject—I will make my decision in accordance with these views, in accordance with what my conscience tells me to be in the national interest, and without regard to outside religious pressure or dictate. And no power or threat of punishment could cause me to decide otherwise.

But if the time should ever come—and I do not concede any conflict to be remotely possible—when my office would require me to either violate my conscience, or violate the national interest, then I would resign the office, and I hope any other conscientious public servant would do likewise.

But I do not intend to apologize for these views to my critics of either Catholic or Protestant faith, nor do I intend to disavow either my views or my church in order to win this election. If I should lose on the real issues, I shall return to my seat in the Senate, satisfied that I tried my best and was fairly judged.

But if this election is decided on the basis that 40,000,000 Americans lost their chance of being President on the day they were baptized, then it is the whole nation that will be the loser in the eyes of Catholics and non-Catholics around the world, in the eyes of history, and in the eyes of our own people.

But if, on the other hand, I should win this election, I shall devote every effort of mind and spirit to fulfilling the oath of the Presidency—practically identical, I might add, with the oath I have taken for fourteen years in the Congress. For, without reservation, I can, and I quote, "solemnly swear that I will faithfully execute the office of President of the United States and will to the best of my ability preserve, protect and defend the Constitution, so help me God."

from The Kennedy Wit

by Bill Adler

I want to say that I have been in on-the-job training for about eleven months and feel that I have some seniority rights.

I am delighted to be here with you and with the Secretary of Labor, Arthur Goldberg. I was up in New York, stressing physical fitness, and in line with that, Arthur went over with a group to Switzerland to climb some of the mountains there. They got up about five and he was in bed. He got up to join them later and when they all came back at four o'clock in the afternoon he didn't come back with them.

So they sent out search parties and there was not a sign that afternoon and night. The next day the Red Cross went out and

around, calling: "Goldberg, Goldberg! It's the Red Cross!" Then
this voice came down from the mountain: "I gave at the office!"
Those are the liberties you can take with members of the cabinet.

AFL-CIO Convention
Bal Harbour, Florida
December 7, 1961

from

Kennedy

by Theodore C. Sorensen

Chapter **XXIII**
The Continuing Crisis

*Theodore Sorensen was John F. Kennedy's first appointee
as President. In his capacity as Special Counsel, Sorensen
was as close to the President during the whole of his
Administration as any man could be. He knew Kennedy well,
having served with him since 1953 as legislative assistant,
advisor, and "intellectual blood-bank." In the section that
follows, Sorensen recounts and analyzes the President's
thoughts and decisions on the knotty problem of South Vietnam.*

It was not possible for John Kennedy to organize his approach to
foreign affairs as arbitrarily as the chapters of this or any book.
Military conflicts required more than military solutions. The Com-

munists exploited genuine non-Communist grievances. The problems of aid and trade, the need for conventional and unconventional forces, the roles of allies and neutrals, all were tangled together. Nowhere were these interrelationships more complex than in those situations in the new and developing nations which Khrushchev somewhat hypocritically called "wars of liberation." The extent of U.S. commitment and of Communist power involvement differed from one to the other, but the dilemma facing John Kennedy in each one was essentially the same: how to disengage the Russians from the "liberation" movement and prevent a Communist military conquest without precipitating a major Soviet-American military confrontation.

On Inauguration Day, 1961, three such dilemmas were on Kennedy's desk, with dire predictions of catastrophe before the year was out: the Congo, Laos and South Vietnam. In none of these cases were those predictions fulfilled, even by the end of Kennedy's term. Supporting the UN in the Congo, seeking a neutral coalition in Laos and trying to broaden the political appeal of the local regime in Vietnam, he rejected the purely militaristic and automatically anti-Communist answer to pursue more meaningful objectives in all three countries. While these objectives also remained unfulfilled, their conflicts were at least adequately managed and confined, partly because of his growing grasp of their nonmilitary implications, partly because the Sino-Soviet split restrained as well as aggravated these situations, and partly because of the lessons John Kennedy had learned since the Bay of Pigs. . . .

VIETNAM

Life was certainly uncertain and full of hazard next door to Laos in South Vietnam. There the prospects of a final, easy answer were even more remote. Unlike Laos, Vietnam was a highly populated and productive country ruled by a central government determined to oppose all Communist aggression and subversion. Unlike the often farcical battles in Laos, the war in Vietnam was brutal on both sides, and the government forces—despite a lack of imaginative and energetic leadership—were sizable, engaged in actual combat and dying in large numbers for their country. Unlike their situation in Laos, the great powers were more firmly committed on both sides in Vietnam, and the struggle was over not merely control of the government but the survival of the nation.

Kennedy's basic objective in Vietnam, however, was essentially the same as in Laos and the rest of Southeast Asia. He sought neither a cold war pawn nor a hot war battleground. He did not insist that South Vietnam maintain Western bases or membership in a Western alliance. As in Laos, his desire was to halt a Communist-sponsored guerrilla war and to permit the local population peacefully to choose its own future. But South Vietnam was too weak to stand alone; and any attempt to neutralize that nation in 1961 like Laos, at a time when the Communists had the upper hand in the fighting, and were the most forceful element in the South as well as the North, would have left the South Vietnamese defenseless against externally supported Communist domination. The neutralization of both North and South Vietnam had been envisioned by the 1954 Geneva Accords. But when a return to that solution was proposed by Rusk to Gromyko, the latter not surprisingly replied that the North was irrevocably a part of the "socialist camp."

We would not stay in Southeast Asia against the wishes of any local government, the President often said. But apart from that local government's interest, free-world security also had a stake in our staying there. A major goal of Red China's policy was to drive from Southeast Asia—indeed, from all Asia—the last vestiges of Western power and influence, the only effective counter to her own hegemony. Southeast Asia, with its vast population, resources and strategic location,[1] would be a rich prize for the hungry Chinese. Kennedy, as shown by his reversal of our policy in Laos, saw no need to maintain American outposts in the area. The Kennedy Southeast Asia policy respected the neutrality of all who wished to be neutral. But it also insisted that other nations similarly respect

---

[1] Lying across the air and sea lanes between the Pacific and Indian oceans, it had served as a staging area in World War II for Japanese attacks on the Philippines.

that neutrality, withdraw their troops and abide by negotiated settlements and boundaries, thus leaving each neutral free to choose and
fulfill its own future within the framework of its own culture and
traditions. To the extent that this required a temporary U.S. military presence, American and Communist objectives conflicted. The
cockpit in which that conflict was principally tested was hapless
South Vietnam, but neither Kennedy nor the Communists believed
that the consequences of success or failure in that country would be
confined to Vietnam alone. . . .

In 1961 all the evidence was not yet in on the extent to which
the antigovernment forces in the South were the creatures of the
Communist North. But it was reasonably clear that many of them
were trained in the North, armed and supplied by the North, and
infiltrated from the North through the Laotian corridors, across the
densely wooded frontier and by sea. The North supplied them with
backing, brains and a considerable degree of coordination and control. Their food and shelter were largely provided at night by South
Vietnamese villagers, who were sometimes wooed—with promises
of land, unification and an end to political corruption, repression
and foreign troops—and sometimes terrorized, with demonstrations
of kidnaping, murder and plunder, before the guerrillas vanished
back into the jungle at daybreak. A considerable portion of the
insurgents' arms, American-made, were captured from the South
Vietnamese forces.

By early 1961 these "Vietcong" guerrillas, as they were labeled
by the government in Saigon, were gradually bleeding South Vietnam to death, destroying its will to resist, eroding its faith in the
future, and paralyzing its progress through systematic terror against
the already limited number of local officials, teachers, health workers,
agricultural agents, rural police, priests, village elders and even
ordinary villagers who refused to cooperate. Favorite targets for
destruction included schools, hospitals, agricultural research sta-
tions and malaria control centers.

The Eisenhower administration—in the creation of SEATO, in
statements to President Diem and in commenting on the 1954

Geneva Accords—had pledged in 1954 and again in 1957 to help resist any "aggression or subversion threatening the political independence of the Republic of Vietnam." Military as well as economic assistance had begun in 1954. This country in that year drew the line against Communist expansion at the border of South Vietnam. Whether or not it would have been wiser to draw it in a more stable and defensible area in the first place, this nation's commitment in January, 1961—although it had assumed far larger proportions than when it was made nearly seven years earlier—was not one that President Kennedy felt he could abandon without undesirable consequences throughout Asia and the world.

Unfortunately he inherited in Vietnam more than a commitment and a growing conflict. He also inherited a foreign policy which had identified America in the eyes of Asia with dictators, CIA intrigue and a largely military response to revolution. He inherited a military policy which had left us wholly unprepared to fight—or even to train others to fight—a war against local guerrillas. Our military mission had prepared South Vietnam's very sizable army for a Korean-type invasion, training it to move in division or battalion strength by highways instead of jungle trails. Nor had the United States encouraged a build-up in the local Civil Guard and Self-defense Corps which bore the brunt of the guerrilla attacks.

Under Kennedy the earlier commitment to South Vietnam was not only carried out but, as noted below, reinforced by a vast expansion of effort. The principal responsibility for that expansion belongs not with Kennedy but with the Communists, who, beginning in the late 1950's, vastly expanded their efforts to take over the country. The dimensions of our effort also had to be increased, unfortunately, to compensate for the political weaknesses of the Diem regime.

In that sense, Eisenhower, Ho Chi Minh and Ngo Dinh Diem all helped to shape John Kennedy's choices in Vietnam. His essential contribution—which is reviewed here as the situation then appeared, not to pass judgment on subsequent developments—was both to raise our commitment and to keep it limited. He neither permitted the war's escalation into a general war nor bargained away Vietnam's security at the conference table, despite being pressed along both lines by those impatient to win or withdraw. His strategy essentially was to avoid escalation, retreat or a choice limited to those two, while seeking to buy time—time to make the policies and programs of both the American and Vietnamese governments more appealing to the villagers—time to build an anti-guerrilla capability sufficient to convince the Communists that they could not seize the country militarily—and time to put the Vietnamese themselves in a position to achieve the settlement only they could achieve by bringing terrorism under control.

That it would be a long, bitter and frustrating interval he had no doubt. Ultimately a negotiated settlement would be required. But the whole fight was essentially over a return to the basic principles (if not the letter) of an earlier negotiated settlement, the Geneva Accords of 1954. The North Vietnamese and Chinese showed no interest in any fair and enforceable settlement they did not dictate; and they would show no interest, the President was convinced, until they were persuaded that continued aggression would be frustrated and unprofitable. Any other settlement would merely serve as a confirmation of the benefits of aggression and as a cover for American withdrawal. It would cause the world to wonder about the reliability of this nation's pledges, expose to vengeance all South Vietnamese (and particularly those the U. S. had persuaded to stand by their country) and encourage the Communists to repeat the same tactics against the "paper tiger" Americans in Thailand, Malaysia and elsewhere in Asia—until finally Kennedy or some successor would be unalterably faced with the choice he hoped to avoid: withdrawal or all-out war.

Almost immediately upon his assumption of office, Kennedy created a State-Defense-CIA-USIA-White House task force to prepare detailed recommendations in Vietnam. Those recommendations were considered in late April and early May of 1961 simultaneously with the Joint Chiefs' recommendations for intervening in Laos. The two reports, in fact, resembled and were related to each other.

Both called for a commitment of American combat troops to Vietnam.

The President—his skepticism deepened by the Bay of Pigs experience and the holes in the Laos report—once again wanted more questions answered and more alternatives presented. The military proposals for Vietnam, he said, were based on assumptions and predictions that could not be verified—on help from Laos and Cambodia to halt infiltration from the North, on agreement by Diem to reorganizations in his army and government, on more popular support for Diem in the countryside and on sealing off Communist supply routes. Estimates of both time and cost were either absent or wholly unrealistic.

Finally, a more limited program was approved. The small contingent of American military advisers was tripled, with officers assigned at the battalion level as well as to regiments, to advise in combat as well as training and to aid in unconventional as well as conventional warfare. American logistic support was increased, and money and instructors were made available to augment the size of South Vietnam's Civil Guard and Self-defense Forces as well as her army. To demonstrate his support, to obtain an independent first-hand report and to make clear to Diem his insistence that Diem's own efforts be improved, the President dispatched Vice President Johnson on a tour of Southeast Asia, including a lengthy stopover at Saigon.

But throughout 1961 the situation in Vietnam continued to deteriorate. The area ruled by guerrilla tactics and terror continued to grow. American instructors—accompanying Vietnamese forces in battle and instructed to fire if fired upon—were being killed in small but increasing numbers. The Vice President's report urged that the battle against Communism be joined in Southeast Asia with strength and determination. The key to what is done by Asians, he said, is confidence in the United States, in our power, our will and our understanding. In late October a new high-level mission to Vietnam, headed by Maxwell Taylor and Walt Rostow, visited Vietnam preparatory to a major Presidential review.

A new set of recommendations proposed a series of actions by the American and Vietnamese governments. Once again, the most difficult was the commitment of American combat troops. South Vietnam's forces already outnumbered the enemy by ten to one, it was estimated, and far more could be mobilized. But many believed that American troops were needed less for their numerical strength than for the morale and will they could provide to Diem's forces and for the warning they would provide to the Communists. The President was not satisfied on either point. He was unwilling to commit American troops to fighting Asians on the Asian mainland for speculative psychological reasons.

Nevertheless, at this moment more than any other, the pressures upon the President to make that commitment were at a peak. All his principal advisers on Vietnam favored it, calling it the "touchstone" of our good faith, a symbol of our determination. But the President in effect voted "no"—and only his vote counted.

The key to his "vote" could be found in his speech on the Senate floor on the French-Indochinese War on the sixth of April, 1954:

> . . . unilateral action by our own country . . . without participation by the armed forces of the other nations of Asia, without the support of the great masses of the peoples [of Vietnam] . . . and, I might add, with hordes of Chinese Communist troops poised just across the border in anticipation of our unilateral entry into their kind of battleground—such intervention, Mr. President, would be virtually impossible in the type of military situation which prevails in Indochina . . . an enemy which is everywhere and at the same time nowhere, "an enemy of the people" which has the sympathy and covert support of the people.

That year he had watched the French, with a courageous, well-equipped army numbering hundreds of thousands, suffer a humiliating defeat and more than ninety thousand casualties. Now the choice was his. If the United States took over the conduct of the war on the ground, he asked, would that not make it easier for the

Communists to say we were the neo-colonialist successors of the French? Would we be better able to win support of the villagers and farmers—so essential to guerrilla warfare—than Vietnamese troops of the same color and culture? No one knew whether the South Vietnamese officers would be encouraged or resentful, or whether massive troop landings would provoke a massive Communist invasion—an invasion inevitably leading either to nuclear war, Western retreat or an endless and exhausting battle on the worst battleground he could choose.

What was needed, Kennedy agreed with his advisers, was a major counterinsurgency effort—the first ever mounted by this country. South Vietnam could supply the necessary numbers—and would have to supply the courage and will to fight, for no outsider could supply that. But the United States could supply better training, support and direction, better communications, transportation and intelligence, better weapons, equipment and logistics—all of which the South Vietnamese needed, said his advisers, if they were to reorient their effort to fight guerrilla battles.

Formally, Kennedy never made a final negative decision on troops. In typical Kennedy fashion, he made it difficult for any of the prointervention advocates to charge him privately with weakness. He ordered the departments to be prepared for the introduction of combat troops, should they prove to be necessary. He steadily expanded the size of the military assistance mission (2,000 at the end of 1961, 15,500 at the end of 1963) by sending in combat support units, air combat and helicopter teams, still more military advisers and instructors and 600 of the greenhatted Special Forces to train and lead the South Vietnamese in antiguerrilla tactics. . . .

Kennedy recognized far more clearly than most of his advisers that military action alone could not save Vietnam. As a congressman back from Indochina in 1951, he had warned that the southward drive of Communism required its opponents to build "strong native non-Communist sentiment within these areas and rely on that as a spearhead of defense rather than upon . . . force of arms." As a Senator in 1954, he had cited the dangers and inaccuracies inherent in the long years of assurances given by French and American officials that the Vietnamese people were truly free and independent.

But as President, unfortunately, his effort to keep our own military role in Vietnam from overshadowing our political objectives was handicapped by the State Department's inability to compete with the Pentagon. The task force report in the spring of 1961, for example, had focused almost entirely on military planning. A five-year economic plan, "a long-range plan for the economic development of Southeast Asia on a regional basis," a diplomatic appeal to the United Nations and other miscellaneous ideas were somewhat vaguely and loosely thrown in to please the President. But there was no concrete definition of the civil effort essential to the success of the military effort, nor was there in the months and years that followed. Economic aid and a rural rehabilitation program were increased. But the guerrillas kept much of the countryside too frightened or hostile to cooperate, repeatedly ambushed health and education workers, and burned schools and other government centers. "You cannot carry out a land reform program," Secretary McNamara said, "if the local peasant leaders are being systematically murdered." No amount of social and economic assistance in South Vietnam would end the ambitions of North Vietnam. American assistance, moreover, was not accompanied by the internal reforms required to make it effective.

A full-scale articulation by the President of this country's long-range political and economic aims for Southeast Asia might have strengthened this neglected nonmilitary side of his Vietnam policy. The Taylor report recommended a major television address. But unwilling to give Vietnam a status comparable to Berlin, the President chose to keep quiet. Even his news conference statements on Vietnam were elusive. Moreover, the new military efforts mounted in late 1961 and early 1962 seemed initially to be paying off. The rapid disintegration taking place in the fall of 1961 was stemmed, especially in the coastal provinces where the Vietcong had threatened to cut the country in two. American helicopters in particular provided a new and effective challenge to the guerrillas. From time to time the building of U. S. forces in the area continued, particularly with the addition of more airpower early in 1963. The President hopefully reported to the Congress in January of that year that "the spear point of aggression has been blunted in Vietnam."

In fact, the neglected civilian side of the effort had already begun to handicap the military side, and in 1963 these handicaps would become evident. Taylor's 1961 report had warned Kennedy —and Kennedy had politely warned Diem—that the people around the Presidential palace in Saigon were often corrupt and ambitious, that Diem's army was weakened by politics and preference, that his treatment of political opponents had stifled the nation's nationalism and that Diem's own lack of popularity in the countryside was handicapping antiguerrilla efforts. The ever suspicious and stubborn Diem had promised reform, but few reforms were forthcoming. American military advice was requested, but it was still often disregarded—in an overexpansion, for example, of the "strategic hamlet" program which sought to clear areas of all guerrillas and then protect the inhabitants in newly constructed and fortified settlements. Antiguerrilla tactics were taught but ignored. Funds were sought for additional Vietnamese battalions, but those battalions were too stationary, too cautious about going out to meet the enemy. Diem and his family still meddled deeply in army politics.

As President Diem became more and more remote from the people, his government was increasingly dominated by an increasingly unbalanced man, the President's brother, Ngo Dinh Nhu. The Catholic Diem, his brother and his brother's wife—the sharp-tongued Madam Nhu—were accused of religious persecution by powerful Buddhist leaders, many of whom for political reasons fanned small instances of personal discrimination into national crises.

In mid-1963 the picture worsened rapidly. Diem's troops broke up a demonstration of Buddhists protesting a ban on their banner. Nhu's Special Forces raided Buddhist pagodas. Pictures of Buddhist monks burning themselves to death in protest—as well as Madame Nhu's cruel remarks on the "barbecue show" sacrifice of "so-called holy men"—brought calls in Congress to cut off all aid. Vietnamese students rioted against the government. Officials not personally committed to the family—including Madame Nhu's father, the Ambassador to Washington—resigned in protest against new repressions. The maintenance of internal security, employing the most arbitrary means and the most valuable troops, began to occupy the full attention of the shaky Diem regime. The prosecution of the war inevitably faltered. Nhu was reported ready to make a secret deal with the North, and both he and his wife publicly castigated the United States for its efforts to broaden the government and get back to the war.

The religious persecutions deeply offended John Kennedy. "Human . . . rights are not respected," he pointedly said in his September, 1963, UN speech, "when a Buddhist priest is driven from his pagoda." He further bristled when brother Nhu, angered at American interference, said publicly there were too many U. S. troops in Vietnam. "Any time the government of South Vietnam would suggest it," said the President, "the day after it was suggested we would have some troops on their way home." But while publicly deploring "repressive actions," he at first paid too little attention to those members of the Congress and American press— particularly the heavily restricted correspondents in Saigon—who complained that we were aiding a dictator. He had generally been more careful than his subordinates to talk of our support for the aspirations of the country, not the individual regime. But sometimes the national security required this country to aid dictators, particularly in the newer nations unprepared for true democracy. He knew that we were dangerously dependent on one man, but there was no simple way to force a broadening of that man's government or the development of more representative civilian leaders without endangering the entire war efforts.

By late summer, 1963, he had become more concerned. Growing disunity and disorder within the non-Communist camp in

Saigon further handicapped the national war effort. Countering guerrilla warfare, as he had stressed in 1961, was more of a political than a military problem; and a government incapable of effective political action and popular reform would continue to lose ground steadily throughout the country.

In a long letter to Diem, the President reviewed frankly the troubled relations between the two governments. Some of the methods used by some members of your government, he wrote Diem, may make it impossible to sustain public support in Vietnam for the struggle against the Communists. Unless there can be important changes and improvements in the apparent relation between the government and the people in your country, he added, American public and Congressional opinion will make it impossible to continue without change their joint efforts. American cooperation and American assistance will not be given, he stressed, to or through individuals whose acts and words seem to run against the purpose of genuine reconciliation and unified national effort against the Communists. . . .

Kennedy's advisers were more deeply divided on the internal situation in Saigon than on any previous issue. The State Department, by and large, reported that the political turmoil had seriously interfered with the war effort outside of Saigon, and that one of the many coups rumored almost weekly was certain to succeed if we kept hands off. The military and the CIA, on the other hand, spoke confidently of the war's prosecution and Diem's leadership, and questioned the likelihood of finding any equally able leader with the confidence of the people who could prosecute the war as vigorously.

There were bitter disputes, with each side often trying to commit the President in the other's absence. As a result recommendations to the President differed sharply regarding the continuing or conditioning of our aid and what changes should be sought in the regime. Whichever way he turned—continuing to support Diem or interfering in his internal affairs—Kennedy foresaw the United States losing respect in the eyes of many Vietnamese. Through a series of meetings (and missions to Saigon) in September and October, he hoped to move the administration away from its total dependence on Diem without causing South Vietnam to fall or his own team to split wide open.

Finally, on November 1, 1963, as corruption, repression and disorder increased, a new effort by the Vietnamese military to take command of the government was launched and succeeded. It received no assistance from the United States, nor did this country do anything to prevent or defeat it. While all the reports of all the various plots and proposed coups had regularly reached American ears, neither the timing nor the scale of this one was known in the U.S. when it was launched (much less to Kennedy, who had previously planned for Lodge to be out of Saigon at that time reporting to Washington). The generals seized control of the government and assassinated Diem and Nhu, who had refused the offer of sanctuary in the American Embassy.

Kennedy was shaken that Diem should come to such an end after his long devotion to his country, whatever his other deficiencies, remarking that Diem's bitterest foes, the Communists, had never gone that far. An uncertain military junta took over in Saigon. The new leaders had no more deep-rooted popularity or administrative skill than their predecessors. Constant top-to-bottom changes in personnel, to be succeeded in time by still more changes, further impaired whatever momentum and morale were left in the war effort, and permitted still further Communist gains.

Obviously, then, in November of 1963 no early end to the Vietnam war was in sight. The President, while eager to make clear that our aim was to get out of Vietnam, had always been doubtful about the optimistic reports constantly filed by the military on the progress of the war. In his Senate floor speech of 1954, he had criticized French and American generals for similar "predictions of confidence which have lulled the American people." The Communists, he knew, would have no difficulty recruiting enough guerrillas to prolong the fighting for many years. The struggle could well be, he thought, this nation's severest test of endurance and patience. At times he compared it to the long struggles against guerrillas in Greece, Malaya and the Philippines. Yet at least he had a major counterguerrilla effort under way, with a comparatively small commitment of American manpower. He was simply going to weather it out, a nasty, untidy mess to which there was no other acceptable solution. Talk of abandoning so unstable an ally and so costly a commitment "only makes it easy for the Communists," said the President. "I think we should stay."

He could show little gain in that situation to pass on to his successor, either in the military outlook or the progress toward reform. His own errors had not helped. But if asked why he had increased this nation's commitment, he might have summed up his stand with the words used by William Pitt when asked in the House of Commons in 1805 what was gained by the war against France: "We have gained everything that we would have lost if we had not fought this war." In the case of Vietnam, that was a lot. . . .

Address to the General Assembly of the United Nations

New York
September 25, 1961

Mr. President [Mongi Slim], *honored delegates, ladies and gentlemen:*

We meet in an hour of grief and challenge. Dag Hammarskjold is dead. But the United Nations lives. His tragedy is deep in our hearts, but the task for which he died is at the top of our agenda. A noble servant of peace is gone. But the quest for peace lies before us.

The problem is not the death of one man—the problem is the life of this organization. It will either grow to meet the challenges of our age, or it will be gone with the wind, without influence, without force, without respect. Were we to let it die, to enfeeble its vigor, to cripple its powers, we would condemn our future.

For in the development of this organization rests the only true alternative to war—and war appeals no longer as a rational alternative. Unconditional war can no longer lead to unconditional victory. It can no longer serve to settle disputes. It can no longer concern the great powers alone. For a nuclear disaster, spread by wind and water and fear, could well engulf the great and the small, the rich and the poor, the committed and the uncommitted alike. Man must put an end to war—or war will put an end to mankind.

So let us here resolve that Dag Hammarskjold did not live, or die, in vain. Let us call a truce to terror. Let us invoke the blessings of peace. And, as we build an international capacity to keep peace, let us join in dismantling the national capacity to wage war.

II.

This will require new strength and new roles for the United Nations. For disarmament without checks is but a shadow—and a community without law is but a shell. Already the United Nations has become both the measure and the vehicle of man's most generous impulses. Already it has provided—in the Middle East, in Asia, in Africa this year in the Congo—a means of holding man's violence within bounds.

But the great question which confronted this body in 1945 is still before us: whether man's cherished hopes for progress and peace are to be destroyed by terror and disruption, whether the "foul winds of war" can be tamed in time to free the cooling winds of reason, and whether the pledges of our Charter are to be fulfilled or defied—pledges to secure peace, progress, human rights and world law.

In this hall, there are not three forces, but two. One is composed of those who are trying to build the kind of world described in Articles I and II of the Charter. The other, seeking a far different world, would undermine this organization in the process.

Today of all days our dedication to the Charter must be maintained. It must be strengthened first of all by the selection of an outstanding civil servant to carry forward the responsibilities of the Secretary General—a man endowed with both the wisdom and the power to make meaningful the moral force of the world community. The late Secretary General nurtured and sharpened the United Nations' obligation to act. But he did not invent it. It was there in the Charter. It is still there in the Charter.

However difficult it may be to fill Mr. Hammarskjold's place, it can better be filled by one man rather than three. Even the three horses of Troika did not have three drivers, all going in different directions. They had only one—and so must the United Nations executive. To install a triumvirate, or any panel, or any rotating authority, in the United Nations administrative offices would replace order with anarchy, action with paralysis, confidence with confusion. . . .

III.

Today, every inhabitant of this planet must contemplate the day when this planet may no longer be habitable. Every man, woman and child lives under a nuclear sword of Damocles, hanging by the slenderest of threads, capable of being cut at any moment by accident or miscalculation or by madness. The weapons of war must be abolished before they abolish us.

Men no longer debate whether armaments are a symptom or a cause of tension. The mere existence of modern weapons—ten million times more powerful than any that the world has ever seen, and only minutes away from any target on earth—is a source of horror, and discord and distrust. Men no longer maintain that disarmament must await the settlement of all disputes—for disarmament must be a part of any permanent settlement. And men may no longer pretend that the quest for disarmament is a sign of weakness—for in a spiraling arms race, a nation's security may well be shrinking even as its arms increase.

For 15 years this organization has sought the reduction and destruction of arms. Now that goal is no longer a dream—it is a practical matter of life or death. The risks inherent in disarmament pale in comparison to the risks inherent in an unlimited arms race.

It is in this spirit that the recent Belgrade Conference—recognizing that this is no longer a Soviet problem or an American problem, but a human problem—endorsed a program of "general, complete, and strictly an internationally controlled disarmament." It is in this same spirit that we in the United States have labored this year, with a new urgency, and with a new, now statutory agency fully endorsed by the Congress to find an approach to disarmament which would be so far-reaching yet realistic, so mutually balanced and beneficial, that it could be accepted by every nation. And it is in this spirit that we have presented with the agreement of the Soviet Union—under the label both nations now accept of "general and complete disarmament"—a new statement of newly agreed principles for negotiation.

But we are well aware that all issues of principle are not settled, and that principles alone are not enough. It is therefore our intention to challenge the Soviet Union, not to an arms race, but to a peace race—to advance together step by step, stage by stage, until general and complete disarmament has been achieved. We invite them now to go beyond agreement in principle to reach agreement on actual plans.

The program to be presented to this assembly—for general and complete disarmament under effective international control—moves to bridge the gap between those who insist on a gradual approach and those who talk only of the final and total achievement. It would create machinery to keep the peace as it destroys the machinery of war. It would proceed through balanced and safeguarded stages designed to give no state a military advantage over another. It would place the final responsibility for verification and control where it belongs, not with the big powers alone, not with one's adversary or one's self, but in an international organization within the framework of the United Nations. It would assure that indispensable condition of disarmament—true inspection—and apply it in stages proportionate to the stage of disarmament. It would cover delivery systems as well as weapons. It would ultimately halt their production as well as their testing, their transfer as well as their possession. It would achieve, under the eyes of an international disarmament organization, a steady reduction in force, both nuclear and conventional, until it has abolished all armies and all weapons except those needed for internal order and a new United Nations Peace Force. And it starts that process now, today, even as the talks begin.

In short, general and complete disarmament must no longer be a slogan, used to resist the first steps. It is no longer to be a goal without means of achieving it, without means of verifying its progress, without means of keeping the peace. It is now a realistic plan, and a test—a test of those only willing to act.

Such a plan would not bring a world free from conflict and greed—but it would bring a world free from the terrors of mass destruction. It would not usher in the era of the super state—but it would usher in an era in which no state could annihilate or be annihilated by another. . . .

IV.

The logical place to begin is a treaty assuring the end of nuclear tests of all kinds, in every environment, under workable controls. The United States and the United Kingdom have proposed such a treaty that is both reasonable and effective, and it is ready for signature. We are still prepared to sign that treaty today.

We also proposed a mutual ban on atmospheric testing, without inspection or controls, in order to save the human race from the poison of raidoactive fallout. We regret that that offer has not been accepted.

For 15 years we have sought to make the atom an instrument of peaceful growth rather than of war. But for 15 years our concessions have been matched by obstruction, our patience by intransigence. And the pleas of mankind for peace have met with disregard.

Finally, as the explosions of others beclouded the skies, my country was left with no alternative but to act in the interests of its own and the free world's security. We cannot endanger that security by refraining from testing while others improve their arsenals. Nor can we endanger it by another long, uninspected ban on testing. For three years we accepted those risks in our open society while seeking agreement on inspection. But this year, while we were negotiating in good faith in Geneva, others were secretly preparing new experiments in destruction.

Our tests are not polluting the atmosphere. Our deterrent weapons are guarded against accidental explosion or use. Our doctors and scientists stand ready to help any nation measure and meet the hazards to health which inevitably result from the tests in the atmosphere.

But to halt the speed of these terrible weapons, to halt the contamination of the air, to halt the spiralling nuclear arms race, we remain ready to seek new avenues of agreement; our new Disarmament Program thus includes the following proposals:

—First, signing the test-ban treaty by all nations. This can be done now. Test-ban negotiations need not and should not await general disarmament.

—Second, stopping the production of fissionable materials for use in weapons, and preventing their transfer to any nation now lacking in nuclear weapons.

—Third, prohibiting the transfer of control over nuclear weapons to states that do not own them.

—Fourth, keeping nuclear weapons from seeding new battlegrounds in outer space.

—Fifth, gradually destroying existing nuclear weapons and converting their materials to peaceful uses; and

—Finally, halting the unlimited testing and production of strategic nuclear delivery vehicles, and gradually destroying them as well.

V.

To destroy arms, however, is not enough. We must create even as we destroy—creating a worldwide law and law enforcement as we outlaw worldwide war and weapons. In the world we seek, the United Nations Emergency Forces which have been hastily assembled, uncertainly supplied, and inadequately financed will never be enough.

Therefore, the United States recommends that all member nations earmark special peace-keeping units in their armed forces— to be on call of the United Nations, to be specially trained and quickly available, and with advance provision for financial and logistic support. . . .

VI.

As we extend the rule of law on earth, so must we also extend it to man's new domain—outer space.

All of us salute the brave cosmonauts of the Soviet Union. The new horizons of outer space must not be driven by the old bitter concepts of imperialism and sovereign claims. The cold reaches of the universe must not become the new arena of an even colder war.

To this end we shall urge proposals extending the United Nations Charter to the limits of man's exploration in the universe, reserving outer space for peaceful use, prohibiting weapons of mass destruction in space or on celestial bodies, and opening the mysteries and benefits of space to every nation. We shall propose further cooperative efforts between all nations in weather prediction and eventually in weather control.

We shall propose, finally, a global system of communications satellites linking the whole world in telegraph and telephone and radio and television. The day need not be far away when such a system will televise the proceedings of this body to every corner of the world for the benefit of peace.

VII.

But the mysteries of outer space must not divert our eyes or our energies from the harsh realities that face our fellow men. Political sovereignty is but a mockery without the means of meeting poverty and illiteracy and disease. Self-determination is but a slogan if the future holds no hope.

That is why my Nation, which has freely shared its capital and its technology to help others help themselves, now proposes officially designating this decade of the 1960's as the United Nations Decade of Development. Under the framework of that Resolution, the United Nations' existing efforts in promoting economic growth can be expanded and coordinated. Regional surveys and training institutes can now pool the talents of many. New research, technical assistance and pilot projects can unlock the wealth of less developed lands and untapped waters. And development can become a cooperative and not a competitive enterprise—to enable all nations, however diverse in their systems and beliefs, to become in fact as well as in law equal nations.

VIII.

My country favors a world of free and equal states. We agree with those who say that colonialism is a key issue in this Assembly. But let the full facts of that issue be discussed in full.

On the one hand is the fact that, since the close of World War II, a worldwide declaration of independence has transformed nearly 1 billion people and 9 million square miles into 42 free and independent states. Less than two percent of the world's population now lives in "dependent" territories.

I do not ignore the remaining problems of traditional colonialism which still confront this body. Those problems will be solved, with patience, good will, and determination. Within the limits of our responsibility in such matters, my Country intends to be a participant and not merely an observer in the peaceful, expeditious movement of nations from the status of colonies to the partnership of equals. That continuing tide of self-determination, which runs so strong, has our sympathy and our support.

But colonialism in its harshest forms is not only the exploitation of new nations by old, of dark skins by light, or the subjugation of the poor by the rich; my Nation was once a colony, and we know what colonialism means: The exploitation and subjugation of the weak by the powerful, of the many by the few, of the governed who have given no consent to be governed, whatever their continent, their class, or their color.

And that is why there is no ignoring the fact that the tide of self-determination has not reached the Communist empire where a population far larger than that officially termed "dependent" lives under governments installed by foreign troops instead of free institutions—under a system which knows only one party and one belief—which suppresses free debate, and free elections, and free newspapers, and free books and free trade unions—and which builds a wall to keep truth a stranger and its own citizens prisoners. Let us debate colonialism in full—and apply the principle of free choice and the practice of free politics in every corner of the globe.

IX.

Finally, as President of the United States, I consider it my duty to report to this Assembly on two threats to the peace which are not on your crowded agenda, but which cause us, and most of you, the deepest concern.

The first threat on which I wish to report is widely misunderstood: the smoldering coals of war in Southeast Asia. South Viet-Nam is already under attack—sometimes by a single assassin, sometimes by a band of guerrillas, recently by full battalions. The peaceful borders of Burma, Cambodia, and India have been repeatedly violated. And the peaceful people of Laos are in danger of losing the independence they gained not so long ago.

No one can call these "wars of liberation." For these are free countries living under their own governments. Nor are these aggressions any less real because men are knifed in their homes and not shot in the fields of battle.

The very simple question confronting the world community is whether measures can be devised to protect the small and the weak from such tactics. For if they are successful in Laos and South Viet-Nam, the gates will be opened wide. . . .

Secondly, I wish to report to you on the crisis over Germany and Berlin. This is not the time or the place for immoderate tones, but the world community is entitled to know the very simple issues as we see them. If there is a crisis it is because an existing island of free people is under pressure, because solemn agreements are being treated with indifference. Established international rights are being threatened with unilateral usurpation. Peaceful circulation has been interrupted by barbed wire and concrete blocks.

One recalls the order of the Czar in Pushkin's *Boris Godunov:* "Take steps at this very hour that our frontiers be fenced in by barriers. . . . That not a single soul pass o'er the border, that not a hare be able to run or a crow to fly."

It is absurd to allege that we are threatening a war merely to prevent the Soviet Union and East Germany from signing a so-called "treaty" of peace. The Western Allies are not concerned with any paper arrangement the Soviets may wish to make with a regime of their own creation, on territory occupied by their own troops and governed by their own agents. No such action can affect either our rights or our responsibilities.

If there is a dangerous crisis in Berlin—and there is—it is because of threats against the vital interests and the deep commitments of the Western Powers, and the freedom of West Berlin. We cannot yield these interests. We cannot fail these commitments. We cannot surrender the freedom of these people for whom we are responsible. A "peace treaty" which carried with it the provisions which destroy peace would be a fraud. A "free city" which was not genuinely free would suffocate freedom and would be an infamy.

For a city or a people to be truly free, they have the secure right, without economic, political or police pressure, to make their own choice and to live their own lives. And as I have said before, if anyone doubts the extent to which our presence is desired by the people of West Berlin, we are ready to have that question submitted to a free vote in all Berlin and, if possible, among all the German people. . . .

The Western Powers have calmly resolved to defend, by whatever means are forced upon them, their obligations and their access to the free citizens of West Berlin and the self-determination of those citizens. This generation learned from bitter experience that either brandishing or yielding to threats can only lead to war. But firmness and reason can lead to the kind of peaceful solution in which my country profoundly believes. . . .

X.

The events and decisions of the next ten months may well decide the fate of man for the next ten thousand years. There will be no avoiding those events. There will be no appeal from these decisions. And we in this hall shall be remembered either as part of the generation that turned this planet into a flaming funeral pyre or the generation that met its vow "to save succeeding generations from the scourge of war."

In the endeavor to meet that vow, I pledge you every effort this Nation possesses. I pledge you that we shall neither flee nor invoke the threat of force, that we shall never negotiate out of fear, we shall never fear to negotiate.

Terror is not a new weapon. Throughout history it has been used by those who could not prevail, either by persuasion or example. But inevitably they fail, either because men are not afraid to die for a life worth living, or because the terrorists themselves came to realize that free men cannot be frightened by threats, and that aggression would meet its own response. And it is in the light of that history that every nation today should know, be he friend or foe, that the United States has both the will and the weapons to join free men in standing up to their responsibilities.

But I come here today to look across this world of threats to a world of peace. In that search we cannot expect any final triumph —for new problems will always arise. We cannot expect that all nations will adopt like systems—for conformity is the jailor of freedom, and the enemy of growth. Nor can we expect to reach our goal by contrivance, by fiat or even by the wishes of all.

But however close we sometimes seem to that dark and final

abyss, let no man of peace and freedom despair. For he does not stand alone. If we all can persevere, if we can in every land and office look beyond our own shores and ambitions, then surely the age will dawn in which the strong are just and the weak secure and the peace preserved.

Ladies and gentlemen of this Assembly, the decision is ours. Never have the nations of the world had so much to lose, or so much to gain. Together we shall save our planet, or together we shall perish in its flames. Save it we can—and save it we must—and then shall we earn the eternal thanks of mankind and, as peacemakers, the eternal blessing of God.

On November 26, 1963, a special commemorative meeting of the General Assembly of the United Nations was convened, at which many delegates took the opportunity to express their sentiments and those of their countrymen on the death of President Kennedy. Eloquent and sometimes impassioned tributes, the three speeches reprinted here manifest a feeling seemingly held by people the world over—that each one of us had lost a very dear friend.

from

Homage to a Friend:
A Memorial Tribute
by The United Nations

H. E. U Thant

Secretary-General of the United Nations

Today we are gathered in this Assembly of one hundred and eleven
Member Governments to pay solemn tribute to the memory of a
martyr. I feel bound to participate in this occasion not only on my
own behalf, but also on behalf of the entire Secretariat.

On 20 September 1963, John F. Kennedy, President of the
United States of America, addressed the General Assembly of the
United Nations. He said, inter alia:

> ". . . we meet today in an atmosphere of rising hope, and at a
> moment of comparative calm. My presence here today is not a sign
> of crisis but of confidence. . . . I have come to salute the United Na-
> tions and to show the support of the American people for your
> daily deliberations."

Exactly nine weeks later, President Kennedy fell a victim to an assassin's bullet, and all of us at the United Nations felt that we had lost a friend—not only a friend of the Organization, not only a friend of peace, but a friend of man.

I recall, with equal vividness, a time some two years ago when the United Nations was plunged in gloom because of the sudden death of its Secretary-General. At that time President Kennedy made a special appearance before the General Assembly of the United Nations, and in the course of his address he said:

"So let us here resolve that Dag Hammarskjold did not live— or die—in vain. Let us call a truce to terror. Let us invoke the blessings of peace. And, as we build an international capacity to keep peace, let us join in dismantling the national capacity to wage war."

Although we all know that man is born under sentence of death with but an indefinite reprieve, death is a tragedy whenever it comes. It is human to feel sorrow at the passing of anyone dear to us, even when death comes as a merciful release from chronic suffering and pain. But when a young and dynamic leader of a great country, with his brilliant promise only half fulfilled, is felled in the prime of life by an utterly incomprehensible and senseless act, the loss is not only a loss to the bereaved family, whose head he was, nor even the country over whose destiny he presided with rare ability and distinction as Head of State. It is a loss suffered by the entire world, by all humanity, for the late President embodied a rare and quite remarkable combination of intellect and courage, of vigour and compassion, of devotion to the arts and sciences, which was focused on serving his basic concern for the well-being of all mankind.

It is a strange irony that President Kennedy, like President Lincoln—I note that some have already begun to speak of Kennedy as a younger Lincoln, dedicated as both were to the paths of peace and reconciliation—should have come to that violent end at the hands of an assassin. I have the feeling that President Kennedy was sincerely seeking to carry forward to fulfillment the monumental task which began in this country a hundred years ago.

Throughout his public career President Kennedy sought to reduce tension, to uphold the law and to discourage violence, whether in word or deed. On 10 June 1963 he observed:

"And if we cannot end now our differences, at least we can help make the world safe for diversity. For in the final analysis, our most basic common link is that we all inhabit this planet. We all breathe the same air. We all cherish our children's future. And we are all mortal."

President Kennedy was mortal like the rest of us. Not so his place in history, where he will live as a great leader who sought peace at home and abroad and who gave his life as a true martyr in the service of his country and of all mankind.

Let us all, here and now, draw inspiration from his example, and let us resolve that he did not live, or die, in vain. Let us call a truce to terror. Let us invoke the blessings of peace.

H.E. Mr. Nikolai Trofimovich Fedorenko

Union of the Soviet Socialist Republics
Vice-President of the General Assembly

. . . The Soviet Union shares the grief of the people of the United States of America at this terrible loss. The feelings of the Soviet people are expressed in the following cable which **Mr. Khrushchev**, Chairman of the Council of Ministers of the USSR, sent to President Johnson:

I am deeply grieved by the news of the tragic death of an outstanding statesman, President John Fitzgerald Kennedy of the United States of America.

The death of Mr. Kennedy is a hard blow to all people who cherish the cause of peace and Soviet-American co-operation.

The heinous assassination of the United States President at a time when, as a result of the efforts of peace-loving peoples, signs of a relaxation of international tensions have appeared and a prospect of improving relations between the USSR and the United States of America has opened, evokes the indignation of the Soviet people against those guilty of this base crime.

From my personal meetings with President Kennedy, I shall remember him as a man of broad outlook who realistically assessed the situation and tried to find ways to reach negotiated settlements of the international problems which now divide the world.

The Soviet Government and the Soviet people share the grief of the people of the United States of America at this great loss and express the hope that the search for settlements of disputed questions, a search to which President Kennedy made a tangible contribution, will be continued in the interest of peace, for the benefit of mankind.

The Soviet delegation expresses the hope that efforts to achieve a peaceful settlement of problems, to reduce international tension and to initiate Soviet-American co-operation—one manifestation of which is the Moscow Treaty banning nuclear weapons tests, so highly prized by the President who has been tragically assassinated —will be carried on both here in the United Nations and outside the Organization. This will be the best memorial to President John Fitzgerald Kennedy.

H. E. Mr. Adlai E. Stevenson

United States of America

. . . President Kennedy was so contemporary a man, so involved in our world, so immersed in our times, so responsive to its challenges, so intense a participant in the great events and the great decisions of our day, that he seemed the very symbol of the vitality and exuberance that is the essence of life itself. Never once did he lose his way in the maze; never once did he falter in the storm of spears; never once was he intimidated. Like the ancient prophets, he loved the people enough to warn them of their errors; and the man who loves his country best will hold it to its highest standards. He made us proud to be Americans.

So it is that after four sorrowful days we still can hardly grasp the macabre reality that the world has been robbed of this vibrant presence by an isolated act conceived in the strange recesses of the human mind.

We shall not soon forget the late President's driving ambition for his own country—his concept of a permanently dynamic society spreading abundance to the last corner of this land and extending justice, tolerance and dignity to all its citizens alike.

We shall not soon forget that as the leader of a great nation he met and mastered his responsibility to wield great power with great restraint. "Our national strength matters," he said just a few weeks ago, "but the spirit which informs and controls our strength matters just as much."

We shall not soon forget that he held fast to a vision of a world in which the peace is secure; in which inevitable conflicts are reconciled by pacific means; in which nations devote their energies to the welfare of all their citizens; and in which the vast and colorful diversity of human society can flourish in a restless, competitive search for a better society.

We shall not soon forget that by word and by deed he gave proof of profound confidence in the present value and the future promise of this great Organization, the United Nations.

We shall never forget these ambitions, these visions and these convictions that so inspired this remarkable young man and so quickened the quality and tempo of our times in these fleeting past three years. And our grief is compounded by the bitter irony that he who gave his all to contain violence lost his all to violence.

Now he is gone. Today we mourn him. Tomorrow and tomorrow we shall miss him. So we shall never know how different the world might have been had fate permitted this blazing talent to live and labor longer at man's unfinished agenda for peace and progress for all. . . .

Finally, let me say that John Kennedy never believed that he or any man was indispensable. As several speakers have reminded us this afternoon, he said of Dag Hammarskjold's death: "The problem is not the death of one man—the problem is the life of this Organization." But he did believe passionately that peace and justice are indispensable and he believed, as he told this Assembly in 1961, ". . . in the development of this Organization rests the only true alternative to war. . . ."

So, my friends, we shall honor him in the best way that lies open to us—and the way he would want—by getting on with the everlasting search for peace and justice, for which all mankind is praying.

from

A Nation of Immigrants

by John F. Kennedy

Chapter 5
The Immigrant Contribution

John F. Kennedy originally published A Nation of
Immigrants *in 1958, after playing an instrumental role
in the Senate's passage of a 1957 bill to bring immigrant
families together. At the time of his death he was working
on a revision, for use in his campaign for the complete
revocation of existing immigration law. Published posthumously,
the revision in many ways typifies John Kennedy's
historical writing with, as Allan Nevins has written, its
"eloquence, sound historical knowledge, and a true comprehension
of the requisites of American greatness."*

Oscar Handlin has said, "Once I thought to write a history of the
immigrants in America. Then I discovered that the immigrants

were American history." In the same sense, we cannot really speak of a particular "immigrant contribution" to America because all Americans have been immigrants or the descendants of immigrants; even the Indians, as mentioned before, migrated to the American continent. We can only speak of people whose roots in America are older or newer. Yet each wave of immigration left its own imprint on American society; each made its distinctive "contribution" to the building of the nation and the evolution of American life. Indeed, if, as some of the older immigrants like to do, we were to restrict the definition of immigrants to the 42 million people who came to the United States *after* the Declaration of Independence, we would have to conclude that our history and our society would have been vastly different if they had stayed at home.

As we have seen, people migrated to the United States for a variety of reasons. But nearly all shared two great hopes: the hope for personal freedom and the hope for economic opportunity. In consequence, the impact of immigration has been broadly to confirm the impulses in American life demanding more political liberty and more economic growth.

So, of the fifty-six signers of the Declaration of Independence, eighteen were of non-English stock and eight were first-generation immigrants. Two immigrants—the West Indian Alexander Hamilton, who was Washington's Secretary of the Treasury, and the Swiss Albert Gallatin, who held the same office under Jefferson—established the financial policies of the young republic. A German farmer wrote home from Missouri in 1834,

> If you wish to see our whole family living in . . . a country where freedom of speech obtains, where no spies are eavesdropping, where no simpletons criticize your every word and seek to detect therein a venom that might endanger the life of the state, the church and the home, in short, if you wish to be really happy and independent, then come here.

Every ethnic minority, in seeking its own freedom, helped strengthen the fabric of liberty in American life.

Similarly, every aspect of the American economy has profited from the contributions of immigrants. We all know, of course, about the spectacular immigrant successes: the men who came from foreign lands, sought their fortunes in the United States and made striking contributions, industrial and scientific, not only to their chosen country but to the entire world. In 1953 the President's Commission on Immigration and Naturalization mentioned the following:

Industrialist: Andrew Carnegie (Scot), in the steel industry; John Jacob Astor (German), in the fur trade; Michael Cudahy (Irish), of the meat-packing industry; the Du Ponts (French), of the munitions and chemical industry; Charles L. Fleischmann (Hungarian), of the yeast business; David Sarnoff (Russian), of the radio industry; and William S. Knudsen (Danish), of the automobile industry.

Scientists and inventors: Among those whose genius has benefited the United States are Albert Einstein (German), in physics; Michael Pupin (Serbian), in electricity; Enrico Fermi (Italian), in atomic research; John Ericsson (Swedish), who invented the iron-clad ship and the screw propeller; Guiseppe Bellanca (Italian), and Igor Sikorsky (Russian), who made outstanding contributions to airplane development; John A. Udden (Swedish), who was responsible for opening the Texas oil fields; Lucas P. Kyrides (Greek), industrial chemist; David Thomas (Welsh), who invented the hot blast furnace; Alexander Graham Bell (Scot), who invented the telephone; Conrad Hubert (Russian), who invented the flashlight; and Ottmar Mergenthaler (German), who invented the linotype machine.

But the anonymous immigrant played his indispensable role too. Between 1880 and 1920 America became the industrial and agricultural giant of the world as well as the world's leading creditor nation. This could not have been done without the hard labor, the technical skills and the entrepreneurial ability of the 23.5 million people who came to America in this period.

Significant as the immigrant role was in politics and in the economy, the immigrant contribution to the professions and the arts was perhaps even greater. Charles O. Paullin's analysis of the *Dictionary of American Biography* shows that, of the eighteenth- and nineteenth-century figures, 20 percent of the businessmen, 20 percent of the scholars and scientists, 23 percent of the painters, 24 percent of the engineers, 28 percent of the architects, 29 percent of the clergymen, 46 percent of the musicians and 61 percent of the actors were of foreign birth—a remarkable measure of the impact of immigration on American culture. And not only have many American writers and artists themselves been immigrants or the children of immigrants, but immigration has provided American literature with one of its major themes.

Perhaps the most pervasive influence of immigration is to be found in the innumerable details of life and customs and habits brought by millions of people who have never become famous. The impact was felt from the bottom up, and these contributions to American institutions may be the ones which most intimately affect the lives of all Americans.

In the area of religion, all the major American faiths were brought to this country from abroad. The multiplicity of sects established the American tradition of religious pluralism and assured to all the freedom of worship and separation of church and state pledged in the Bill of Rights.

So, too, in the very way we speak, immigration has altered American life. In greatly enriching the American vocabulary, it has been a major force in establishing "the American language," which, as H. L. Mencken demonstrated thirty years ago, had diverged materially from the mother tongue as spoken in Britain. Even the American dinner table has felt the impact. One writer has suggested that "typical American menus" might include some of the following dishes: "Irish stew, chop suey, goulash, chili con carne, ravioli, knackwurst mit sauerkraut, Yorkshire pudding, Welsh rarebit, borsch, gefilte fish, Spanish omelet, vaviarm mayonnaise, antipasto, baumkuchen, English muffins, Gruyère cheese, Danish pastry, Canadian bacon, hot tamales, wiener schnitzel, petits fours, spumone, bouillabaisse, maté, scones, Turkish coffee, minestrone, filet mignon."

Immigration plainly was not always a happy experience. It was hard on the newcomers, and hard as well on the communities to which they came. When poor, ill-educated and frightened people disembarked in a strange land, they often fell prey to native racketeers, unscrupulous businessmen and cynical politicians. Boss Tweed said, characteristically, in defense of his own depredations in New York in the 1870's, "This population is too hopelessly split into races and factions to govern it under universal suffrage, except by bribery of patronage, or corruption."

But the very problems of adjustment and assimilation presented a challenge to the American idea—a challenge which subjected that idea to stern testing and eventually brought out the best qualities in American society. Thus the public school became a powerful means of preparing the newcomers for American life. The idea of the "melting pot" need not mean the end of particular ethnic identities or traditions. Only in the case of the Negro has the melting pot failed to bring a minority into the full stream of American life. Today we are belatedly, but resolutely, engaged in ending this condition of national exclusion and shame and abolishing forever the concept of second-class citizenship in the United States.

Sociologists call the process of the melting pot "social mobility." One of America's characteristics has always been the lack of a rigid class structure. It has traditionally been possible for people to move up the social and economic scale. Even if one did not succeed in moving up oneself, there was always the hope that one's children would. Immigration is by definition a gesture of faith in social mobility. It is the expression in action of a positive belief in the possibility of a better life. It has thus contributed greatly to developing the spirit of personal betterment in American society and to strengthening the national confidence in change and the future. Such confidence, when widely shared, sets the national tone. The opportunities that America offered made the dream real, at least for a good many; but the dream itself was in large part the product of millions of plain people beginning a new life in the conviction that life could indeed be better, and each new wave of immigration rekindled the dream.

This is the spirit which so impressed Alexis de Tocqueville, and which he called the spirit of equality. Equality in America has never meant literal equality of condition or capacity; there will always be inequalities in character and ability in any society. Equality has meant rather that, in the words of the Declaration of Independence, "all men are created equal . . . [and] are endowed by their Creator with certain unalienable rights"; it has meant that in a democratic society there should be no inequalities in opportunities or in freedoms. The American philosophy of equality has released the energy of the people, built the economy, subdued the continent, shaped and reshaped the structure of government, and animated the American attitude toward the world outside.

The *continuous* immigration of the nineteenth and early twentieth centuries was thus central to the whole American faith. It gave every old American a standard by which to judge how far he might go. It reminded every American, old and new, that change is the essence of life, and that American society is a process, not a conclusion. The abundant resources of this land provided the human resources. More than that, it infused the nation with a commitment to far horizons and new frontiers, and thereby kept the pioneer spirit of equality and of hope, always alive and strong. "We are the heirs of all time," wrote Herman Melville, "and with all nations we divide our inheritance."

Remarks in the
Rudolf Wilde Platz

Berlin
June 26, 1963

I am proud to come to this city as the guest of your distinguished Mayor [Willy Brandt], who has symbolized throughout the world the fighting spirit of West Berlin. And I am proud to visit the Federal Republic with your distinguished Chancellor [Conrad Adenauer] who for so many years has committed Germany to democracy and freedom and progress, and to come here in the company of my fellow American, General [Lucius D.] Clay, who has been in this city during its great moments of crisis and will come again if ever needed.

Two thousand years ago the proudest boast was *"civis Romanus sum."* Today, in the world of freedom, the proudest boast is *"Ich bin ein Berliner."*

I appreciated my interpreter translating my German!

There are many people in the world who really don't understand, or say they don't, what is the great issue between the free world and the Communist world. Let them come to Berlin. There are some who say that communism is the wave of the future. Let them come to Berlin. And there are some who say in Europe and elsewhere we can work with the Communists. Let them come to Berlin. And there are even a few who say that it is true that communism is an evil system, but it permits us to make economic progress. *Lass' sie nach Berlin kommen.* Let them come to Berlin.

Freedom has many difficulties and democracy is not perfect, but we have never had to put a wall up to keep our people in, to prevent them from leaving us. I want to say, on behalf of my countrymen, who live many miles away on the other side of the Atlantic, who are far distant from you, that they take the greatest pride that they have been able to share with you, even from a distance, the story of the last 18 years. I know of no town, no city, that has been besieged for 18 years that still lives with the vitality and the force, and the hope, and the determination of the city of West Berlin. While the wall is the most obvious and vivid demonstration of the failures of the Communist system for all the world to see, we take no satisfaction in it, for it is, as your Mayor has said, an offense not only against history but an offense against humanity, separating families, dividing husbands and wives and brothers and sisters, and dividing a people who wish to be joined together.

What is true of this city is true of Germany—real, lasting peace in Europe can never be assured as long as one German out of four is denied the elementary right of free men, and that is to make a free choice. In 18 years of peace and good faith, this generation of Germans has earned the right to be free, including the right to unite their families and their nation in lasting peace, with good will to all people. You live in a defended island of freedom, but your life is part of the main. So let me ask you, as I close, to lift your eyes beyond the dangers of today, to the hopes of tomorrow, beyond the freedom merely of this city of Berlin, or your country of Germany, to the advance of freedom everywhere, beyond this wall to the day of peace with justice, beyond yourselves and ourselves to all mankind.

Freedom is indivisible, and when one man is enslaved, all are not free. When all are free, then we can look forward to that day when this city will be joined as one and this country and this great Continent of Europe in a peaceful and hopeful globe. When that day finally comes, as it will, the people of West Berlin can take sober satisfaction in the fact that they were in the front lines for almost two decades.

All freemen, wherever they may live, are citizens of Berlin, and, therefore, as a free man, I take pride in the words *"Ich bin ein Berliner."*

A Tragedy for the World

The Manchester Guardian
November 23, 1963

President Kennedy was in Texas to gather support for his Civil
Rights Programme. Like Lincoln before him, it has cost him his life.
He believed in it and he fought for it. The best memorial to him
would be a more rapid acceptance of it in the South—and in
Northern communities where the subtler forms of segregation and
discrimination are practiced; and, for that matter, in every country
where equal rights and equal opportunities are not accorded without regard to race or religion. Civil Rights became the foremost part
of his domestic programme. He had to move carefully, both because
haste could so easily bring bloodshed and because he was opposed
by the Southern wing of his own party. While he sought to avert
collisions—even though events in Arkansas and Mississippi made

417

it hard—he conceded nothing to the South. His platform in the 1960 Presidential Campaign came out boldly and explicitly for the Negro's right to share school benches and polling booths with whites, and for the Federal Government's duty to enforce this. He was backed in this by Lyndon Johnson, himself a Southerner and now President in John F. Kennedy's place.

To the world he will be remembered as the President who helped to bring the thaw in the cold war. This, too, was a consistent aim from the earliest days—and to set up the Disarmament Agency in Washington was one of his first acts. The real change came, however, only after Cuba. That crisis, taking the world to the edge of a nuclear war, left its mark on both him and Mr. Khrushchev. Each man in the eight critical days at the end of October, 1962, had looked an unthinkable human disaster in the face. President Kennedy certainly—and Mr. Khrushchev probably—knew that a false move by either of them in those days could have been catastrophic. Although, in a conventional sense, the Americans won the encounter, there was no crowing in the White House. The President recognized how frightening were the consequences of misunderstandings between East and West. He was on his guard against further Soviet expansion, and immediately after the crisis he was not hopeful of an early improvement in relations. But he worked for such improvement, as did Mr. Khrushchev, and it came. It is, today, only at a beginning. The "hot line" has been installed to handle future incidents and frictions; the test ban treaty has been negotiated to end pollution of the earth's atmosphere; the worst tensions in Germany have been eased. He leaves in this a monument —but one on which his successors must build.

President Kennedy respected his allies and worked with them. His last visit to this country was during a lightning tour of Europe —part triumphal and part persuasive—in which he sought to reassure people and Governments that the United States was as deeply committed as ever to the defence of Western Europe. It was a tour undertaken mainly because of the suspicions and uncertainties generated in the spring, after the failure of Britain's endeavor to join the Common Market, and when President de Gaulle seemed to be drawing Western Germany away from its firm ties with the Atlantic Alliance. It was a tour also in which he sounded his allies on methods of securing better consultation—and that, too, is something to be continued today.

But he will be remembered, as much as anything, for his youth and friendliness. "The torch has been passed to a new generation of Americans," he said in his inaugural address. To people in many other countries it was gladdening to see leading the greatest of Western nations a young man, though one matured by war and by years of public service. He and Mrs. Kennedy made the White House what it had hardly ever been before—a place where artists and thinkers of all nations and creeds were welcomed. He was a true liberal, a thinker himself no less than a man of action, and a courageous leader.

from The Kennedy Wit

by Bill Adler

Introducing Astronaut Alan Shepard, Jr.:

We have with us today the nation's number one television performer, who I think on last Friday morning secured the largest rating of any morning show in recent history.

And I think it does credit to him that he is associated with such a distinguished group of Americans whom we are all glad to honor today—his companions in the flight to outer space—so I think we'll give them all a hand. They are the tanned and healthy ones; the others are Washington employees.

I also want to pay a particular tribute to some of the people who worked in this flight: Robert Gilruth, who was director of the Space Task Force Group at Langley Field; Walter Williams, the operations director of Project Mercury; the NASA Deputy Administrator, Dr. Hugh Dryden; Lieutenant Colonel Glenn, Jr., and, of course, Jim Webb, who is head of NASA.

Most of these names are unfamiliar. If the flight had not been an overwhelming success, these names would be very familiar to everyone.

May 8, 1961

A Eulogy:
John Fitzgerald Kennedy

by Arthur M. Schlesinger, Jr.

THE SATURDAY EVENING POST
December 14, 1963

The thing about him was the extraordinary sense he gave to being alive: This makes his death so grotesque and unbelievable. No one had such vitality of personality—a vitality so superbly disciplined that it sometimes left the impression of cool detachment, but imbuing everything he thought or did with an intense concentration and power. He was life-affirming, life-enhancing. When he entered the room, the temperature changed; and he quickened the sensibilities of everyone around him. His curiosity was unlimited. The restless thrust of his mind never abated. He noticed everything, responded to everything, forgot nothing. He lived his life so intensely that in retrospect it almost seems he must have known it would be short, and that he had no time to waste. Or perhaps it was that, having lived closely to death ever since he swam those lonely, terrible hours along Ferguson Passage in 1943, ever since he nearly died after the operation on his back in 1955, he was determined to savor everything of life.

He was a man profoundly in earnest. Yet there was never a moment when his manner was not informal, irreverent, rueful and witty. He took life seriously, but never himself. He cared deeply, but his passion was understatement. No heart ever appeared on his sleeve, though only the unaware could have concluded that this meant there was no heart at all. He mistrusted rhetoric, and he detested histrionics. But the casualness, the dry humor, the sardonic throwaway lines, the cool precision in press conference, the sense of slight distance from emotion, the invariable courtesy and the inextinguishable gaiety—none of this could conceal the profound concern and commitment underneath.

His whole life gave him that concern. He came from a religion and race which had known discrimination and persecution. He came from a family which in its energy, its warmth, its subtle and disparate solidarity had nourished his capacity for competition, for tenacity and for affection. Education developed his intelligence and awakened his historical imagination. This was most important; for he saw the movement of events as an historian sees them, not as a morality play, but as a complex and obscure interaction of men and values and institutions, in which each man's light is often dim but each must do the best he can. As a senior at Harvard he wrote an honors essay to explain why Great Britain was so poorly prepared for the Second World War. The book was published the next year, and he wrote in the introduction: "In studying the reasons why England slept, let us try to profit by them and save ourselves her anguish." He had the insight and the sense of language which could have made him a distinguished historian, but his was the nerve of action.

The hard experience of war deepened and toughened him. He was, of course, an authentic hero, a man of valor and hope. As a young skipper on a PT boat, he displayed his capacity for command, which always meant for him, not the compulsion to bark orders, but the capacity to enlist confidence and assume responsibility. After the war, he was broken in health but lively in spirit. Though his father had been one of the most successful businessmen of his time, something had saved the older Kennedy from the ethos of the business community; he inspired his children with the belief that serving the nation was more important than making money; and it was the natural thing for young Lieutenant Kennedy, pale and shaky from the war, to run for Congress from the 11th District of Massachusetts. I had been a classmate of his older brother's at Harvard and had been aware of John Kennedy who was a sophomore when I was a senior; but I first knew him when he became the congressman from the district in which I lived. One remembers the quick intelligence, the easy charm, the laconic wit. One did not then see the passion and power which lay underneath.

I have always felt that in these years John Kennedy perhaps thought he was going to die because of the unresolved trouble with his back, and that he was therefore determined to have the best possible time in the days left to him. This was his season of careless gaiety, of Palm Beach and Newport, of dances and parties, and he married the most beautiful girl of them all. But the trouble with his back remained; and in 1955 he underwent a long and complicated operation—a double fusion of spinal disks with ensuing complications. He received last rites and nearly died. But he fought through, as he had fought through the waters of Ferguson Passage. When he recovered, he knew that he would live. My guess is that at this point he decided to become President of the United States.

"HE WANTED TO USE POWER"

There used to be a fashion of criticizing John Kennedy for being ambitious, as if anyone ever became President of the United States who had not schemed and labored to that end. Of course he wanted to be President. But he wanted to be President not because he wanted power for its own sake: He wanted to be President because he wanted to use power to advance the purposes of the nation. He was a supreme politician. He loved the flicker of tension and persuasion, the cut and thrust of political infighting, the puzzles of political strategy. He also came to love campaigning. He always seemed a little surprised by the ardor of the crowds which flocked to see him; but he gathered strength from them as they gathered strength from him.

But, overriding everything else, he had a vision of America, of what this country might do and might be, and he had a vision of the world. He saw this nation as a noble nation, rising above mean and ugly motives, subordinating private selfishness to public purpose, raising the standards of existence and opportunity for all its citizens. He was always receptive to new experience, and new experience steadily deepened his sense of what America must do to fulfill the vision. Thus the primary campaign in West Virginia in the spring of 1960 gave his understanding of poverty and his determination to eliminate it new concreteness and urgency. He never could understand the complacent rich who, so long as they had everything they needed for themselves, were content to starve schools, medical services and social services for their less fortunate fellow citizens. In one of the last talks I had with him, he was musing about the legislative program for next January and said, "The time has come to organize a national assault on the causes of poverty, a comprehensive program, across the board."

So too the agony of the Negroes transformed another abstraction into cruel reality, and so he committed himself to the battle for civil rights. He did this not for political reasons, because he always believed it would lose him many more votes than it would gain him. He did this because it was necessary to keep the faith of American democracy and preserve the fabric of American life. He did this because he felt with cold passion that it was the right thing to do.

These things deeply preoccupied him, but what preoccupied him most, I believe, was the peace of the world and the future of mankind. His historian's perspective made him see the conflict with Communism not as a holy war but as a difficult and perilous struggle for adjustment and accommodation. The world, he deeply believed, was in its nature and historical movement a diverse world—

a world which had room for a great diversity of economic systems, of political creeds, of philosophical faiths. He respected the distinctive values and traditions, the distinctive identities, of other nations and other societies. He felt that, as the possessing classes in the American community had an obligation to the weak and defenseless, so the possessing nations had an obligation to the nations struggling to emerge from the oblivion of stagnation and want. And he saw this not just as a moral obligation but as a social necessity. "Those who make peaceful revolution impossible," he once said, "make violent revolution inevitable."

Above all, life must survive on this planet. He knew what nuclear war would mean, and he believed that the avoidance of such a war was the common interest of mankind—a common interest which must transcend all conflicts of ideology and national ambition. This common interest was the bridge across the dark abyss. His deepest purpose was to strengthen that bridge against the storms of suspicion and fear, and to persuade his adversaries that, if each nation and people respected the integrity of the rest and accepted the reality of the world of diversity, if nations abandoned a messianic effort to remake the world in their own image, peace would be possible, and humanity would endure.

These hopes, I believe, guided him in his terrible task. In the midst of his crushing burdens, he moved always with grace, composure and cheer. His office reflected his own serenity in a world of chaos. He was a man born to the exercise of power, but also a man born to the responsibility of power. He immersed himself in the issues, understood what mattered and what did not, mastered the necessary information and dominated the process of government. I have so often seen experts come before him, men who had worked on problems for months or years, and I have seen him penetrate at once to the heart of the issue, and then place it in a wider context, raising questions of significance which the experts had not thought about. His presence pervaded Washington, and he infused the laborious and opaque machinery of government with a sense of his own standards, his own imagination and his own high purpose.

With all this, his kindness, his consideration, his gaiety and his strength were absolute.

He had grown all his life, and he grew even more in the presidency. The ordeal of the first Cuba made possible the triumph of the second Cuba. He broke new paths in a dozen sectors of national policy—in civil rights, in economic policy, in the reorientation of military strategy, in the reconstruction of foreign aid, in the exploration of space, in the encouragement of the arts. But the bright promise of his Administration, as of his life, was cut short in Dallas. When Abraham Lincoln died, when Franklin Roosevelt died, these were profound national tragedies; but death came for Lincoln and Roosevelt in the last act, at the end of their careers, when the victory for which they had fought so hard was at last within the nation's grasp. John Kennedy's death has greater pathos, because he had barely begun—because he had so much to do, so much to give to his family, his nation, his world. His was a life of incalculable and now unfulfilled possibility.

Still, if he had not done all that he had hoped to do, finished all that he had so well begun, he had given the nation a new sense of itself—a new spirit, a new style, a new conception of its role and destiny. He saw America, not as an old nation, self-righteous, conservative, satisfied in its grossness and materialism, but as a young nation, questing, self-critical, dissatisfied, caring for greatness as well as for bigness, caring for the qualities of mind, sensibility and spirit which sustain culture, produce art and elevate society. He was the most civilized President we have had since Jefferson, and his wife made the White House the most civilized house in America. Statecraft was for him not an end in itself; it was a means of moving forward toward a spacious and splendid America.

And so a crazed and political fanatic shot him down. With this act of violence, and with the violence that followed, the idea of America as a civilized nation—the idea which John F. Kennedy so supremely embodied—suffered a grievous blow. The best way to serve his memory is to redeem and revindicate the values of decency, of rationality, of civility, of honor—those values for which he stood through his life and to which in the end he gave his life.